ROOTED
IN SIN RESCUED
BY LOVE

BY PETER MARTIN

PUBISHED FOR RUNNING LIGHT MINISTRIES, INC. BY:

WORD PRODUCTIONS

Rooted in Sin...Rescued by Love

By Peter Martin

Copyright ©2019 by Peter Martin

ISBN 978-0-9978373-8-4

Published for Running Light Ministries, Inc. By:
Word Productions LLC

PO Box 11865, Albuquerque, NM 87192
http://wordproductions.org

Printed in the United States of America.

INTRODUCTION

ROOTED IN SIN...RESCUED BY LOVE

THE WORD "SIN" IS AN INCREDIBLY UNPOPULAR ONE in our culture today. When we hear it we tend to think of something old and outdated that carries with it condemnation and shame. We see it as a word that is only used by overly religious figures that don't know how to have any fun. Even in the church, we tend to primarily focus on things such as God's deep love for us or the victory that Christians can have in this world.

While topics like this are very beautiful to be sure, we can make the mistake of ignoring equally beneficial topics, like *sin,* because they seem a little too depressing. As a result of this negative view, most Christians (myself included) skim over the word "sin" in our Bibles and never really think through what God has to say to us on this issue.

Over the last couple of years, I have seen that I was sorely missing out on a wonderfully rich subject that, if understood correctly, can actually draw us closer to God than we have ever been, cause us to grow deeper in our understanding of His deep and passionate love for us, and help us understand and better combat those sins in our lives.

This book will not go into depth on every single sin issue. Instead, this book is designed to be an introduction to this topic which should spur us on to greater self-reflection and growth.

Proverbs 4:26 tells us to "...ponder the path of your feet, and let all your ways be established..." In order to truly grow in the Christian life, we can't just be told what to do; we *must understand* things for ourselves. That is why I chose to write this book in a workbook format. As you go through the study, please take your time and really think through the questions that are asked of you. The more thought you put into your responses, the more beneficial this time will be for you.

My hope is that as you study through this workbook, God will begin to show you a fresh understanding of sin which will richly bless you in your walk with God, as it has blessed me.

TABLE OF CONTENTS

WHAT IS SIN?

Romans 7:15-19 "I don't really understand myself, for I want to do what is right, but I don't do it. Instead, I do what I hate. But if I know that what I am doing is wrong, this shows that I agree that the law is good. So I am not the one doing wrong; it is sin living in me that does it. And I know that nothing good lives in me, that is, in my sinful nature. I want to do what is right, but I can't. I want to do what is good, but I don't. I don't want to do what is wrong, but I do it anyway...." (NLT)

The first thing that we need to understand about sin is the biblical definition of it. When most of us try to define sin, we think of it as some sort of divine rule breaking. God says, "Thou shalt not..." but we do it anyway, thereby sinning. While this is partially true, the biblical definition of sin is far deeper than that. According to the Bible, sin is not something that we merely do in our thoughts or in our actions, but it is something that is deeply rooted in our very hearts.

According to Paul in Romans 7, where does sin live? _____

_____

Paul admits that the battle he is having with sin is not external, something attacking him from the outside, but rather internal, something happening within his very soul. And more than that, he tells us that sin lives in him and he, by his very nature, is a sinner. Sin is like a tree rooted deep in every human's heart, and from this tree comes the fruit of sin, which are all the wrong and sinful things that we think and do. To put it another way, committing sin isn't what makes us sinners; we are sinners already and that is why we sin. Our default setting is to rebel against God and serve ourselves which is the source of all of our bad decisions and unhappiness. I think Dorothy Sayers, a Christian author, put it best when she said,"Sin is a deep, interior dislocation of the soul."

"As the Scriptures say in Romans 3:11-18, 'No one is righteous— not even one. No one is truly wise; no one is seeking God. All have turned away; all have become useless. No one does good, not a single one. Their talk is foul, like the stench from an open grave. Their tongues are filled with lies. Snake venom drips from their lips. Their mouths are full of cursing and bitterness. They rush to commit murder. Destruction and misery always follow them. They don't know where to find peace. They have no fear of God at all." (NLT)

According to this passage, who is righteous before God? _____

Paul here is talking about humanity's condition in general, not simply people who have sexual issues or drug addicts, but everybody. He says that we are all walking away from God, and it makes no difference if you walk away from God in your sexuality, in your pride, in your greed, etc. We are all by nature walking away from God, and therefore, we can't find true peace.

Why is this so important to understand? First, it is understanding the complexity of sin that enables us to comprehend the true depth of our issues and consequences of our actions. When we have a simplistic view of sin and we want to stop sinning, our only solution will be to "just say no." We won't realize that our behavior is actually growing out of something rooted much deeper in us that must be addressed. I have heard so many sermons where the message is, "If you are viewing porn or engaging in sexual sin, just stop." And I would get so frustrated with myself when I couldn't "just stop." I mean, what was wrong with me that I couldn't stop viewing porn even when I wanted to? You see, I was trying to stop an action without addressing its source. As bad as our outward sins are, they are just symptoms of our real problem, and until we deal with that, we can never be truly free from our issues.

Have you ever tried to "just stop" sinning?

This also means that when we think something to the effect of "I'm going through a lot right now, I will deal with this problem later" or "I'll give in one more time to get it out of my system," we're fooling ourselves. If our sins are growing out of something rooted deeper within us, feeding our sin will only make it stronger. So the longer we wait to deal with our problems and the more we give into our cravings, the more intense our struggle will become and the more difficult it will be stop. *Please read and comment on this passage:*

Galatians 6:7-8 says, "Do not be deceived, God is not mocked; for whatever a man sows, that he will also reap. For he who sows to his flesh will of the flesh reap corruption, but he who sows to the Spirit will of the Spirit reap everlasting life."

_____

_____

 Next, religious people (Christians included) are always trying to clean up their lives from the outside in. We try to stop certain negative behaviors through sheer willpower, and we either fail and get frustrated, or succeed and become severely puffed up and proud. For years I tried to change myself, and in the areas I was "successful" I was becoming more and more proud. I found myself constantly judging those around me with "worse sins" and feeling good about myself because of my accomplishments. But this was a two-edged sword. Whenever I was successful, I felt great; but every time I fell to porn I would slip into a pit of despair, sometimes even doubting my salvation and God's love for me. This kept up until I was constantly unhappy because, no matter how hard I tried, the shameful truth was that I still really enjoyed porn and thought about it constantly. So even when I wasn't indulging, it was always on my mind. I should have known the Words of Jesus:

"Woe to you, scribes and Pharisees, hypocrites! For you cleanse the outside of the cup and dish, but <u>inside they are full of extortion and self-indulgence</u>. Blind Pharisee, <u>first cleanse the inside of the cup and dish, that the outside of them may be clean also</u>. Woe to you, scribes and Pharisees, hypocrites! For you are like whitewashed tombs which indeed appear beautiful outwardly, but inside are full of dead men's bones and all uncleanness. <u>Even so you also outwardly appear righteous to men, but inside you are full of hypocrisy and lawlessness</u>." (Matthew 23:25-28, NKJV, emphasis added).

Can you relate to this?_____

_____

There are so many Christian and secular programs that are aimed at doing exactly this: cleaning the outside but leaving the inside untouched. That is why most Christian programs have taken a much more secular approach to getting rid of our problems. In his article entitled "What Sin Really Is," Charles Spufford, a Christian Pastor, writes: "Everybody knows, that 'sin' basically means 'indulgence' or 'enjoyable naughtiness.' If you were worried (about an issue) you'd use a different word or phrase. You'd talk about 'eating disorders' or 'addictions'; you'd go to another vocabulary cloud altogether."

Does this not sound like Christian culture today? We don't want to use the Word sin anymore, and so we talk about "disorders" or "addictions" being our central problem, trying to convey our Christian values to the world without mentioning Christ. But don't you see? By doing this, we take God out of the focus, and our goal becomes mere behavior modification and not an issue of seeking God and relying on Him. When a Christian has a problem with overeating, we don't immediately focus on their relationship with God but simply label them with an "eating disorder." When someone becomes obsessed with weight loss, we don't focus on their problem with vanity, but instead label them with "body dysmorphia." And when someone views porn, we don't go through the Bible and read about sexual lust, which is a much discussed topic, but instead we label them a "sex addict" or "porn addict."

Now I am not saying that disorders and addictions don't exist. But what I am saying is that when we are quick to label people like this, we immediately exile them from the rest of humanity and put them in a box of negative self-identity. This can fill a person with crushing hopelessness, either feeling like they have done something irreversible to themselves, or that their genes as an addict will always haunt them and they will never be able to escape. Eventually, that negative self-identity can become so much a part of us that it almost becomes an excuse to not even attempt to change because we think that we physically can't do it. It also can become nearly impossible for someone like this to accept a new identity in Christ. Meaning, even though the Bible tells us that we are loved, accepted, and made holy by the love of God, we won't be able to accept these truths because we have embraced our negative identity as "an addict." This can lead to a belief that God's grace is only for other people; it certainly can't be for someone as messed up as us.

Labeling someone with terms such as "addiction" or "disorder" means we are lumping them into a category and ignoring their individual struggle and identity. If I label someone a "sex addict," I am using a loaded term that carries with it a lot of negative connotations and assumptions. I have spoken to parents of teenagers over the years who are truly convinced that their child is already lost and on their way to prison because they have dabbled in porn. I have spoken to wives who believe that their husband must have been sexually abused, and they must be delving into dark types of sexual dysfunction like child pornography and prostitution because they found out that their husband has viewed porn. And I have spoken to men that truly believe that they are beyond hope because they believe that they are sex addicts, and because of that, they have accepted "truths" about themselves that aren't actually true. "Truths" like: they believe that they will escalate to worse and worse types of sexual dysfunction in their addiction, that they will never be able to stop viewing porn, that they will never be able to love their wives, that they must be only using their wives in sexual intimacy, and many other harsh statements like these. These may not be true of them, but they believe it because they have accepted the identity as an addict and all that goes with it. Now it is true that some people who struggle sexually go these directions, but not everyone does. And here is my main point: no matter what our struggle may be, we have to understand that we are individuals and have to be treated as such. We can't lump people into neat little categories because everyone is different in the particular way that they struggle. We have to talk to people and think through our own issues so that we have an idea of exactly how our struggles work and deal with our individual problems.

Instead, by labeling each other we have taken away our ability to communicate in any type of meaningful way about our issues. Because when we label other people like this, it allows everyone who doesn't have these outward "disorders" or "addictions" to feel superior and alienate themselves from those that are diagnosed as such. It can even convince someone like this that because they don't have any outward "addictions" or "disorders" they must not struggle with sin at all. Often even if someone wants to help, they have convinced themselves that they can't relate to the struggles of "those people." And individuals who are labeled like this will feel so disgusting about who they are that they won't even try to communicate about their struggles because they already feel rejected and condemned. I felt this way for years, but while the Bible does say that we are all unique as individuals, it still affirms that we all share a level of commonality in our struggles:

1 Corinthians 10:13 says that "The temptations in your life are no different from what others experience..." (NLT) Did you get that?

According to the Bible, we are all in the same boat; we all struggle with sin because it is rooted in all of our hearts. Not all sin is addiction, but all sin is bondage. We may struggle in different ways and to different degrees, but the root is present for all of us. And if we can't admit that in the church, then those who struggle in sins like these will always feel alienated and like "others." The most tragic part about this is that we were designed for community. No one can be an island. And so, if you feel like a outcast in the church, you will naturally leave the church and gravitate towards a community that understands you. For someone like me, this meant hanging around people who actually encouraged my sin causing me to slip more and more into my sinful behaviors. God intended His church to be a community of believers that would help each other in all of our struggles and issues. It is only through this strong community, beginning with us and God and extending out to the church as a whole, that we can truly change from the inside out.

Galatians 6:1-2 tells us: "Brethren, if a man is overtaken in any trespass, you who are spiritual restore such a one in a spirit of gentleness, considering yourself lest you also be tempted. Bear one another's burdens and so fulfill the law of Christ."

Have you ever felt isolated by your sins before? _____

_____

Also remember, when we discuss our issues in a secular way, it puts the central and primary focus on simply changing our behavior and not on our relationship with God. When we do this, God becomes a means to what we really want and not the end that He deserves to be. But this is so backwards from the way that the Bible speaks to us. 1 Corinthians 10:31 says, "Whether you eat or drink, do all to the glory of God." God alone deserves the glory in our lives, but when we take Him out of the focus and use Him for our own ends, we are falling to pride and self-contentedness. So we might be free from some of our other sins, but if it makes us more proud and more distant from God, was it really worth it?

William Booth, the founder of the Salvation Army, said:

> "I consider that the chief dangers which confront the coming century will be .... religion without the Holy Ghost, Christianity without Christ, forgiveness without repentance, salvation without regeneration, politics without God and heaven without hell."

Do you see the danger that he is talking about, alive in our culture today? _____

For most people in our culture, the belief is that people are naturally good and decent, but through bad circumstances, mental disorders, and unjust societies, people become bad. We tend to think that if we had better programs, legislation, and family structures, people would be perfect. The church has not been immune to this philosophy. We blame our society and upbringings for what is wrong with us as we dream of building a perfect society free from sin. Because of this, when we try to help those who are struggling with "more serious" sins, we automatically assume that their issues must stem from a mental disorder or from past abuse or trauma. So we attempt to label them with some sort of a diagnosable disorder, or we try dig around in their past looking for the source of their sin. We do this thinking that the only way to heal this person is to diagnose their trauma and treat it. This mentality has unfortunately led to people falsely labeling and diagnosing themselves and others in an attempt to explain and fix a sinful behavior.

If we really believed what is taught to us in the Bible, we would see that wicked behavior doesn't need a specific trigger to exist. Sin naturally resides in every human heart, and because of this, we are by nature fallen and so we are innately capable of every form of evil. We are the problem, and so we will never be able to create the solution. While mental disorders and abusive, unjust upbringings certainly can magnify our sin issues (and understanding the impact of our past can help us change), our past pain is not responsible for creating sin in us and it is not what is fundamentally wrong with us. Even with a perfect upbringing, we would still be bent and twisted in our sin. Developing a more just society and better programs to help others is important and can help to reform people from certain bad behaviors, but unfortunately there is no system or program that can change the heart of man, cure us from our sin, or bring us unity with God.

Herein lies the real crux of our problem: if God wants more than a simple change of action, how do you change your very heart? Is it even possible to alter the very core of your nature? The answer in the Bible is that we can't:

> *"Can the Ethiopian change his skin or the leopard its spots? Then may you also do good who are accustomed to do evil." (Jeremiah 13:23)*

This is the bleak picture that we get from the Bible: the best that man can do before God is change the outward, but sin will always dominate our hearts in one way or another. But if this is the case, is there any hope for us?

> *"Oh, what a miserable person I am! Who will free me from this life <u>that is dominated by sin</u> and death? <u>Thank God! The answer is in Jesus Christ our Lord.</u> So you see how it is: In my mind I really want to obey God's law, but because of my sinful nature I am a slave to sin."* (Romans 7:24-25 NLT)

Far from defeating Paul, it was understanding his depravity as a sinner that drove him to Christ; not just to receive forgiveness for his sins (he needed that too) but also to receive a new nature from God. You see, if we don't get to the place where Paul was at, we will continue to try and fix ourselves through programs and our own self-control, and we will be constantly frustrated with the results. It is here in this place of despair that we are finally free to cry out to God and receive His help. That is why so much of the Bible revolves around this topic of sin. It isn't to defeat you, it is designed by God to drive you to Him in humility. God wants to free us from the grips of sin, but the main issue in your life and mine revolves around our relationship with God.

The power of the gospel is that what we could never do in our own strength, God did for us through His Son. We all sit in despair as we see the infinite chasm between the way we know that things should be and the way that things are. And in our flesh, we try to cross that divide in our own strength only to constantly come up short. But what the gospel tells us is that while we could never reach God, God reached us through His Son. And now the righteous life is not based on us being good enough in our own strength, but in trusting the finished work of Christ and allowing Him to transform us into His image and perfect our relationship with Him. The gospel is God's power to save man and bring us to Himself, not man's power to save ourselves and reach God. And the more we realize this, the more free we will become.

Think through the passage below and comment on how this passage relates to our study:

> *Then Jesus said to those Jews who believed Him, "If you abide in My word, you are My disciples indeed. And you shall know the truth, and the truth shall make you free" They answered Him, "We are Abraham's descendants, and have never been in bondage to anyone. How can You say, 'You will be made free?'" Jesus answered them, "Most assuredly, I say to you, whoever commits sin <u>is a slave of sin</u>. And a slave does not abide in the house forever, but a son abides forever. Therefore if the Son makes you free, you shall be free indeed."* (John 8:31-36)

_____

_____

As we finish up the first lesson, I want to address a couple of errors that we can make in light of this teaching. First, we can mistakenly think that once we have this new nature in Christ, living the Christian life becomes simple and free from struggle. I fell into this trap and wondered, "If I am still struggling with sin, does that mean that I am not saved?" This is another lie that can be severely devastating to our walks with God. God promises us a new nature that yearns to pursue Him and do the right thing. And if you have put your faith in Jesus Christ for the forgiveness of your sins, the Bible says that you are saved and have this new nature already. But one thing to understand is that the Bible never teaches us that when we are saved we won't still struggle against our old nature.

> *For the flesh lusts against the Spirit, and the Spirit against the flesh; and these are contrary to one another, so that you do not do the things that you wish.* (Galatians 5:17)

Oh how I wish that I had always understood this passage. God gives us a new nature, but our old sinful nature still remains and will continue to remain until we are face to face with Jesus. If you are struggling against sin, it isn't because you aren't saved, it is actually because you are. Before we were saved, our sinful nature dominated our lives without a fight. But now that we are saved and have a new nature, there is continuous warfare between our old sinful nature and our new nature in Christ. And while we do have a glorious hope that every day we can draw closer and closer to Christ as He delivers us more and more from our sins, we need to understand that our freedom will not be complete until we are with Him in heaven.

Have you fallen into the trap of believing that "real" Christians don't struggle? _____

A second trap that we can fall into is believing that because God has given us this new nature and paid for our sins, the responsibility for living a "good" Christian life rests squarely on our shoulders now. When we do this, we fall into the same mindset that the Galatians did:

> *"O foolish Galatians! Who has bewitched you that you should not obey the truth, before whose eyes Jesus Christ was clearly portrayed among you as crucified? This only I want to learn from you: Did you receive the Spirit by the works of the law, or by the hearing of faith? Are you so foolish? Having begun in the Spirit, are you now being made perfect by the flesh?"* (Galatians 3:1-3)

Notice that they had begun in the Spirit, meaning they were saved in the past, but they had fallen from this foundational teaching and moved into a focus on works and not grace given through trusting and relying on God. This was the mistake that I had made when I was trying to get free from sin in order to please God with my works. But all this did was create a legalistic relationship with Him where I saw Him as more of a disapproving boss than a loving and compassionate Father. This also destroyed my hope because all I saw in myself was failure. Eventually I got to the place where I had nearly given up, thinking that I could ever change. But oh what hope there is for us when we rely on the power of God and not our own!

Being confident of this very thing, that He who has begun a good work in you will complete it until the day of Jesus Christ; (Philippians 1:6)

Have you fallen into this trap? _____

Do you believe that God is able to complete the good work that He began in you? _____

_____

This doesn't mean that our struggle will be easy. It is clear throughout the Bible that our fight against sin will be like actual warfare (2 Corinthians 10:3-6, Ephesians 6:10-20). But when we are fighting, we are fighting in the hope and assurance that the victory is already won. Because of what Jesus did for us, we have confidence in our struggle against sin that, even when we fail, we are still loved and accepted by God. And because He is for us, we will ultimately be victorious through Him. While there are practical steps we can take in our fight against sin, what I am emphasizing is that everything we do in this fight must be built on the foundation of trusting God and believing in His power. He has already saved us and will ultimately be responsible for our freedom from sin. Finally, we must remember that freedom from sin is not the goal of our struggle but intimacy with God is. As we adore and delight in God more and more, the fruit of our relationship with Him will be freedom from sin. As great as freedom from sin is, it is merely a fruit; God alone is worthy of being our ultimate goal and prize. In the next lesson we will talk about the source of our sin and what overcomes it, but here is one last verse to reflect on:

If indeed you have heard Him and have been taught by Him, as the truth is in Jesus: that you put off, concerning your former conduct, the old man which grows corrupt according to the deceitful lusts, and be renewed in the spirit of your mind, and that you put on the new man which was created according to God, in true righteousness and holiness. (Ephesians 4:21-24)

THE SOURCE OF SIN

In Lesson One we talked about how sin isn't merely our actions against God, but it is something that dwells in our very souls. Now we are going to discuss the source of our sin as well as the source of our salvation in Christ.

Now the serpent was more cunning than any beast of the field which the LORD God had made. And he said to the woman, "Has God indeed said, You shall not eat of every tree of the garden?" And the woman said to the serpent, "We may eat the fruit of the trees of the garden; but of the fruit of the tree which is in the midst of the garden, God has said, 'You shall not eat it, nor shall you touch it, lest you die.' Then the serpent said to the woman, "You will not surely die. For <u>God knows</u> that in the day you eat of it your eyes will be opened, and you will be like God, knowing good and evil." So when the woman saw that the tree was good for food, that it was pleasant to the eyes, and a tree desirable to make one wise, she took of its fruit and ate. She also gave to her husband with her, and he ate. (Genesis 3:1-6)

When you read through the account above, what was the temptation of Satan? _____

_____

As you can see from the passage, the temptation of Satan was to eat from the tree of the knowledge of good and evil. Unfortunately, since most of us have heard this story countless times, we gloss over the deeper implications of what happened. The shocking thing to me about this story is that the original sin of man wasn't something major and horrific like rape or murder. It was something as tame and seemingly unimportant as eating a piece of fruit. Why was it so important to God that they never ate from a particular tree? And if it was so important, why plant the tree in the first place? Questions like these used to haunt me and even caused me to doubt the love and wisdom of God. And when I thought about, what seemed to me, the pettiness of the original sin, it made me think about the other commandments, especially those regarding my sexuality. The things in the world just seemed so pleasurable, and I could never understand why God would tell us we couldn't do things that were so much fun.

But in the middle of my doubts, I missed the obvious fact that I was falling for the same temptation of the serpent, and I was missing the point of God's commands. You see, when God created human beings, He didn't create us to merely serve Him but to be in a love relationship with Him. And while love will always include service, service is not the basis for love, trust is. Genuine love requires deep intimacy and therefore deep vulnerability, and in order to do that with someone there has to be genuine trust. The Bible says that mankind was naked and unashamed before both God and each other, signifying that we had the very thing that all of us truly want in our relationships: total vulnerability with total acceptance and love.

The point of the tree was not about mere obedience; God had already filled His creation with countless things in nature that bowed to His every whim without question. The tree was about trust. It was God trusting humanity by giving us a command that we had the power to keep or break, and humanity trusting God by keeping His command and believing that He had our best interests in mind.

Look at the name of the tree: the tree of the knowledge of good and evil. Before the fall, Adam and Eve knew what good and evil were by the Word of God alone. But Satan destroyed our trust in God's spoken word by attacking His character. In essence, Satan was asking, "How do you really know that God is correct when He tells you what is right and what is wrong? God is lying to you and trying to keep you from real pleasure; you should be like God and determine what is good and evil for yourselves." Listen to Satan's actual words and you will see this: "Did God really say?... 'You will not surely die. For God knows that in the day you eat of it your eyes will be opened'?"

Do you see what he was doing? He cast doubt on God's character and motives by subtly suggesting that God is a liar, and that He was withholding true pleasure from them.

Please read and comment on a quote from C.S. Lewis in his book *Mere Christianity:*

> *What Satan put into the heads of our remote ancestors was the idea that they could 'be like gods'—could set up on their own as if they had created themselves—be their own masters—invent some sort of happiness for themselves outside God, apart from God. And out of that hopeless attempt has come nearly all that we call human history—money, poverty, ambition, war, prostitution, classes, empires, slavery—the long terrible story of man trying to find something other than God which will make him happy... God cannot give us a happiness and peace apart from Himself, because it is not there. There is no such thing.*

Because of this initial fall, our default setting is to doubt God. For example, when people use the Word sin we think of something that is pleasurable but is unfortunately forbidden. That's why we title things like Las Vegas "Sin City." We aren't using that terminology because we think of that city as dangerous, but instead we see it as tantalizing and seductive. At the center of our hearts, we believe that true pleasure and satisfaction are found outside the commands of God not within them. It is because of this that I used to think of a relationship with God as an absence of true pleasure. As a result, I followed God out of obligation and fear. However, the more I followed God, the more miserable I felt. As a matter of fact, whenever I read in the Bible that something was wrong, it was immediately more appealing to me. And I know from the record of people in the Bible that I'm not alone.

> *What shall we say then? Is the law sin? Certainly not! On the contrary, I would not have known sin except through the law. For I would not have known covetousness unless the law had said, "You shall not covet." But sin, taking opportunity by the commandment, produced in me all manner of evil desire. For apart from the law sin was dead.* (Romans 7:7-8)

Even Paul says that his sinful nature lusted after what the law forbade him to do. This shows the truth of the fall. We are naturally predisposed to believe that God is withholding true happiness and pleasure from us. And so, even if we do keep His commandments, it can produce in us greater lust, pride, and even resentment towards God.

Have you noticed that this is true for you too? _____

The truly tragic thing about this is that the greatest and most beautiful pleasure is found in God Himself; not in what God can do for you but in Him alone. When I reflect on my own relationship with God, I realize that most of the time I follow God for what He can do for me and not because He Himself is worthy. I demand that He fix my problem with porn, help my marriage, heal my body, protect my relationships, etc. And when He doesn't answer those prayers, I become bitter with Him. This shows my supreme lack of trust in God. I, like Adam and Eve before me, don't believe that God is all that I need, that His commandments are all for my good and betterment, and that His decisions for my life really are for the best. I believe that I must dig out for myself my own joy and happiness apart from God.

> *And now, Israel, what does the LORD your God require of you, but to fear the LORD your God, to walk in all His ways <u>and to love Him</u>, to serve the LORD your God with all your heart and with all your soul, and to keep the commandments of the LORD and His statutes which I command you today <u>for your good</u>?* (Deuteronomy 10:12-13)

Do you struggle believing that God's commandments are good and pleasurable for you? _____

_____

> *And we know that <u>all things</u> work together for good to those who love God, to those who are called according to His purpose. For whom He foreknew, He also predestined to be conformed to the image of His Son, that He might be the firstborn among many brethren.* (Romans 8:28-29)

Do you struggle trusting in God's will for your life, especially when His will for you includes suffering?

_____

_____

_____

And the results of our sin go even deeper than all of this. Not only does our doubt in God's word and character impact our peace and happiness because we rebel against His good commandments for us, but we have also lost trust in our value as human beings. Our value was determined by God. He alone declared us "good" in the beginning, and we always trusted His Word and His love, which gave us an unshakable foundation of self-worth that enabled Adam and Eve to be naked with no shame. But after the fall, they immediately became ashamed and insecure. We no longer trusted God's word for our value and worth, so we had cover our own shame in order to give ourselves a new sense of worth.

Most of the sin in our lives is done in order to cover this horrible feeling of inadequacy in us and to make us feel "worthy." We will talk more about this as we get into more specific sins, but for all of us most of our sin issues stem from this insecurity. Maybe you find your worth and value through your looks or your talents, so you struggle with vanity. Or maybe you find that worth in your job, so you struggle with greed. Or you find all your value in your relationships, so you struggle with sexual lust. But no matter what, all of these pursuits are found in a deep well of insecurity and self-doubt. No matter how much we strive, our insecurities will never fully go away. If we continue in this pattern, those insecurities will always be there because the only rest that exists for us is found in the affirmation and love of our Father. However, through the fall we all turned from the one source of validation that could have given us rest and we turned to coverings that could never silence our guilt and shame.

Have you seen this insecurity alive in your life? _____

_____

These insecurities also isolate us and keep us from the joys and freedoms of confession and accountability not just with God, but with other believers.

> *Confess your trespasses to one another, and pray for one another, that you may be healed. The effective, fervent prayer of a righteous man avails much.* (James 5:16)

It has unfortunately become more important in church to appear good than to actually be good. Because of this, we miss out on the joys and strengths of being vulnerable without shame. I remember coming to church for years and feeling completely isolated and alone in my struggles. So even though I looked happy at church, I didn't dare confess my struggles for fear of being judged. And so my shame isolated me from other believers and made me feel more alone at church than anywhere else. But the intent of God in creating the church was not to assemble a group of people together to be fake and pretend to be holy, but instead to bring us together so that we might be real and help each other towards holiness in God. We have fallen a long way from the comfort of Eden where Adam and Eve were so convinced of their beauty in their Father's eyes that they could be vulnerable without shame. Now we are so convinced of our ugliness that we are terrified of vulnerability, and so we attempt to cover up our faults and hide from our failures. But all this does is fill the church with hypocrisy, grow our shame, and keep us from experiencing growth and freedom in Christ.

Can you relate to this shame and isolation? _____

_____

_____

So what is the solution to this trust issue? Unfortunately, a trust issue like this can never be healed through works. If I don't trust someone, serving them certainly won't help at all. Many Christians try their best to serve God, but never realize the source of their problems is their distrust of God. For years I tried to get free from porn, but while I was trying to stop, my craving for porn increased even more and my love for God continued to shrink. If you are trying to stop any sin without first confronting this issue, your fight will bring you further from God not closer. You see, the only way to build trust with another person is to demonstrate faithfulness. Not surprisingly, the issue of trust was one of the central missions of Jesus' first coming. While He did come to pay the debt we could never pay, one of the major reasons He came was to demonstrate supreme faithfulness and love toward mankind in order to set us free from our doubts and teach us to trust God again.

Jesus lived a life submitted completely to the commandments of God, even when those commandments cost Him His very life. And yet, in spite of all of His suffering, He was the most joyous person that ever lived. By doing this, Jesus was able to demonstrate to us that the joy of God is so supreme that even in the midst of the most intense suffering, following God is still better than any pleasure that is apart from God. Even though Moses didn't have this demonstrated to him through Christ, he was able to see this truth in his own life:

> *By faith Moses, when he became of age, refused to be called the son of Pharaoh's daughter, <u>choosing rather to suffer affliction</u> with the people of God than to enjoy <u>the passing pleasures of sin</u>, esteeming the reproach of Christ <u>greater riches than the treasures in Egypt</u>; for he looked to the reward.* (Hebrews 11:24-26)

In the cross we can trust in the love of God. Knowing that God didn't just tell us that He loved us, but He showed us His love at the cost of His own life. And because Jesus died for us in the midst of our sins, we can trust that even when we are falling to sin, God's love for us remains. Through the cross we as Christians have an unshakable foundation in the love God has for us.

> *Very rarely will anyone die for a righteous person, though for a good person someone might possibly dare to die. But God demonstrates his own love for us in this: While we were still sinners, Christ died for us. Since we have now been justified by his blood, how much more shall we be saved from God's wrath through him!* (Romans 5:7-9 NIV)

Finally, though more painful than anything we will ever experience, the cross of Jesus was purposed and fashioned by God for the supreme glory of Jesus and the salvation of all who would come to Him. This shows us that even in suffering, God is working out His good purposes, and we can trust Him because He chose not to be immune to our pain.

What, then, shall we say in response to these things? If God is for us, who can be against us? He who did not spare his own Son, but gave Him up for us all—how will He not also, along with Him, graciously give us all things? (Romans 8:31-32 NIV)

Can you see that God is worthy of your trust? _____

Please read through and comment on this quote from John Stott:

> *For the essence of sin is man substituting himself for God [Gen. 3:1-7], while the essence of salvation is God substituting Himself for man [2 Cor. 5:21]. Man asserts himself against God and puts himself where only God deserves to be; God sacrifices Himself for man and puts Himself where only man deserves to be.*

_____

_____

_____

Because our doubt in God is the source of our sin, it is faith alone that saves us and pleases our Creator.

> *Abram believed the LORD, and he credited it to him as righteousness.* (Genesis 15:6)

> *But without faith it is impossible to please Him, for he who comes to God must believe that He is, and that He is a rewarder of those who diligently seek Him.* (Hebrews 11:6)

Many people in our culture misunderstand this issue of faith and foolishly demand for God to show Himself so they can believe in Him. But when they do this, they are missing the point. Our original sin wasn't doubting the existence of God but the character and the Word of God. Believing that God exists doesn't mean you trust in Him or love Him. James warns us in James 2:19, "You believe there is one God, you do well, the demons believe and tremble." James is saying that it is a basic thing to believe in His existence because even the demons do and they tremble!

God doesn't just want our obedience and basic belief in His existence. God desires to have a loving relationship with us built on trust. If we lack this faith in God, especially in His love for us, all of our works are going to be for the purpose of earning our place with Him. This kind of legalistic worship is despised by God because it only serves to puff up our egos and has nothing to do with truly loving Him. If you don't first trust God and accept His salvation for yourself by faith alone, then all of your works will be built on your own insecurity and not on the love of God.

This legalism will steal all of your love and adoration for God and bring you into a joyless service of God that is built on fear. It's unbearable to be in the presence of someone that we feel is constantly judging us, and most of us see God in this way. We think that He is sitting on His throne looking down and demanding that we live up to His standards or else He will crush us in His wrath.

There is no fear in love; but perfect love casts out fear, because fear involves torment. But he who fears has not been made perfect in love. We love Him because He first loved us. (1 John 4:18-19)

God loves us and delights in us in spite of our sins not because of our works. Therefore, it is only when we accept this by faith that we will be moved to want to serve God out of love and joy. But we must always remember that it is our faith that saves us not our works. Read and comment on this quote from Richard Lovelace:

"It is an item of faith that we are children of God; there is plenty of experience in us against it. The faith that surmounts this evidence and that is able to warm itself at the fire of God's love, instead of having to steal love and self-acceptance from other sources, is actually the root of holiness... We are not saved by the love we exercise, but by the love we trust."

_____

_____

_____

C.S. Lewis rightly said that faith is the key to every locked door in the Christian life. It is by our faith alone in what Jesus did for us that we are made right with God. It is by faith in God's worth and pleasure that we can leave our sin for the greater joy that is in Christ. It is faith in God's love for us that enables us to overcome our insecurities so that we will no longer strive for value in this world. It is by faith in the completed work of Christ that we can be free from all of our guilt, shame and regret from our past. It is by faith in the example of Jesus that we can learn to live lives that honor God in every way. It is by trusting God's sovereignty that we are able to experience peace in every circumstance. But this kind of faith that surmounts every issue in life is something that takes lots and lots of time to grow. This is one of the biggest things we will wrestle with throughout our lives. None of us will achieve perfect faith this side of heaven. Even though we are saved and believe in the loving character of God to some extent, there are always those parts of us that still doubt God's love and goodness.

This issue of faith is something that God is working on in all of our hearts, and He alone will finish this work. But there are some practical tools that God has given us that can help us grow in this area. For one thing we can read God's word and see His faithfulness there:

So then faith comes by hearing, and hearing by the Word of God. (Romans 10:17)

As previously mentioned, faith can only be grown through seeing faithfulness. God's word shows us the beauty of His faithfulness and love towards His people throughout history. As we see God's faithfulness at work in the Bible, we can also reflect on God's faithfulness in our own lives. It is such a vital thing for us to spend time in prayer thanking God for His faithfulness towards us. If we don't do this, our default setting is to complain about God and forget all of His goodness. But when we spend time reflecting on God's goodness towards us in our own lives, and we spend time reading about God's faithfulness in His Word, our minds will be renewed and our trust and love for God will grow.

21

But we all, with unveiled face, beholding as in a mirror the glory of the Lord, are being transformed into the same image from glory to glory, just as by the Spirit of the Lord. (2 Corinthians 3:18)

This concept might seem really odd to us, but it is only when we spend time beholding the glory of God that we can grow in our faith for Him and, by doing this, be transformed to be more and more like Him.

It is also important that when we have doubts, we need to be honest about them with God and ask Him to help us with our faith. God is the only One who can give us faith. So when we hide our doubts out of shame, not only does this demonstrate our lack of trust in His love, but it also alienates us from the only One who can actually help us with our problems. We need to learn to pray just as the man in Mark 9:24 prayed: "Immediately the boy's father exclaimed, 'I do believe; help me overcome my unbelief!'" (NIV).

I love this prayer because sometimes I can be discouraged by my lack of faith and believe that I have no faith at all, and other times I can be arrogant and believe that I have perfect faith. But this prayer shows us the truth that while I have some faith towards God, it isn't perfect and it needs to grow. When we don't pray like this, our doubts and distrust will only grow. But when we confess this to God and ask for help, He will be faithful to continuously grow our faith in Him.

Take this time to reflect on your faith toward God and pray to Him.

As we wrap up this lesson, remember it isn't our perfect faith that saves us but God's perfect faithfulness. The source of our eternal salvation from hell is faith in God, and the source of our salvation from all of our particular sins is that same faith. Over time our faith will become richer and fuller as we learn to be honest with God and meditate on His love for us. As our faith and love for God grow, our works should organically grow with them. The issue that we get into as Christians is that we get the cart before the horse, focusing on works as a means to faith and love, and not faith and love as a foundation for works. Next, we will talk about the root of our sin, which is our pride and selfishness, but let's end this lesson by reflecting on a quote from pastor Timothy Keller's book on prayer: "You are in Christ. You are adopted into the Father's family. You have the very divine life in you, the Holy Spirit. You are loved and accepted in Christ. You know about these things, and yet at another level you don't know them, you don't grasp them. You are still dogged by your bad habits, often anxious or bored or discouraged or angry. You may have many specific problems and issues that need to be faced and dealt with through various specific means. Yet the root problem of them all is that you are rich in Christ but nevertheless living poor."

For by grace you have been saved through faith, and that not of yourselves; it is the gift of God, not of works, lest anyone should boast. For we are His workmanship, created in Christ Jesus for good works, which God prepared beforehand that we should walk in them. (Ephesians 2:8-10

THE ROOT OF SIN

God resists the proud, but gives grace to the humble. (James 4:6)

Now we are going to study the sin of pride, which according to the Bible is the root of all of our sin issues and the number one sin that separates us from God. Once again, this was a shocking truth for me. I thought certainly the Bible would say that sexual sin was the worst sin you could commit. I never thought that pride would be the central sin issue. But when you look through the Bible, this is the truth that we see. The above quote from James is just one example of a myriad of passages that speak of God's hatred toward pride. When you look at the ministry of Jesus, this truth is played out for us in amazing clarity. Jesus seemed more than happy to hang out with thieves, liars, drunks, prostitutes, racists, and even murderers. And while He did challenge all these people to change, it is astounding to me that the only people that He rejected were the proud. Take a look at this story and answer the following questions: What was it that justified the tax collector, and what alienated the Pharisee?

Also He spoke this parable to some who trusted in themselves that they were righteous, and despised others:

> *Two men went up to the temple to pray, one a Pharisee and the other a tax collector. The Pharisee stood and prayed thus with himself, "God, I thank You that I am not like other men—extortioners, unjust, adulterers, or even as this tax collector. I fast twice a week; I give tithes of all that I possess." And the tax collector, standing afar off, would not so much as raise his eyes to heaven, but beat his breast, saying, "God, be merciful to me a sinner!" I tell you, this man went down to his house justified rather than the other; for <u>everyone who exalts himself will be humbled, and he who humbles himself will be exalted.</u>* (Luke 18:9-14)

_____

_____

_____

It was the sin of pride that separated this Pharisee from God, while the wicked and sinful tax collector was received and forgiven because of his humility and honesty. From this we can see that men like C.S. Lewis were right when they said things such as, " ...the essential vice, the utmost evil, is pride. Unchastity, anger, greed, drunkenness, and all that are mere flea bites in comparison: it was through pride that the devil became the devil: pride leads to every other vice: it is the complete anti-God state of mind."

But when we see this, we have to ask the question—why is pride the worst sin and the root of all my other sins? In order to understand this, we have to go back to Genesis 1-2 and see God's original intent for mankind. When God created man in Genesis, He said that He made us in His image and likeness. This doesn't signify that we look like God, but instead it shows us our ultimate purpose and meaning for existence. When an artist makes a sculpture in someone's image, it doesn't mean that the sculpture is exactly like that person. It means that the artist formed the sculpture for a specific purpose: to reflect part of that person's nature and being to others. Take the Lincoln Memorial for example. When we look at that memorial, we aren't supposed to assume that Abraham Lincoln was 20 feet tall and made of marble. Instead, when we look at it, we see that just like this statue, Lincoln himself was larger than life. It is made out of marble to show that he was a hard man when he needed to be, and yet he is seated depicting that he wasn't a bloodthirsty warrior but was first and foremost a diplomat. You see, when something is made in the image and likeness of someone else, we can see pieces of that person's character and likeness by looking at the image.

God is awesome and completely beyond our understanding, so in His creation He designed things to reflect His nature and being. When we look at the vastness of space we see the greatness of God; when we see the power of a hurricane we see might of God; when we see the brightness of the sun we see the majesty and the glory of God. Human beings are the peak of His good creation, meaning that in us is the greatest reflection of God's being and glory.

We were created expressly by God to bring Him glory in a way that is unique to us over any other created thing. Unlike the rest of creation, we have increased abilities to love, think, reason, have community, exercise authority, and create. We also have free will, which enables us to choose to follow God as opposed to the rest of the creation that obeys out of necessity. All of these blessings and abilities were given to us by God so that we could live to show His glory. But in the fall, we rejected that purpose and chose to live for ourselves rather than for God.

What we failed to realize though was that there was a heavy price for rejecting our intended purpose. We are not only rejecting our greatest potential by doing this, but we are damaging ourselves by misusing that which God had intended for other purposes. A simpler example of this would be a car. Cars were designed to function in a specific way and for a specific purpose. If I use my car in the proper way and for the proper purpose, my car will run beautifully and reach its full potential as it fulfills its intended purpose. But if I decide that I know better than the creators of that car and start putting the wrong type of fuel in it or try to drive it through water, I will ruin that car. We were created by God to serve a specific purpose, but in the fall we rejected that purpose and chose to live for ourselves. However, by doing this, we went against our own design. So we are not only damaging ourselves, but we are denying ourselves the deepest source of fulfillment and joy.

God is the greatest being in existence. Therefore, there is no higher purpose in all of creation than glorifying Him. God didn't create us for His glory because He is arrogant or mean. He did this because He loves us and wants the best for us, and there is nothing greater that we could possibly live for than Him. But in our pride, we thought that living for ourselves was better. We foolishly thought that we knew better than God and so we cut ourselves off from the only pursuit that would actually satisfy us, and sentenced ourselves to a life away from our true purpose.

This is why all other sins come from pride itself. In denying God, we created a hole in ourselves that only He could fill. Now we spend our lives trying to fill that vacuum with worldly pleasures, but we never quite find what we are looking for. We may all be bent toward sin in different ways and to different degrees, but whether you are trying to find your value in your looks, sexuality, wealth, relationships, or pleasure, unless God does a work in our hearts to turn us away from our own self interests and towards our intended purpose of glorifying Him, we won't see any real victory in our fight against sin.

Please read and comment on the following passage in James 4:1-4, NIV:

> What causes fights and quarrels among you? Don't they come from your desires that battle within you? You desire but do not have, so you kill. You covet but you cannot get what you want, so you quarrel and fight. You do not have because you do not ask God. When you ask, you do not receive, because you ask with wrong motives, that you may spend what you get on your pleasures. You adulterous people, don't you know that friendship with the world means enmity against God? Therefore, anyone who chooses to be a friend of the world becomes an enemy of God.

_____

_____

_____

What James tells us here is that all of the issues that we have in our lives come from our own desires that war within us. It is our pride and selfishness that lead us towards all the errors and sins that we commit every day. His rebuke for us is that we are trying to find our own pleasure through sin when all we would have to do is ask God and find that our true joy and pleasure are freely given to us in a relationship with Him. But James also recognizes that we are so proud that even when we come to God, we might be coming to Him to make Him our servant rather than our master. We are so twisted in our culture today that we totally miss this danger, and we actually believe that God's ultimate purpose in the universe is to serve us. When we look at the Christian culture today, it is astounding that we have huge branches of Christianity given over to what we call "the prosperity gospel." This is a belief that teaches that God's whole purpose in our lives is to make us happy and bless us materially. So when we want a good marriage, an amazing career, help with our finances, better health, or any other physical blessing, we suddenly turn to God with an expectation that He ought to help us with these things. And so at best, we receive the blessing we want, turning God into a genie that we use for our own ends. At worst, we don't receive the blessing we want, and so we blame God and turn away from Him. Either way, with this belief system, we follow God not because we love Him, but in order to get from Him what we really want.

But this belief system runs so contrary to what we see in the Bible. Throughout the Bible, the constant message is that all of creation is for the glory of God not for human prosperity. There is one section in particular in John 9 where Jesus comes across a man that was born blind. When He was asked why this man was born blind, He responded by saying that the man was born blind so that "the works of God should be revealed in him." In our pride we reject this response. We believe that either that man deserved his blindness or that God was being unjust. At our core, we think that life is about what is good for us not what is honoring to God. We can't accept that God would allow suffering and hardship into our lives, and so we try different prayers and techniques to get blessings and avoid trials. But this teaching won't ever bring us to the place where we seek God because He alone is worthy. This teaching feeds our pride and convinces us more and more that our lives are all about us and not about God. This belief blinds us from the glory of God and keeps us from seeing that God is so worthy, that even if we lost every blessing and suffered the very tragedy that we fear the most, God would be enough for us. Always remember that the men and women in the Bible who most sought their own desires ended up being the most miserable, and the men and women that most sought the glory of God, even when His glory cost them dearly, were the most joyous people who ever lived.

> *Jesus said: He who finds his life will lose it, and he who loses his life <u>for My sake</u> will find it.* (Matthew 10:39)

Have you seen yourself follow God for what He can do for you? _____

_____

_____

The root of our pride runs so deep that even when we are earnestly trying to seek God and do the right thing, we are still consumed by our own selfishness. Martin Luther used to spend 6 hours every day confessing sins to his priest, until one day his priest told him he couldn't take it anymore, that he was being far too sensitive. But Luther responded famously by saying that he was, "curved in on himself." He said that he used to live only for himself in sin, but now that he had come to God, he had become a monk and denied himself all of his past pleasures only to find that he did this because he reveled in the praise he got from man. He read the Bible, but now he felt superior as a result. He gave to the poor, all the while judging those who didn't. He resisted sin, but felt that God loved him more than other people because of his own righteousness. Luther accepted the truth that so many of us are determined not to see, that we are all eaten up by our pride and selfishness. And this is so rooted in us, that even if we try to do right things, it is ultimately for selfish purposes. So while we might become outwardly better people, unless we are addressing pride, this sin issue is only getting worse as a result of our efforts.

Pride Is Like A Spiritual Cancer

Please read and comment on this quote from C.S. Lewis: "Pride can often be used to beat down the simpler vices. Teachers, in fact, often appeal to a boy's pride, or, as they call it, his self-respect, to make him behave decently: many a man has overcome cowardice, or lust, or ill-temper, by learning to think that they are beneath his dignity—that is, by pride. The devil laughs. He is perfectly content to see you becoming chaste and brave and self-controlled provided, all the time, he is setting up in you the dictatorship of pride—just as he would be quite content to see your cold cured if he was allowed, in return, to give you cancer. For pride is spiritual cancer: it eats up the very possibility of love, or contentment, or even common sense."

_____

_____

_____

You see, all of our sins, whether they are sexual or not, are rooted in pride because we are seeking our own desires above God and others. But even when we are trying to get free from sin, we are so rooted in pride that all of our noble efforts are corrupt and ultimately selfish. You see I can resist the sin of vanity by telling myself that I don't care what other people think of me. But in doing so I may defeat vanity, but only by elevating my opinions above everyone else's. I can beat my sexual sin, my eating problems, my substance abuse, my anger... all by telling myself that these things are disgusting and beneath me, or by seeing these sins as obstacles to my goals of doing well at school, or having a successful career, or having a good marriage...But by doing so I am appealing to my own desires and self respect. Which means that even in my moral pursuits I can be feeding my pride.

And the scariest part of this is, that while our pride is bad enough when it is feeding our other sins, the worst thing that can possibly happen to us is not that we would be stuck in our outward sins, but that we would free ourselves from our outward sins, only to be consumed with pride. Look at the pharisees. These were righteous and holy men, they weren't committing sexual sin, or getting drunk, or robbing people... They were men who were reading, memorizing, and even teaching the Scriptures , they tithed, fasted, and shared their faith consistently and were ministers in their communities. And yet, Jesus called them whitewashed tombs, meaning that they were beautiful on the outside, but were only filled with death on the inside. Jesus even had the audacity to say to the self-righteous pharisees: "..the tax collectors and the prostitutes are entering the kingdom of God ahead of you (NLT)."

This is so unbelievable for us to read. Prostitutes are people who are actively engaging in sexual sin on a daily basis and the tax collectors in His day were thieves and traitors to their fellow Jews. Jesus intentionally picked out the two most offensive types of sinners in His day and said to the proud pharisees, "As bad as they are, you are far worse." Because as bad as they were, at least they were humble enough to realize they needed help, the pharisees thought they were good as is.

For years I was so frustrated at God for not delivering me from my struggles with porn, but now I see that my worst struggle wasn't my sexual sin, but my pride. I am so proud and arrogant that even in the midst of my struggles with porn, I was constantly judging everyone around me whom I considered "worse sinners." I would say to myself, "Yeah, I view porn but at least I'm not as bad as the people who commit adultery, or get drunk, or abuse their kids…" I was just like the Pharisee in the first passage we read at the beginning of the lesson, boasting in my own accomplishments and comparing myself to people I saw as being worse than me. And to top it all off, I didn't want freedom from porn so that I could better honor God. I wanted freedom from porn because I was worried that other people would find out about my struggle, because I thought that doing this was beneath me, because I thought that viewing porn would prevent me from having a successful marriage, and other self-centered reasons that had nothing to do with God. I was like a spoiled child, selfishly demanding that God would serve my interests, and when He didn't "come through" for me, I would become more bitter towards Him. If God would have removed all my struggles with sexual sin, I would have immediately stopped pursuing Him and become a complete pharisee. In other words, God would have saved me from my sexual sin, only to damn me to my pride.

Can you see how big an issue your pride is? _____

_____

When you look at pride this way, you see how subtle and deadly it really is. Please read and comment on this quote from Jonathan Edwards in his essay on spiritual pride: "Alas, how much pride the best have in their hearts! It is the worst part of the body of sin and death; the first sin that ever entered into the universe and the last that is rooted out. It is God's most stubborn enemy! Spiritual pride takes many forms and shapes, one under another, and encompasses the heart like the layers of an onion: when you pull off one, there is another underneath. Therefore, we have need to have the greatest watch imaginable over our hearts with respect to this matter and to cry most earnestly to the great Searcher of hearts for His help. He that trusts his own heart is a fool."

_____

_____

_____

Another problem with pride is that it keeps you foolish as it says in Proverbs 11:2: "When pride comes, then comes shame; but with the humble is wisdom."

Our pride refuses to admit when it's wrong and it refuses to admit that we need correction and change. And even if we can admit that we were wrong, we won't be able to see just how wrong we have been, or just how much we really need to change. It is your pride that keeps you in denial about your issues, that keeps you from asking for help even though you need it, that gets offended at advice from others, that cares so much about your reputation that you can't be honest with others, that keeps you from self reflection because you would rather believe that you are a good person than think through your issues.... It is ironic, your pride is what wants to learn and do better in these areas, but ultimately your pride keeps you from growing and learning. How can we possibly grow and learn if we can't admit our mistakes and receive correction?

Proverbs 12:1 tells us, "Whoever loves instruction loves knowledge, but he who hates correction is stupid" (NIV).

It's also possible for pride to affect us in a negative way, as opposed to positive. Sometimes we can struggle with pride in the common way of thinking that we are better than other people. But, sometimes our pride turns inward and we can think that we are worse than everyone else. When this happens we become massively insecure about who we are. And when someone offers us even the slightest correction we become severely wounded in our hearts. This will also keep us from gaining wisdom and changing because we become so obsessed with our own failure, and convinced of our own worthlessness that we won't have the courage or the hope to humbly receive correction and grow as a result. Instead we will just sulk in our depression and self-pity and become even more self absorbed than we were before. When we do this, we forget the joys of correction, and the love that our Father has for us that can actually change us and bring us to Him. We must always remember what the Bible teaches us:

> And have you forgotten the encouraging words God spoke to you as his children? He said, "My child, don't make light of the Lord's discipline, and don't give up when he corrects you. For the LORD disciplines those he loves, and he punishes each one he accepts as his child." As you endure this divine discipline, remember that God is treating you as his own children. Who ever heard of a child who is never disciplined by its father? (Hebrews 12:5-7 NLT)

Conviction and correction are never fun in the moment, but when our pride is out of the way, we can receive this correction and change as a result. But when pride clouds our judgment, it will make us more stubborn and arrogant, or more depressed and shame ridden. Either way, pride will keep us from true growth and wisdom. That is why it is an act of love that God corrects His children. He doesn't convict us of sin because He is horribly disappointed with us and wants to make us feel bad, He does this because He loves us too much to leave us in the sins that are killing us.

Before we move on, I do want to clarify something quickly. A question that someone could have while reading this is: But, there are a lot of proud people who are very smart and successful, so how can we say that pride will definitely make you foolish? This misunderstanding comes from a misunderstanding of the Word wisdom. Wisdom is not the same thing as knowledge, wisdom is the practical application of knowledge not just intellectually understanding something. It's the difference between reading a book on how to drive [knowledge], and then actually getting behind the wheel and practically learning how to drive for yourself [wisdom].

Because of this, there are many really smart people out there that are very foolish. There have been many very intelligent Christians who have known the Bible front to back, who could have long conversations about theology and morality, but haven't really applied any of that to their own lives. You see, our pride likes to keep things vague and philosophical, we don't like making things practical because when we start talking practically we begin to become convicted in how we are actually living. So you might be someone who is very smart, and has an incredible knowledge of the Bible, but this doesn't mean that you are actually applying the Bible in your life. The ultimate example of all of this, would be Solomon. Solomon wrote the Proverbs. He was so wise that people came from around the world to see his wisdom. And as long as he was applying that wisdom, he had a great life. But eventually, he became overcome by his own pride and arrogance and he started thinking that he actually knew better than God. Because of this, he began to ignore his own advice and he started breaking all of the laws that God had for His kings and eventually introduced idol worship to Israel. You see, knowing something is not the same as applying it. I have said some very profound things to other people in counseling and teaching, but then I can look at my own life and realize with shame that I haven't been doing what I just told someone else to do. We might be very smart, but our pride has kept us very foolish. We need to take the advice of James and not just be hearers of the Word, but doers as well.

Can you see how your pride has kept you foolish? _____

_____

Pride will also severely damage your relationships. Proverbs 13:10 tells us, "By pride comes nothing but strife, But with the well-advised is wisdom."

Pride makes everything about our own goals and desires. So as long as everyone around me is helping me towards what I want, I am happy, but the second someone becomes an obstacle to my goals, I become frustrated with them. A simple example is traffic, why am I so upset in traffic? It's because I have a goal to get somewhere, so I see everyone else as being in my way. And this is not just true for traffic, but it applies to every relationship in our lives. We get frustrated with friends and family members for not doing what we want them to and we blame them for our issues. And when fighting starts, pride keeps us from apologizing and admitting that we were wrong while we instead sulk in our bitterness and demand that other people apologize to us first. It also keeps us from trusting others. In pride we always assume that we are right, so we don't like putting our faith in other people or even God. Instead we choose to trust in our own instincts and strength, always believing that we know best. It seems so much easier and safer to be skeptical of others instead of being trusting and vulnerable, but this ultimately leaves us alone.

Proverbs 18:1-2 also says, "A man who isolates himself seeks his own desire; he rages against all wise judgment. A fool has no delight in understanding, but in expressing his own heart."

Pride is also the source of our jealousy. Desiring to look like other people, act like other people, have what other people have, wishing our spouses looked different, treated us differently... all stemming from our own selfish assessment of what would make us happy. It is this that breeds our discontentment with life, blaming those around us for our problems, and inflaming our lust for more. As we seek our own happiness at the expense of others, we never actually find it. It also makes us feel like we are in competition with everyone around us, constantly comparing our lives to others, always trying to be the best. And ultimately, when we make decisions to sin, even when those decisions hurt those around us, it shows us how selfish we really are. When push comes to shove, our desires are more important than the betterment of those we love.

Can you see how pride has hurt your relationships?_____

_____

Pride will also steal all of our joy. The reason for this is because pride is so self focused that it can only think about what it thinks it deserves. That means that when a proud person receives good things, they can't be thankful because they legitimately think that they earned it. And when bad things happen, the proud person is deeply disturbed because they think that life is being unfair. Because of this, the proud person will lash out at the people closest to them, blaming them, and most often, blaming God for all their problems because they can't possibly be to blame. In our pride we begin to expect praise, love, and service from those closest to us, and when we don't receive it, we become frustrated and bitter at those who we think are letting us down. As we talked about earlier, pride can also be a two edged sword as it causes us to be so self focused that we can slip into despair. This happens when pride turns in on itself, instead of thinking too highly of ourselves, we think too low. When this happens, we will not expect good things to come our way because we feel undeserving. And when good things do come we will think, "It's only a matter of time before I lose this too." And when bad things happen we think, "This is what I deserve."

Can you see how your pride has kept you from joy? _____

_____

Something else that we also have to be aware of is the effect of social media on our pride. Now, some older ministers talk about social media and the Internet as if they caused our issues with pride. And while they are wrong about that, social media has certainly amplified narcissism in our culture to previously unseen heights. Social media has made it easier than ever to make our lives completely about ourselves. We are constantly promoting ourselves, while seeking likes and followers for our accomplishments and endeavors. Because of this, we now have completely photo-shopped our lives, pretending to live a far better and more carefree existence than we actually have in reality. Now we have a source to constantly compare our lives with other peoples' in such an incessant way. This has made us far more covetous and selfish than ever before, all the while isolating us from any real and meaningful relationships built on vulnerability, love, and trust. Because we have the anonymity of talking through a website, as opposed to face to face conversation, people express themselves in the most aggressive and damaging ways. In short, while the Internet didn't create sin and brokenness, it is the ultimate tool for amplifying our pride, sexual lust, vanity, greed, anger, depression, laziness, and anxiety. And the truly tragic thing about this is never before have we had a more beautiful tool for loving others. We can be constantly connected with people around the world as we pray for them, encourage them, reach out to them, and help them in tangible ways. And while many of us do use the Internet for a lot of great purposes, in our pride we have twisted this powerful tool into something incredibly destructive. As Christians, we shouldn't be seeking to shut down the Internet, because even without it we are still fallen and horribly proud. But we should be willing to address the real issue in our hearts so that we can use this powerful tool for God's glory.

Can you see how social media can amplify our issues with sin? _____

_____

_____

Finally, pride will keep us from God for two main reasons. Number one, pride is always in competition with others, that is why we are constantly comparing ourselves with other people. And if there is one thing that pride hates, it is to be in the presence of someone truly greater than itself. God is a being who is ultimately greater than us in every way, so the pride in us will naturally hate to be in His presence.

> *For the wicked boasts of his heart's desire; he blesses the greedy and renounces the LORD. The wicked in his proud countenance does not seek God; God is in none of his thoughts.* (Psalm 10:4)

Read and comment on this quote from C.S. Lewis: "As long as you are proud you cannot know God. A proud man is always looking down on things and people: and, of course as long as you are looking down, you cannot see something that is above you. This raises a terrible question. How is it that people who are quite obviously eaten up with pride can say they believe in God and appear to themselves very religious? I am afraid it means they are worshiping an imaginary God. They theoretically admit themselves to be nothing in the presence of this phantom God, but are really all the time imagining how He approves of them and thinks them far better than ordinary people."

_____

_____

_____

Pride also hates to obey. We tell ourselves that we are obedient toward God, but we are actually only obedient to what we think is proper. A simple example in my life is when I am driving on the road, I have no problem keeping the speed limit as long as I agree with the speed limit. But, if I think that the speed limit isn't fair, I justify my speeding by telling myself, "That speed limit is for people who don't know how to drive like me..." And I do the same thing in my relationship with God. For years I would just gloss over all the many passages in the Bible that told me to confess my sins to other believers. I would come up with so many different excuses for why that didn't apply to me, even quoting and citing scripture to feel "holy" while I ignored advice from God. I would say things like, "God is my accountability partner, I don't need to tell anyone else..." or, "My struggle isn't that big of a deal, plus I'll never do it again so there is no reason to tell anyone else..." These are just a few examples, but my walk with God is filled with self-justification and flat out ignoring my Father's words. Because I follow certain commands, I think I am obedient, when in reality I am burdened under my pride.

This is an issue that is especially prevalent in our culture today. We come to the Bible not out of humility to hear God, instead we come to it like its a self-help book that is supposed to show us better solutions to our problems. I have had countless conversations with students over the years about commands in the Bible. They say things like, "I know that marriage is important, but if I really love someone and I am committed to them, do we still have to wait for marriage to have sex?" Or, "I know the Bible says not to be unequally yoked with a non-believer, but we have such a good relationship and we have so many shared values does it really matter?" Or, "I know the Bible talks about homosexuality, but this is more for people who weren't committed in same sex relationships, why can't I have this relationship if I intend to walk in love?" Or, "Why can't I get drunk or high for fun if I make sure to stay safe?" There are many more questions in this same vein, but I hope you see the underlying issue in all of these questions. All of these questions assume that the commands of God are only given for our benefit, and the only time I am doing something wrong is if I am doing something physically harmful to myself or others. To put it another way, these questions are all centered around pride; they aren't concerned with God's glory, but instead with self-benefit. Now it is true that all the commands of God are good for us in the long run, but they won't necessarily be immediately beneficial for us. We need to remember that our ultimate good isn't found in our physical benefit, but in God's glory.

God wants us to follow His commands because of our love for Him, not because His commands are convenient for us. I remember as a kid, my parents would give me all sorts of commands that I disagreed with. As I got older I would pester my parents with constant questions of why. You see, in my pride, I assumed that I knew better than my parents and I was so selfish that if what my parents were asking of me didn't line up with my own views for what was good for me, I would rebel. My parents used to answer one or two of my "why" questions, but after a time, they would just say, "Do it because I said so." This answer used to infuriate me because I thought that this answer was a cop-out and that they must not have a good reason for what they were telling me. Whenever they did this, I would see my parents as stubborn and oppressive. But now looking back I understand that answer. My parents were hurt by my "why" questions because when I asked them "why," it showed first that I didn't trust them, and second it showed that I would only listen to them if it made sense to me. They wanted me to be obedient because I loved and respected them. Our walk with God is the same way. In our pride we demand to know why God has asked us to do certain things, but when we do this we demonstrate that we don't trust God. Often we express that we are so self absorbed, we won't follow God unless it benefits us.

Can you see how you are disobedient in your pride? _____

_____

_____

The second reason why pride keeps us from God is that in our pride, whether we think too highly of ourselves or too low of ourselves, we will reject the message of the gospel. People who think too highly of themselves can easily accept the fact that God loves them and died for them, but will struggle greatly with the fact that they need a Savior. We would like to believe that God sent Jesus mainly for other people and that we do just fine on our own, but we appreciate the assist. We can't abide in the truth that we are so fallen and sinful, that without God saving us, we can never make it to heaven. None of our good deeds could get us there and therefore we are in the same boat spiritually as everyone else. The person that thinks too low of himself, finds it easy to believe they are a sinner, but won't be able to accept that they are loved by God and forgiven. Someone like this might say, "I know that God forgives me, but I can never forgive myself." I used to think that this was humility, but then I realized that it was just pride inverted. I was valuing my perspective about my life over God's. If God loves me and has forgiven me, I am not being holy and righteous by rejecting that, I am being intensely proud.

Read and comment on Habakkuk 2:4-5:

> Behold _the proud_, his soul is not upright in him; But the just shall live by his faith. Indeed, because he transgresses by wine, he is a proud man, and he does not stay at home. Because he enlarges his desire as hell, and he is like death, and cannot be satisfied, he gathers to himself all nations and heaps up for himself all peoples.

———————————————————————————————

———————————————————————————————

So what is the solution, how can we escape from pride? Unfortunately, pride is rooted so deep in the human heart, that there will always be a battle between us and pride as long as we live. In heaven we have the glorious hope of being fully delivered from sin. Here on earth we get the down payment as God does begin to remove sin from us in this life. But the first thing that we have to do in order to begin to be freed from our pride is admit to ourselves and to God that we are proud. Unless you can do that, pride is keeping you blinded to its presence and you won't make any headway. If you are reading this and honestly believe that you are humble and don't really struggle with pride, I suggest that you are so consumed by pride that you can't see your own faults. In which case, by faith you must admit that you are far more proud than you understand and begin to consistently pray that God would reveal your pride to you so that you can be humbled before Him.

Also, only God has the power to uproot our pride, and simply admitting this to Him is a crucial step toward crushing pride because our pride hates to admit our helplessness.

> _"Blessed are the poor in spirit, for theirs is the kingdom of heaven."_ (Matthew 5:3)

Next, it is important to confess sin to other Christians, read this quote from Dietrich Bonhoeffer in his book Life Together and comment below: "The root of all sin is pride, superbia. I want to be my own law, I have a right to my self, my hatred and my desires, my life and my death. The mind and flesh of man are set on fire by pride; for it is precisely in his wickedness that a man wants to be God. Confession in the presence of a brother is the profoundest kind of humiliation. It hurts, it cuts a man down, it is a dreadful blow to pride. To stand there before a brother as a sinner is an ignominy that is almost unbearable. In the confession of concrete sins the old man dies a painful, shameful death before the eyes of a brother. Because this humiliation is so hard we continually scheme to evade confessing to a brother. Our eyes are so blinded that they no longer see the promise and glory in such abasement."

———————————————————————————————

———————————————————————————————

———————————————————————————————

We also must pursue God. I know that sounds basic, but it is so crucially important. We are beings obsessed with our own importance, and simply thinking to ourselves, "pride is wrong," will never be enough to destroy that supreme self focus. Our hearts must be captured by a greater beauty. We must, through the Spirit, begin to grab ahold of the supreme worthiness and beauty of our God so that we begin to focus more on Him, and less on ourselves. This happens through the simple things that we already know to do as Christians: praying to God, reading His Word, worshiping and adoring Him, and fellowshipping with other believers. Our pride will want a more grand solution that will breed faster results, but that is precisely why pursuing God has to be like this. In our pride we want to pursue God in order to be delivered from our problems, but we need to be pursuing God because of who He is. God wants a real, loving relationship with us. He doesn't want to just be our "problem solver." And all true loving relationships are built on faithfulness and simplicity. No one loves their spouse because of one grand gesture, or one moment of happiness. They love their spouse because of the daily conversations, affirmation, and quality time that is spent together. The grand gestures and moments of passionate joy will come out of this consistency, but they are not the source. When we pursue God, we need to know that we aren't doing this just to have some intense experience, or because we need help with an issue; we are, instead, supposed to pursue God for His sake and glory. In humility we need to learn to daily pursue God, faithfully, because of His worthiness and not for what He can give to us.

This is also why trust in God must be the foundation. One of the primary reasons for our self focus is our fear and our need to feel in control of our own lives. But the more we try to stay in control of things, the more out of control we will feel. It is only in the face of the supreme love and sovereignty of our God, that we can trust Him with our life and discover peace.

We must desire to see God as He truly is, which is terrifying because in His presence we will see ourselves as we truly are. As we get closer to Him, we will become like Isaiah in Isaiah 6, and we will cry out, "I am undone!" For in the presence of God, we see just how unlike Him we really are. We naturally want to distance ourselves from God so that we can feel good about ourselves in comparison to other people. But we can never be freed from our pride until we are humbled in the reality of the greatness of God. And when we do this, it won't lead us to despair, but glorious hope as we learn to receive God's love. We truly are nothing in His presence, but the only One in the universe whose opinion really matters, loved you enough to die for you while you were at your worst. And God not only died for you, but He lives in you, delights in you, and desires to spend eternity with you. Yes, the Bible does say that you are more sinful than your pride would like to see, but you are also more loved than your despair could ever believe. Always remember, as C.S. Lewis famously put it, "humility isn't thinking less of yourself, but thinking of yourself less."

In thinking of ourselves less, we can finally let go of what we think we deserve, and discover a vital truth:

> *...And what do you have that you did not receive? Now if you did indeed receive it, why do you boast as if you had not received it?* (1 Corinthians 4:7)

The Bible tells us the opposite of what our pride says. For those times when we get too full of ourselves, it tells us that everything good we have was given to us by our Father. We may have worked hard to get the things we have, but we can only work hard with what we already had to begin with. We didn't earn our personality, our gender, the year of our birth, the place of our birth, our intelligence, our aptitudes… You can use those things to build a better life, but you never earned those things in the first place. You see, we didn't work hard to get all we have, we work hard with what we already had. We also must remember that because of sin, the only thing that we truly deserve from God is separation from Him. Every good thing that we do have comes by grace, not by what we deserve. This sets us free to enjoy the good things that come our way, because we remember, "I don't deserve this, but because of the goodness of my Father, I have it." This kind of understanding will lead to amazing praise and thanksgiving.

And when bad things happen, we can understand that this is not divine judgment from God, because my relationship with Him is based on grace not on what I deserve. But it is also not unjust for God to allow trials into my life. In my pride I can get frustrated at God for allowing bad things to happen to me, and when I do this, I am judging God as if He is my employee. I have to remember that all things in creation, including my life, are in His control and for His glory. It isn't about me. But I couple that hard truth with the beautiful truth that while God is the sovereign Lord of all creation, because of His grace, He is also my Father. And if my loving Father has allowed a trial into my life, there must be a purpose behind it. Maybe it's to teach me from my mistakes, maybe it's to learn to trust Him in my trials, maybe it's to learn compassion for others going through something similar, or many other possible options. But ultimately, we have confidence to know that our pain is not a sign of God's hatred towards us, but it is something that He has allowed into our lives and will ultimately be for our good and His glory.

And when people aren't acting the way I think they should, I can learn to be patient and kind to them because I remember that life isn't about me getting my way, it is about glorifying God. It is my pride that is frustrated at not getting my way, because I assume that my way is what is best. True humility teaches us to evaluate and see that maybe our way isn't the best way and we need to learn to be patient and understanding of where other people are coming from. I also remember that, even though I don't deserve it, God has infinite patience and love for me. We need to always remember, God loves us in spite of our faults, not because of our good deeds; and as we love Him and abide in His love for us, we can learn how to love others with that same level of patience and understanding.

When our pride turns to despair, we remember that we may not deserve anything good from God, but by His love we are given grace freely. That means, that the only thing that really matters in this world, a loving relationship with God, is given to us freely. So when good things happen, we can learn to enjoy them and live in the moment, instead of cynically thinking about when our "good luck" will end. And we do this because we know that God is the one who gave us this good gift, and it is in His control what happens to us next. And when bad things happen, we can know that it isn't because God hates us or has abandoned us, but we know from Psalm 34:18, "The LORD is near to those who have a broken heart…" Even if it is our mistakes that have brought us to this place, God is with us and for us because our relationship with Him is based on His love and not our perfection. This is the only mentality that will help us learn from our mistakes, change from the inside out, receive good things with joy, and maintain hope and peace within severe trials.

Do you see how humility and drawing near to God can give you joy in any circumstance?

_____

_____

This is a vital truth for our relationships as well. Sometimes in my depression I can push away people who are loving me and trying to help me. I tell them things like "I just need space right now…" When in reality I feel undeserving of their love and so I push them away thinking that I am doing them a favor by getting out of their lives. In this low place I will think things like "I am not worth their time…" Or, "They are better off without me…" But when I do this, I am damning myself in my pride, because in my isolation, my depression will snowball because the only 'voice' I will be listening to is my own condemning thoughts. I think that I am doing this to help myself and others, but in reality I am making everything far worse for everyone. The people in my life are not far better without me; they will feel rejected when I push them away, and because of this my attempts to "help" them, will hurt them even more. I need to be vulnerable when I am hurting and receive their help so that they will be able to receive mine when they are hurting.

When I draw near to God I can see the truth that all of my relationships are given to me by grace. I don't deserve them and that's the point, no one deserves to have loving relationships, but by the grace of God we have them. And even though I am a mess, I can trust in God to change me. I think that I am no good for others, so in my pride I push people away. I don't realize that we are all a mess and the loving thing for all of us to do is to remain in our relationships, while we look to God to change us and help us in our relationships. However, there are times that we need to use discernment and see that some relationships are just bad influences on our relationship with God.

1 Corinthians 15:33 tells us: "Do not be deceived: 'Bad company corrupts good morals.'"

But ultimately, when we learn to love other people, and receive love, encouragement, and correction from others, we will be able to draw far closer to God and further away from our pride.

Do you struggle with pushing other people away from you? _____

_____

This leads to my final point, while humility is the absence of pride, the true opposite of pride is love. Pride is self focused and self interested, but God's love is always focused on the betterment of others. As we grow in our love for God and others, our pride will wither accordingly. We need to spend time focusing on the supreme love and humility of Jesus, and this will impact and change us so that we can begin to grow in our love for God and others.

Read and comment on the below passage:

> Let _nothing_ be done through selfish ambition or conceit, but in lowliness of mind let each esteem others better than himself. Let each of you look out not only for his own interests, but also for the interests

of others. Let this mind be in you which was also in Christ Jesus, who, being in the form of God, did not consider it robbery to be equal with God, but made Himself of no reputation, taking the form of a bondservant, and coming in the likeness of men. And being found in appearance as a man, He humbled Himself and became obedient to the point of death, even the death of the cross. Therefore God also has highly exalted Him and given Him the name which is above every name, that at the name of Jesus every knee should bow, of those in heaven, and of those on earth, and of those under the earth, and that every tongue should confess that Jesus Christ is Lord, to the glory of God the Father. (Philippians 2:3-11)

It is because of this truth, that in the twelve step program of Alcoholics Anonymous, the twelfth and final step is:

Having had a spiritual awakening as the result of these steps, we tried to carry this message to alcoholics, and to practice these principles in all our affairs.

For Bill Wilson, (the author of this material and who was himself a Christian), the main problem for the alcoholic is not their substance, but their pride and their narcissism that continually drives them to self-destructive behavior whether they are sober or not. That is why, for him, *an alcoholic isn't fully clean unless they have a spiritual awakening before God, and have learned how to dedicate themselves towards helping others get free from their issues as well.*

We all know how to start relationships that are convenient for us, but unless we learn to truly love others, and begin relationships with them based on serving them, helping them, and putting their needs before our own, our deadly root of pride will continue to suffocate us in all that we do. That is why we look to Jesus and see that He was someone who loved us, not from a selfish desire to gain, but through a humility and love that caused Him to freely give up His glory and to suffer and die in our place and for our sakes. This is the love that will set us free from pride, *nothing else can.*

Because pride is such a personal and deeply rooted issue, I feel I could write an entire book just on this one topic! There is much more that can be said of pride, but I believe that is enough for now. This is a subject that we will have to continually go back to throughout our lives, and one that we will never be truly freed from this side of heaven.

Even as we seek freedom from our specific issues, we must always return to the root of our sickness and seek to grow in our humility and our love, otherwise even our pursuit of God and our good deeds will be polluted by this wicked root of sin. In our next lesson we will begin to talk about God's true love and how that delivers us. But to finish things off, here is one final quote from C.S. Lewis in his book *Mere Christianity:*

We must not think pride is something God forbids because He is offended at it, or that humility is something He demands as due to His own dignity—as if God Himself was proud. He is not in the least worried about His dignity. The point is, He wants you to know Him: wants to give you Himself. And He and you are two things of such a kind that if you really get into any kind of touch with Him you will, in fact, be humbled—delightedly humbled, feeling the infinite relief of having for once got rid of all the silly nonsense about your own dignity which has made you restless and unhappy all your life.... I wish I had got a bit further with humility myself... To get even near it, even for a moment, is like a drink of cold water to a man in a desert.

God's Love

...That Christ may dwell in your hearts through faith; that you, being rooted and grounded in <u>love</u>, may be able to comprehend with all the saints what is the width and length and depth and height—to <u>know</u> the love of Christ which passes knowledge; that you may be filled with all the fullness of God. (Ephesians 3:17-19)

In the last lesson we talked about the root of our sin, which is our pride and selfishness. And in looking at pride we also saw that while humility is the absence of pride, the true opposite of pride that will set us free from our selfishness, deliver us from all of our other sins, and bring us closer to God is the virtue of love. So now, let's take some time to study and understand God's love, and see how it ultimately changes us.

Notice in the passage above, that Paul says that the key to being filled with all the fullness of God is to "know" the love of Christ. Now, to a legalist, this statement seems really fluffy and counter-intuitive. They would think the key to becoming more godly isn't about studying love, but by action. Someone like this would argue that loving God is all about obeying Him and serving Him and not so much about passion or emotional warmth.

As someone who is very hard-headed and not very emotional, I can relate to this mentality. I used to think that following God was not about experiencing love and affection for Him or others, but just about following His commands. Because of this, I never really spent time focusing on love, instead I redefined love in the Bible to just mean obedience. What I have found over the years though is that this is a very dangerous, and unbiblical mentality to have. And if you do it, it will actually keep you away from God.

Though I speak with the tongues of men and of angels, but have not love, I have become sounding brass or a clanging cymbal. And though I have the gift of prophecy, and understand all mysteries and all knowledge, and though I have all faith, so that I could remove mountains, but have not love, I am nothing. And though I bestow all my goods to feed the poor, and though I give my body to be burned, but have not love, it profits me nothing. (1 Corinthians 13:1-3)

In this passage Paul describes some of the most loving actions someone could perform towards God and their neighbor, and yet Paul tells us that you can do all these things and still not have love. I missed this truth growing up in the church, but now I see it clearly that while service and obedience will come out of love, they are not synonymous with love. When we make this error, Paul tells us that even though we might be doing all these loving actions that are benefiting others, unless we already have love and are acting out of that love, we are profiting nothing in God and our actions are actually unattractive towards Him.

When we ignore the reality of God's love, we can become much more legalistic in our relationship with God and we can also be more harsh and emotionally cold towards others. We can also lack compassion and affection for others even while serving them. The years that I thought I was right in this, I never really had the opportunity to experience the beauty and warmth of God's love. I would usually just get the idea from God that He was apathetic towards me at best, and frustrated and disappointed with me at worst. I would serve Him constantly, but I never found myself delighting in God or having affection for Him. I was also very cold towards others. I thought that I was loving people because I would serve them and talk about God with them. But I realize now that I had a very selfish outlook towards my relationships, which is why I never let anyone get that close to me, why I never really opened up or became vulnerable with anyone else, and why I usually only reached out to others when it was convenient for me. I thought I was being godly by acting this way, but I see now just how filled the Bible is with commands to love God and people first, and then serve them out of that love. I also see that the love that God desires for His people isn't passionless obedience, but deep and intimate love for Him and others, just like the love that He has for us. When you read through the Bible, you can't escape the truth that the most important virtue that we need to strive for is love.

Please read and comment on the following passages:

Jesus said to him, "You shall love the LORD your God <u>with all your heart, with all your soul, and with all your mind.</u> This is the first and great commandment. And the second is like it: You shall love your neighbor as yourself. On these two commandments hang all the Law and the Prophets." (Matthew 22:37-40)

"Let all that you do be done with love." (1 Corinthians 16:14)

_____

_____

_____

For most people in our culture today, we agree that the greatest virtue someone could have is love. Both inside the church and outside of it, we are all encouraging one another to walk in love and we are all inundated by movies and songs that speak of the beauty and the power of love. In fact, most of us really do think that anything that is done for the sake of love is morally excellent and even godly to do. But here is the issue, even though most people think that love is the most important virtue, it seems that different people have very different definitions of what love is and what it should look like. This is where the danger lies, if we can't adequately define love and yet we hold it up as the pinnacle of virtue, we are setting ourselves up for unbelievable amounts of abuse and heartache.

For most of us, some of the most damage that has ever been done to us was done by people who claimed that they were loving us; and we have done the most damage to the people that we claim to have been loving. We justify lying, manipulation, jealousy, abuse, and even abandonment all through the claim that we are "loving" the other person. The truth is, we all define love through our own views and the beliefs of our society. We learn how to love in the same way we first learned how to talk. Babies don't learn how to talk through lessons or taking a class, they more acquire language through listening to those talking around them. Love works the same way, we don't "learn" how to love through studying and thinking through it, we have "acquired" love through our families and society.

And because we ourselves are fallen and corrupt, and we come from families and societies that are fallen and corrupt, the way we love has been polluted and brought away from the perfect love that Jesus has commanded us to walk in. Even though we all have noble intentions in our attempts to love others, we lack the ability and the knowledge to actually love the way that God intended us to. It isn't that we can't love at all, it's just that the love that we do exercise is ultimately a corrupt version of God's perfect love, and unless we can recognize that, we are going to be blind to the damage that we are doing to other people. I have talked to so many people who have been utterly devastated by parents, romantic partners, and friends who thought, and even still think, that they were walking in love. And I'm not just talking about people who tried to love but fell short, I am talking about people who have irrevocably damaged others while living up to their own standard of what love should look like. And because they did all this damage in the name of "love," they are completely unapologetic; they really believe that they were following God in what they did because they were walking in their own definition of "love."

For instance I have seen kids who are utterly spoiled, and who lack the ability to understand the concept of personal responsibility, all because their parents "loved" them by doing everything for them and never disciplining them. Because of this, these kids grow up physically, but remain completely dependent on their parents for everything and will be unable to grow up or move on in any other way. I have even seen parents legitimately physically and emotionally abuse their children and attempt to justify their behavior by saying they were "loving" their kids. I have also seen countless romantic relationships devastated by one partner's secret past that they hid for years, all the while telling themselves they were "loving" their partner by hiding painful information from them. The truth inevitably comes out, however, and the damage done to their partner is exponentially increased because now, not only do they have to deal with a painful truth, but they also have to deal with shattered trust. There are many such examples, but the central point is that while we are all capable of exemplifying truly beautiful love towards one another, we must also accept that our ability to love has been corrupted by sin and by our false understanding of what love really is. Unless these issues are being dealt with, we are doomed to walk in our own versions of love, which will ultimately damage those around us.

Take some time to reflect on your own views of love. How did you learn how to love? Where did you get your views on love from? Have you been hurt by people who claimed to be loving you?

Most people would believe that "love" is an abstract concept; they would never even try to come up with a specific definition. But the Bible utterly rejects this abstract view of love. When God commands us to love, He didn't leave defining it to our own devices. The Bible provides us with a clear and concrete view of what true love is, and what it isn't:

He who does not love does not know God, for God is love. (1 John 4:8)

That is such a radical statement. John doesn't just say that "God is loving," which would be beautiful enough, but he goes even further and says that God is love in His very nature and being. Meaning that God doesn't "fall in love" like we do. We "fall in love" with people because of their worth to us and our adoration of them. We love those who love us back, we love those we are attracted to, we love those we respect, we love those we need, we love our family... So our love naturally grows as we become more attracted toward others, while God's love grows out of His very being and therefore is unconditional, eternal, and infinite. This is why God has the unique ability to love those who hate Him, and why He was even willing lay down His life for those who wanted to kill Him. In our weak love, we can only love those that we think deserve it and even then only to a limited extent. But God infinitely loves the unlovable, and that includes you and me.

Read and comment on Matthew 5:43-48, "You have heard that it was said, 'You shall love your neighbor and hate your enemy.' But I say to you, love your enemies, bless those who curse you, do good to those who hate you, and pray for those who spitefully use you and persecute you, that you may be sons of your Father in heaven; for He makes His sun rise on the evil and on the good, and sends rain on the just and on the unjust. For if you love those who love you, what reward have you? Do not even the tax collectors do the same? And if you greet your brethren only, what do you do more than others? Do not even the tax collectors do so? Therefore you shall be perfect, just as your Father in heaven is perfect."

The Words of Jesus should catch us all short. Jesus is not giving us a standard of love that we have to live up to in order to be with Him. Instead, He is showing us through His perfect love that our love is lacking and in need of Him. Jesus is telling us that even the most selfish and arrogant people on earth can love those who benefit them and love them back, but only God can love everyone equally, even though none of us deserve it. To put it another way, only God can truly love unconditionally and selflessly, while all of our loves have conditions on them and are rooted in selfishness.

So why can't we love like God? What is preventing us from loving perfectly, and can we ever be like Him? Like everything else in the Bible, there is wonderful hope for our despair. We can grow in the love of God. But we can never pursue that hope with passion if we don't understand our need for it. This is why Jesus is giving us this impossible standard for love; He isn't saying this to make us feel better about ourselves, or encourage us to be better versions of who we already are. Jesus tells us what His love is like so that we can see the gap that exists between our kind of love and His, and understand that He has bridged that gap and has given us a way to grow in loving perfectly. There are two major things that Jesus has done for us that can begin to enable us to love like Him. John lays them out for us in 1 John 3:16: "By this we <u>know</u> love, because He laid down His life for us. And we also ought to lay down our lives for the brethren."

In the Greek, there are multiple words that we translate "know," and this particular word has a pretty deep meaning. It is the Greek word ginosko, and it means to understand something relationally through experience. This is not the word someone would use for knowing a mere fact, this is a relational word that is used primarily for knowing people, and it is so intimate that it is sometimes used as a euphemism for sexual intimacy. So what does this mean for us? It means that we can only love after we have first begun to experience and receive His love for us. You cannot give to others what you don't already have. We are all trying desperately to love others, but we are trying to give love out of an empty bucket. It is only as we are filled with the perfect love of God, that we can begin to give that love to others out of complete selflessness. And through experiencing God's perfect love we can understand His love, for you can't practice what you don't understand. We end up trying to practice God's kind of love through mere instinct, and we have to humbly accept that the ways that we think we should love are incomplete at best. We need to be re-taught how to properly love by God. He doesn't expect us to automatically know how to love, He desires for us to admit our helplessness before Him so that He can teach us the proper way. We will spend the next two lessons looking at both of these points in detail, but for today, it is important to reflect on the nature of God's love and spend time praying and confessing to God our lack of love and need for Him.

> *Beloved, let us love one another, for love is of God; and everyone who loves is born of God and knows God. He who does not love does not know God, for God is love. In this the love of God was manifested toward us, that God has sent His only begotten Son into the world, that we might live through Him. In this is love, not that we loved God, but that He loved us and sent His Son to be the propitiation for our sins. Beloved, if God so loved us, we also ought to love one another. No one has seen God at any time. If we love one another, God abides in us, and His love has been perfected in us.* (1 John 4:7-12)

He Loved Us First

Now, let's begin to look at God's love more deeply. We ended the last study talking about two things that Jesus has done for us that enable us to grow in His love. The first is that He loves us, and in experiencing His love first hand, we are able to show that same love to others. And the second is that He teaches us how to love like He does, and in understanding this, we can relearn how to truly love. In this lesson, we are going to focus on the fact that it is only through experiencing Jesus' perfect love for us that we are able to truly love Him and others.

> *In this is love, <u>not that we loved God, but that He loved us</u> and sent His Son to be the propitiation for our sins.* (1 John 4:10)

In C.S. Lewis' book *The Four Loves,* he lays out two large categories of love, and calls them "give love" and "need love." "Need love" is the kind of love a child has for their parents. As a child you are unable to take care of yourself, and so you lean on your parents and develop deep intimacy with them through having your needs met. This is the love that causes a child to hold on to their parent when they have a nightmare, finding comfort and safety in their embrace. And "give love" would be the parent receiving their child, giving them protection, care, and compassion freely and without cost. So, to put it another way, "need love" is finding what you need met in another person, while "give love" is expressed out of a fullness and a desire to meet the needs of another.

What C.S. Lewis notes after this is that the major difference between God and us is that God is the only One who can truly demonstrate "give love." While we as humans do have a capacity to demonstrate this love to an extent, God is the only being in the universe who doesn't need anything and, therefore, is the only One who can fully express this kind of love. We, on the other hand, are in constant need. Just because we are independent adults and not needy children doesn't mean that we have ceased to need things. And the primary thing that we need is real love.

Because of this, all of our relationships are expressions of this need. In all of our relationships there is a required balance of giving love and needing love that we experience. When I think through the relationships in my life, I see this painful truth played out. This takes some real honesty on our parts, but if we reflect, we will see that in our attempts to love others selflessly, we also have expectations and needs. I need validation; I need to feel important; I need to be needed; I need to be cared for; I need community because I fear loneliness; I need companionship; I need stability through love; I need freedom in love; I need pleasure; I need comfort; I need understanding, and the list goes on. Even though I am attempting to love others, even in my most loving moments I am ultimately being moved by these needs in my heart.

It is amazing how I have come to simply expect my relationships to meet my needs. This is true to such an extent in my own life, that when I don't get my needs met, I immediately blame those that love me and even feel entitled to use people to get what I want. I will shut down emotionally or even leave those who aren't meeting my needs. I am also prone to fall into depression, fearfulness, and frustration when I don't receive from my relationships what I feel that I deserve. I don't know how many times I have had depressed thoughts about how "nobody understands me, no one is reaching out to me, nobody spends time with me, nobody needs me," and so on. When I think things like that I am expressing my selfish expectation that my relationships exist to meet my needs, not so I can meet the needs of others. I can easily look back and see how many relationships have fallen by the wayside because of my selfishness and neediness. Even though we are sincerely trying to love and escape our selfishness, we remain rooted in our pride and all of our love becomes an expression of our own needs.

Can you see your own neediness in your loves? _____

_____

Ernest Becker was an atheist who wrote a book called *The Denial Of Death* (1973). In it he argued that humanity has a gnawing emptiness inside of them put there by our deep fear of death. Because of this we are all trying to fill this hole with our worldly endeavors, but to no avail. (It is eerie to see how close he came to the truth of the Bible, Ecclesiastes 3:11: " ...He has put eternity in their hearts...")

Becker said that one of the most common ways we try to fill our emptiness is with love, both in trying to give perfect love, and in seeking to be loved perfectly. Please read and comment on his quote:

> *After all, what is it that we want when we elevate the love partner to the position of God? We want redemption—nothing less. We want to be rid of our faults, of our feeling of nothingness. We want to be justified, to know that our creation has not been in vain. We turn to the love partner for the experience of the heroic, for perfect validation; we expect them to "make us good" through love. Needless to say, human partners can't do this. The lover does not dispense cosmic heroism; he cannot give absolution in his own name. The reason is that as a finite being he too is doomed, and we read that doom in his own fallibilities, in his very deterioration...*

> *...On the other hand, what partner could ever want to give redemption—unless he was mad? Even the partner who plays God in the relationship cannot stand it for long, as at some level he knows that he does not possess the resources that the other needs and claims. He does not have perfect strength, perfect assurance, secure heroism. He cannot stand the burden of godhood, and so he must resent the slave. Besides, the uncomfortable realization must always be there: how can one be a genuine god if one's slave is so miserable and unworthy?"*

_____

_____

_____

Now the really interesting thing, is that in his quote of despair there is a gospel shaped hole right in the center. Meaning, that he speaks of the meaninglessness of pursuing this type of love with another human, saying (rightfully so), that no human love can give us this "redemption" because of the frailty of our own love, and the frailty of theirs. So many of us spend our lives struggling under the weight of this problem. We go from relationship to relationship, desperately seeking this love that will set us free. Some of us might even turn to pets to try to fill this void, but none of these relationships can actually satisfy what we are longing for. Because of this, many of us give up the fight altogether like he did, simply saying that such a love doesn't exist. But, what if there was a pure, powerful, passionate, perfect, eternal love that could finally satisfy the human heart? What if there was a love that could forgive all of our mistakes, love us in all of our faults, and actually teach us to reflect its beauty? And what if that love wasn't something that we had to struggle for, but something that was freely given? This is what I meant when I said there is a gospel shaped hole in his argument. It is only in the gospel, the good news of Jesus Christ, that we learn that this perfect love not only exists, but it is freely given to any who would receive it by faith. This is why John said, "We love because He first loved us." It is only the person that is filled and satisfied by this love that can be free to love both God and others, becoming a conduit for God's perfect love. Or, to put it another way, it is only when we are complete, finding all our needs met in God's love for us, that we become free to selflessly give love.

Please comment on Colossians 2:10, which says "And you are complete in Him, who is the head of all principality and power."

_____

_____

_____

I'm not saying that we are only capable of being selfish in how we love. There certainly is a lot of beauty and sincerity in the way we love others. But it doesn't matter how sincere we may be. If we are empty we only know how to take, and ultimately even when we do give, it is only so that we can receive something in return. We can spend our entire lives attempting to love God and others with the most sincere of hearts, but unless the emptiness in our hearts is addressed first, all of our love will ultimately be based on selfishness. In the Bible we run into many people who exemplify this truth, but the most clear example for me is in the relationship between Jacob, Rachel, and Leah.

Leah was someone in the Bible that we don't read much about, but someone who certainly felt the sting of being unloved. We are introduced to her in Genesis 29, and her name literally means "burden." Her father, Laban, named her this because in that culture, a woman's only worth to her parents was in the dowry she would bring home when she was married off. We are told in this section that Leah was considered an unattractive woman who had a very beautiful little sister named Rachel. Because of this, men were always clawing after her little sister, but never gave her the time of day. This made Laban afraid he would never be able to marry her off, and so he treated her more and more as he had named her—as a burden. Lacking the love of her father, and seemingly everyone else, this hole in Leah became larger every day, making her desperate for anyone to love her. Finally, a man arrived named Jacob, but just like every man before him, he only had an attraction for Rachel. But Laban saw that Jacob was desperate for Rachel, so he tricked Jacob into marrying Leah, by switching the girls on the wedding night. Right there, I see her desperation. She allowed a man to sleep with her, while he thought he was with her sister. And she never revealed the truth to him because she was so desperate for any type of attention, that she would rather have affection that was based on a lie, than no affection at all.

The following morning, Jacob finds out. He is furious with Laban and wants the first offer restored, but instead Laban offers his new son-in-law the option to marry both Rachel and Leah. And Jacob accepts. As the story goes on, Leah continues to compete with her little sister for the love of her husband and she does this in her childbearing. In that culture, a woman's main value in marriage was through bearing children for her husband, especially male children. Therefore, Leah began having children for Jacob in order to earn his affection. She named the first son Reuben, which means, "see, a son." After she has him she says in Genesis 29:32, "Now, therefore, my husband will love me." She literally named her son after her desires, that maybe if Jacob saw that she bore him a son he would finally see her and love her, but he didn't.

So, she had another son and named him Simeon which means, "heard." She hoped that maybe having a second son would get her husband to hear her and pay attention to her. The third son, she named Levi which means, "attach," thinking—maybe now my husband will be attached to me. As you can see, all the love she gave to Jacob was out of a huge emptiness in her heart. She thought that the emptiness she felt would finally go away if she could only have a husband that cared for her, but in her relationship with Jacob that emptiness only grew. And even though Leah was trying to serve her husband in everything that she did, all of this service came from her emptiness and a need for validation; none of her actions were done out of selfless love.

Can you relate to Leah? _____

So many of us, including me, know the sting of feeling unloved and uncared for. And in our desperation we can become like Leah and believe that if only we could find someone who really loved us and cared for us, we would be happy. Some might believe this so fervently, that they would read this story and think the real reason why Leah wasn't happy was because she was never loved by Jacob or her father. And if only her father and Jacob would have loved her, she would have been happy. While this fact did magnify the emptiness in Leah, having the love of Jacob and her father wouldn't have truly healed her.

For proof of this fact, we just have to look at her sister Rachel. Rachel was said to have been very beautiful, and even though she had the love of her father, attention from countless men, and even the love of Jacob, it was never enough for her. Rachel fell into a bitter feud with her sister over the attention of Jacob. And even though

Jacob gave her all of his attention and love while he ignored Leah, Rachel was still jealous of her sister. She craved still more love and attempted to obtain it through having children. When she found that she was barren, she became deeply depressed and so desperate for this love that she even asked Jacob to marry her maid, so that the maid could have children in her stead. Her expectation was that this would finally get her the attention and value that she craved so much. But this only fueled a very sad battle between the two sisters to see who could have the most children. By the time you get to the end of the story, you can see that neither sister got what they were looking for from Jacob. Rachel shows us that even when we are loved and wanted by others, it still won't be enough to fill our true hearts' desire. We can have the praise and affection of countless people and still long for a greater love.

Can you relate to Rachel? _____

But what about Jacob? Jacob was also a man who knew what it meant to be unloved by his father. Jacob had an older brother that got all the affection and approval from his father, while Jacob was overlooked. It was so bad, that Jacob actually deceived his dad to try to gain the family blessing from him. But far from winning his dad over, this upset his father, and drove his brother into a murderous rage. So, when Jacob met Rachel and Leah, he was literally fleeing for his life. Jacob was also someone who was empty and looking for satisfaction in love. Even though he married Rachel, Leah, and both of their maids, and he had all four of these women fighting for his attention, he wasn't happy either. In many instances in this story you can tell that Jacob is frustrated with all of his wives and is really unhappy with his marriages.

Because of his emptiness, Jacob felt entitled to these women. He never saw the wickedness of using all of these women to fill his needs. And even though he was a victim of being overlooked by his father, he never saw how much pain he caused these women by marrying all of them and then favoring one over the others. He was so blind to this, that he perpetuated the cycle by favoring his son Joseph over all of his brothers. Jacob shows us that even if we live out our wildest romantic and sexual fantasies, this will also leave us feeling hollow in the end and will only root us deeper into our selfishness. So many men and women even if they are in happy marriages with full sex lives, still find themselves feeling unfulfilled and wanting to stray. They may turn to another person to fill this hole, or pornography, or prioritize their career over their marriage, or spend more time with friends than with their spouse, or idolize their children, or they neglect their spouse for various hobbies. We all need to learn from Jacob and understand the truth that no matter how great a loving relationship can be, it still isn't enough for the human heart.

Can you relate to Jacob? _____

In the middle of this story, we find tremendous hope in Leah as she becomes the first one to discover the fulfillment that is in the love of God. In the midst of her despair, she conceived a fourth son, and in that pregnancy she realized a beautiful truth. Her dad didn't love her, her husband didn't love her, her sister didn't love her, but God did. God was the only One that loved her for who she was; He was the One who had been providing for her and taking care of her. He was the only One that she didn't need to please before He would love her, because He loved her unconditionally (in spite of her ignoring Him). And as she began to see this beautiful truth she named her child Judah which means, "praise," saying, "'Now I will praise the LORD.' Therefore she called his name Judah." (Genesis 29:35) . It would be great to say that her struggle ended there, unfortunately like the rest of us, she continued to battle in her insecurities and self-doubts, but in that moment she got her first taste of freedom in the love of God.

What God is trying to show us through stories like this, is that there is no human love that will ever fill that void in your heart. You were made for His perfect love, and so even though some relationships are better than others, none of them are perfect and none of them can fully satisfy you. We pursue relationships in an attempt to fill our emptiness, but in doing so, we never find what we are looking for and we end up consumed by our selfishness because our deepest motivation is to fulfill our own need for real love. However, when we see what Leah did, and we begin to receive the perfect love of God and delight in Him above all others, we too will begin to be set free from our emptiness and from our selfishness.

Take some time to reflect on your own struggles to find love in your life. Can you see your need for God's love?

_____

_____

Not only can I see the damage I have done to myself and others in pursuing this love, but I can also see how so much of my sin is born out of this gaping hole in my heart. Proverbs 27:7 says: "A satisfied soul loathes the honeycomb, but to a hungry soul every bitter thing is sweet."

You see, the reason why we keep going back to our empty sins is because we are broken. We are empty inside and we are in pain. So we are looking for things to make us feel better or even numb us. But these fillers merely produce temporary satisfaction, followed by more pain and brokenness. And the reason why we can't stop, is because in a weird way, we love these things. It is hard for me to admit, but in a sense, I do love pornography. It is there for me in my stress and pain, and I have used it so frequently to feel pleasure and to mask my emptiness that I instinctively crave it whenever I am struggling. A recovered drug addict once said to me, "Drugs weren't my problem, they were my solution. You take drugs away from me, then I have a problem." You see, the emptiness in us is what is driving us to these things. Which is why it is essential to first experience God's love in order to change. I need to reflect and see that so much of my efforts to 'love' (or even my 'good works' that I do) are just more hollow attempts to struggle for real love, And they end up making me struggle for love in my relationship with God.

We can't be set free from our emptiness by more empty attempts; we must first be filled. It is our nature to go right back to the same bitter things that we are used to, unless we truly taste something better. David understood this and after failing in one of the worst sins of his life he prays in Psalm 51:12, "Restore to me the joy of Your salvation, and uphold me by Your generous Spirit."

David had the boldness to pray like this even in the midst of his failure, because he believed fervently that his relationship with God wasn't dependent on his faithfulness. Even after his big fall, he knew that God's love never fails. And he knew that if God didn't become his joy and salvation again, he would go right back to his old sins, even if he didn't want to.

Can you see how your own emptiness keeps drawing you back to sin? And can you see how sin makes you feel more empty? _____

Your passion will always trump your logic. That is why simply knowing the right thing to do, doesn't mean you will do it. We must begin to experience God's great love for us and see Him as our everything, or we won't be able to change. The pursuit of freedom is the pursuit of beauty and all-satisfying joy in God's great love. Only when our hearts begin to be captured by His supreme love can we begin to be set free from our selfishness and sins. It is from this wholeness and satisfaction that we will be able to love others for their sake as opposed to loving others for what we can get from them.

So how do we do this? The first step is by simply trusting that this love of God is enough for you and it is freely available. If we can't believe this, then all of our works will be done in order to earn God's love. The love of God can only be received, it can never be achieved. As we work on that foundation through asking God to give us faith to believe this, we firm up this foundation through studying His Word and seeing His love for us written out.

Confessing to other Christians will also help us establish the truth that God's love is unconditional. I find that when I slip out of the practice of confession, I quickly fall back into my old pattern of walking the Christian life in order to win God's love instead of going after God because of His great love for me.

For the love of Christ compels us… (2 Corinthians 5:14)

One of the clearest ways for me to see this is when I am struggling with temptations, and even falling to those temptations. In times like this, I will instinctively alienate myself from God thinking that He wants nothing to do with me. When I do this it reveals my belief that God only loves me when I am worthy, instead of believing that God loves me as I am and His love is making me worthy. "But God demonstrates His own love toward us, in that while we were yet sinners, Christ died for us…" (Romans 5:8) . However, when I stay in consistent accountability, I can be reminded of God's love through my brothers in Christ, and they help build my faith in His perfect love.

Also, we should spend time praying like David did. Boldly asking to experience the joy of God's salvation, to taste and see that the Lord is good and that His lovingkindness truly is better than life. I will tell you that we won't always feel the warmth of His love, and we certainly shouldn't live only for that feeling. But we can live on the solid foundation of God's undeserved and supreme love for us, and in so doing, we can have peace and confidence that will quiet all of our doubts and we can begin to love as God does.

Just like any other relationship, we will have amazingly beautiful and passionate moments with God. But, these intimate moments aren't the goal. Quality time is the fruit of a quantity of time. I can't just talk to my wife tonight for an obligatory 5 minutes and expect any amount of warmth to come out of that. But as I see her and learn to adore her, appreciate her, and love her, I will spend more and more time with her naturally. I will desire to change more for her, and quality time will be a result. That is how we must walk with God. And as God's love for us becomes the foundation of our love for others, we will grow more and more in selflessness in all of our relationships. We will notice that we are loving people more and more out of our joy in God, and not out of our empty hearts. This is something that we grow in daily and understand more as we walk in it. I encourage you to immerse yourself in God's word, spend time praying to God and build your intimacy with Him. Talk to other believers about this, and seek to grow more in receiving God's love for you. It may seem counterintuitive, but the only way to love, is to first be loved.

Oh, taste and see that the Lord is good. (Psalm 34:8)

The LORD your God is in your midst, a mighty one who will save; He will rejoice over you with gladness; He will quiet you by His love; He will exult over you with loud singing. (Zeph. 3:17, ESV)

THE COMPLEXITY OF GOD'S LOVE

We have been studying the love of God and seeing how it is God's love alone that can set us free from our selfishness and sin. Today we are going to focus on the complexity and beauty of God's perfect love. We tend to think of love as something that is abstract and simple, or something that is spontaneous and instinctive that grows out of passionate emotion. But what we see demonstrated to us in the Bible is that, God's love is anything but simple; and it most certainly does not always come from intense emotion. As Americans, we have a pretty large disadvantage when it comes to the topic of love, because we only have one word for "love." Because of this, we tend to have an overly simplistic view of love that causes us many problems. We have to understand that a truth that is made too simple can be just a damaging as a lie. As we talked about in an earlier lesson, when we don't fully understand love, we can cause damage to our relationships out of our ignorance. We need to gain a deeper understanding of God's love if we are going to be able to love as God has commanded us, but where do we go to gain this knowledge?

Obviously the Bible is the primary source that we have to study the love of God. And as we read through the Scriptures , and study the way that God acts and cares for people practically, we can begin to understand the complexity and the beauty of His perfect love. However, the Bible was originally written in other languages that had more nuanced definitions of love than the English language. And as a result, we can miss out on some of these complex pictures. First, we are going to focus on the Greek understanding of love in order to better understand the new testament depiction of God's perfect love, then we will move on to the Hebrew understanding of love.

The way that the Greeks understood love was mainly through its differences between types of relationships, and that is why they had 4 primary words for "love." These words were Phileo, which means 'brotherly love,' and speaks mainly of the deep love that is shared between friends and siblings; Eros, which is the love that is shared romantically between lovers; Storge, which is the affectionate love shared between parents and their children; and Agape, which is the divine love. When early Christians wrote about love, they used these words to help people understand the complexity of the love they were discussing and differentiate one kind of love from another. They frequently tell Christians to demonstrate different types of love. They encouraged husbands and wives to share passionate romantic love with one another. They encouraged the church to grow in brotherly love, and they told parents and children to grow in their affectionate love for each other, and so forth. Even though these 'loves' are beautiful, they have been corrupted by the fall and are incomplete in themselves. These loves need to be filled and governed by a greater love, and that love is God's perfect love. And it was this love that they defined as Agape. When John said "God is love" in 1 John 4:8, he used this Word "agape," and when Paul defined love in his very famous letter to the Corinthians, he used the Word agape:

> *Love [agape] suffers long and is kind; [agape] does not envy; [agape] does not parade itself, is not puffed up; does not behave rudely, does not seek its own, is not provoked, thinks no evil; does not rejoice in iniquity, but rejoices in the truth; bears all things, believes all things, hopes all things, endures all things. [Agape] never fails…* (1 Corinthians 13:4-8)

You see, it isn't that our natural loves are sinful, it's that, like everything else in this universe, they are fallen and need to be redeemed and made new again. God's love does this. As I read the description of God's love above I can see how inadequate my love really is. I might be able to do some of those things some of the time, and toward certain people, but God demonstrates this type of love all of the time and toward all people. Our loves certainly fall short, don't they?

Can you see how much greater and complex God's love is than your own? _____

THE HEBREW VIEW OF LOVE

We can easily spend multiple lessons on this passage alone, and it is good for all Christians to continuously go over 1st Corinthians 13 to see clearly how we need to grow. And I would encourage anyone who wants to delve deeper into this topic to read C.S. Lewis' book, *The Four Loves,* to get a better understanding of these four words. But for today I would like to spend some time focusing on the Hebrew view of love.

This view of love is really beautiful and if we can grab a hold of it, it can change our lives. In the Hebrew language, there are 6 primary words for love. Unlike the Greek language, the Hebrews didn't define their words based on relationships. Instead, they imagined love as being kind of like a pie chart, with each word making up a specific piece of the pie. Let me explain.

First, there is the Hebrew word *Dowd,* this Word literally meant "to boil over" and was a description of passionate love. This wasn't a word that was exclusive to romance, you can have passionate love in a friendship or between a parent and their child. This Word doesn't necessitate sexual passion, but just describes that wonderful, passionate feeling that deep love can give you. The next word was *Chabad.* This Word spoke of "protective love." This is the kind of love that causes a person to want to protect someone that they care for, even if it costs them their life. Then there is *Chasaq,* which literally means "to fasten two hooks together." It is the Word that describes beautiful committed love. This is the love that says, "I will be with you no matter what, for the rest of my life." It is a love that rises above emotion and circumstance and expresses dedication. *Racham,* is the Word in the Old Testament that is translated "lovingkindness." It is the kind of love that enables someone to look past another's faults and forgive their mistakes. This is also the kind of love that makes service a true delight. When someone has this kind of love, service is never a chore or an obligation, but a wonderful joy.

Rea speaks of a type of friendship love. This is not a love that is exclusive to friends, but instead it describes the kind of love that arises out of shared interests and experience. This is the love that sees someone as an equal and simply delights in spending time with the other person and enjoying their company. Throughout the *Song of Solomon,* Solomon sometimes uses this word to describe his love for his bride, meaning that he not only had a passionate romantic love for her, but he also enjoyed her as a person and liked spending time with her. The final word that they used was *Ahavah.* This was kind of a generic word for love and was used in the same kind of ways that the English word for love is used. But, in certain instances, the writers of the Old Testament used this word to describe God's perfect love, and in those instances you see the fullness of it's meaning. When this word is used to describe God, it shows the wonderful balance and harmonization of all the aspects of love.

Something that the Hebrews understood all too well though was that while each aspect of love is good in proper balance and harmony, when you allow one of these loves to become engorged in your life, you are in for serious trouble.

Because of the fall all of our loves are out of balance. Our loves are unbalanced in different ways, to different extents, towards different people, and at different times. But none of us can love in perfect balance like God. What would happen if someone's passionate love became unbalanced?

What's important to note, is that when our loves become unbalanced, it isn't as if the other loves go away. It's just that one may become too big and start to outweigh the others to our harm. For me, passionate love is the main area that I fail. I constantly crave that passionate feeling that love provides and so I seek it primarily in my sexuality. This means, that instead of loving someone for who they are or what I can give to them, I love them for what they can give me. That is why porn appeals to me so much. I don't like the idea of "committed love,"or "protective love," or "merciful love," or "friendship love" near as much as I like the simple pleasure I can get when I use others for my own selfish gratification. That is why I was able to spend so much of my time scrolling through countless images of women for my selfish fulfillment. In those moments I don't care about the other aspects of love, and I don't care about the people that I am using, I only want the pleasurable feeling that this form of passionate love can give to me.

Please read and comment on the quote from C.S. Lewis in his book, *The Four Loves:*

> *"The thing [sex] is a sensory pleasure; that is, an event occurring within one's own body. We use a most unfortunate idiom when we say, of a lustful man prowling the streets, that he "wants a woman." Strictly speaking, a woman is just what he does not want. He wants a pleasure for which a woman happens to be the necessary piece of apparatus. How much he cares about the woman as such may be gauged by his attitude to her five minutes after fruition (one does not keep the carton after one has smoked the cigarettes). Now Eros (romantic love) makes a man really want, not a woman, but one particular woman. In some mysterious but quite indisputable fashion the lover desires the Beloved herself, not the pleasure she can give."*

_____

_____

_____

PASSION OF CHRISTIAN LOVE?

I never thought that Christian love could have this level of passion, and this problem was damaging to me. I was not interested in committed relationships, because I thought that passion was only alive in highly sexual, uncommitted types of romance. I also had a misunderstanding of God's view of sex; I thought He was against it and that He was ultimately against pleasure. I never understood that God was the Creator of sex and all the pleasures that surround it. God isn't against sex, He designed it and finds it very beautiful in the correct context. (For more on this, see our pamphlet on _God's Purpose and Design for Sex)_. I never understood that God's love includes this passionate love. But unlike what I was doing, God's love balances passion with the other aspects of love in such a way that brings greater overall depth and even brings deeper passion. I didn't understand that true passion requires depth of intimacy, commitment, and vulnerability. I kept all my loves at a shallow level and only sought my own benefit. Not only did this mistake make me far more self-absorbed, but it also kept me from the far greater passion of God's love. That brought greater separation between me and God as I sought this kind of passion outside of Him, and not with and through Him.

Can you relate to this?_____

I will quickly mention that for some who choose this path, it isn't born out of incredible selfishness like me, but instead out of pain. After being vulnerable with someone in love, (whether it is with a parent, a friend, or a lover) to have that vulnerability betrayed and trampled on can turn someone cold and unloving. The prospect of opening yourself up after having something traumatic like this happen to you is so painful that in order to protect yourself, you might put your walls up and simply use other people so that you remain in control and can't be used and abused again.

C.S. Lewis in _The Four Loves_ said this about love:

> _To love at all is to be vulnerable. Love anything and your heart will be wrung and possibly broken. If you want to make sure of keeping it intact you must give it to no one, not even an animal. Wrap it carefully round with hobbies and little luxuries; avoid all entanglements. Lock it up safe in the casket or coffin of your selfishness. But in that casket, safe, dark, motionless, airless, it will change. It will not be broken; it will become unbreakable, impenetrable, irredeemable. The alternative to tragedy, or at least to the risk of tragedy, is damnation. The only place outside of Heaven where you can be perfectly safe from all the dangers of love is Hell._

To wall yourself off like this is the quickest path to emptiness and pain. You might be able to avoid the pains of love, but you will never be able to experience its pleasures either, not even in your relationship with God. I'm not saying that you should knowingly put yourself in an abusive situation. But I am saying that in order to experience the joys that God has for you in love, you need to be willing to make yourself vulnerable again. You must be willing to experience all aspects of love, not just the passionate parts. And this takes trusting God with your heart. Please read and comment on the passage below.

> *My health may fail, and my spirit grow weak, <u>but God remains the strength of my heart</u>; He is forever mine.* (Psalm 73:26 NLT)

_____

_____

This error isn't just present for people who seek their pleasure in their sexuality, it can also express itself in many other unhealthy ways. For the sake of time, I will just mention two more. This can also be present in a person that is enchanted by toxic relationships. They are attracted to relationships that are incredibly dysfunctional, but they can't leave because, in spite of all the horrible moments that they must endure, the drama and the passion are so intoxicating to them that they can't leave. What they do is they mistake passion and drama for real love and they don't see that all the other aspects of true love are diminished or even non-existent. This type of drama isn't present only in romantic relationships, but also in friendships and even relationships between children and their parents. We have to understand that God's love goes deeper than mere passion, or else we can fall victim to confusing drama with genuine love and affection.

Finally, it can be the mistake of the person who always dreams of that perfect relationship. The person who reads romance novels, or watches romantic movies, dreaming about having the fairytale romance that will finally sweep them off their feet. This kind of person may not even like porn, but can express this lust in online relationships, fantasizing about that "perfect romance," in overly flirtatious behavior, or even in just quiet, consuming fantasies. This kind of individual is also not interested in the person, but only in the love that they crave so much. Because of this, they might also find themselves constantly in and out of relationships and being overly picky towards the people that they are with. Because when they first enter into a relationship they will feel this fire and passion, but after a while the passion fades and they look for it somewhere else. Or they might fall in love with the first person who pays attention to them and ignore a myriad of red flags because they want to be married so badly that they don't care who it's with (again this can also apply in non-romantic relationships).

Please read and comment on this quote from C.S. Lewis:

> *Our experience is colored through and through by books and plays and the cinema, and it takes patience and skill to disentangle the things we have really learned from life for ourselves. People get from books the idea that if you have married the right person you may expect to go on 'being in love' forever. As a result, when they find they are not, they think this proves they have made a mistake and are <u>entitled to a change</u>—not realizing that, when they have changed, the glamour will presently go out of the new love just as it went out of the old one.*

_____

STRUGGLES OF OUR CULTURE

I believe, the vast majority of our culture struggles primarily in this way. If you asked someone in our culture how they know that they are in love, they tend to describe a powerful emotional experience. This is also why so few people today want to get married. They are afraid that passion will dry up and they don't want to get stuck in a marriage that has no passion. Because we don't want to miss out on 'true love,' we become very noncommittal. In Christianity, we try to make it sound a little more holy by saying something like, "I'm waiting for the one that God has for me." But the root of this mentality isn't love, but supreme selfishness. When we have this mentality, we are using other people to get what we want from them but, "love does not seek its own" (1 Corinthians 13). When we do this, we are focusing on seeking our own, not on the betterment of the other person.

Anyone who has been in a relationship where the other person won't commit or open up knows how incredibly dehumanizing it can be. It makes you feel like you are constantly having to live up to a standard, to be "the one" for this person or else they will leave you. This makes you feel like an object, and more than this, it leaves you feeling constantly unstable and insecure. God's love is incredibly passionate, but it is passionate because it includes the wonderful security of commitment, protection, mercy, and the joy of friendship. Jesus teaches us that true passion comes from serving and seeking the betterment of others, not seeking only what you want. So while "passionate love" is beautiful and important in any loving relationship, it is just one small piece of love, it isn't the whole thing, when we make it the main point of love, we become very selfish and unloving. When this facet of love is in balance, we can love others better by using all of the other facets as well. The more we learn how to do this, the more loving we become, and the deeper our love roots will go, which will actually cause more powerful and significant passion to grow.

Have you seen "passionate love" become unbalanced in your life? Can you see how this has made you selfish in your relationships? _____

HOW ABOUT *CHASAQ* (COMMITTED LOVE)?

Surely someone who is focused not on feelings, but on commitment would be nearer to God's perfect love, right? Unfortunately, this type of imbalance is just as destructive as the last. Someone who struggles in this way, isn't focused on what a relationship can give them, but they become obsessed with the person themselves. The Bible does have multiple examples of people who struggled in this way, Leah being one of them. In the world, we call this type of person "codependent." A codependent person is someone whose primary need is to be needed, and they naturally elevate this type of committed love above all others because they gain their sense of worth through their relationships and how much people need them.

Common Traits of the Struggle

There are some common traits of someone who struggles this way. Their greatest fear is to be abandoned; they will struggle with insecurity and find validation only through what others think of them. They don't like asserting their own needs because they feel selfish when they do it. However, when others don't meet their needs they become resentful and bitter, possibly even acting out in passive aggressive ways because they fear confrontation. Their personality and mood are dependent on those around them. They can't set healthy boundaries in their relationships and so they frequently entangle themselves in toxic relationships and don't know how to say "no." They are attracted to broken people because "fixing" people makes them feel more loving and important. They will even allow themselves to be used in unhealthy relationships, all the while thinking about how loving they must be to stay with this person who is such a mess. They find their greatest amount of worth in others needing them, so as a parent they might even "cripple" their child by doing everything for them which will make their child permanently dependent on them. They will actually enable others in bad behavior thinking that they are loving them. They have compulsive, almost instant, loyalty, which means that they can fall in love at the drop of a hat. They are quick to sacrifice personal values for someone else, sex for this type of person might not be so much about an orgasm as it is about feeling "wanted," "connected," "intimate," and so on.

We All Have Struggles

It is important to remember that we all struggle with all of these imbalances to different degrees. So even though I don't relate as strongly to this, I can still relate at some level. You may not find yourself completely described in this category, *but can you see some of these traits in your life?*

As you can see, while this type of love seems very much like God's love, it is actually unbalanced and very unhealthy. Although it looks selfless, it is rooted in selfishness and insecurity. Having this imbalance could lead someone into terrible relationships where they will let themselves be used, and they enable the horrible behavior of the one using them because they think it is loving not to confront. Not only that, but because this person is trying so desperately to love others, love itself has become their idol above God. Because of this, they won't be able to be filled first by God, so out of their emptiness they will try to love, but ultimately will fall short. A person like this can also miss out on the wonderful beauty of "passionate love" thinking that to feel passionate or express their desires would make them selfish. For some, they might become so nurturing to their spouse, that their sensuality totally shuts off and they become more of a parent than a spouse. They might even have a martyr complex, meaning they find secret joy in being used and ignored. If so, this makes it very hard for them to ever receive genuine love and affection from another person. Someone like this might even run from a healthy relationship because they have no idea how to simply receive love from someone that is undeserved. As you can see, this will also hurt their relationship with God, because God doesn't need anything from us. Someone like this will most likely struggle with intense amounts of legalism in their relationship with God. Always striving to be good enough for Him, they will not realize that His love must be freely received, not worked for. It's much like the story of Mary and Martha.

As Jesus and the disciples continued on their way to Jerusalem, they came to a certain village where a woman named Martha welcomed him into her home. Her sister, Mary, sat at the Lord's feet, listening to what he taught. But Martha was distracted by the big dinner she was preparing. She came to Jesus and said, "Lord, doesn't it seem unfair to you that my sister just sits here while I do all the work? Tell her to come and help me." But the Lord said to her, "My dear Martha, you are worried and upset over all these details! There is only one thing worth being concerned about. Mary has discovered it, and it will not be taken away from her." (Luke 10:38-42 NLT)

You see, it was Mary, not Martha who was praised in this story. Martha thought she was in the right because she was serving, but Mary was praised by Jesus because she knew how to sit, be still, and simply receive the love of Christ. That doesn't mean that Mary was lazy and never served Jesus, in fact just a little after this event, all the gospels record that Mary poured out an incredibly expensive flask of perfume on Jesus' head before His crucifixion. This was a tremendous act of service that Jesus again praises, because unlike Martha, Mary's service wasn't out of a co-dependence. Mary was not serving in order to feel wanted or important, but instead because she was already immersed in the undeserved love that Jesus had for her and wanted to serve out of that joy. Mary served Jesus not from insecurity, but from security in love.

When we struggle like Martha did, constantly sacrificially serving others but allowing this service to be rooted in insecurity and emptiness, we are being selfish in our love toward others. We think it is somehow holy to refuse being served and to give all of ourselves to other people, but we need to carefully scrutinize our motives. It is so easy to slip into this co-dependence. Remember, no matter how much we might want to love like God, if we don't receive His love for us first, the love that we are demonstrating is unbalanced and rooted in selfishness.

Please read and comment on this quote from C.S. Lewis *The Four Loves,* where he describes a codependent woman that he knew:

She continued all [of her service] because if she had dropped it she would have been faced with the fact that she was determined not to see; would have known that she was not necessary. That is the first motive. Then too, the very laboriousness of her life silenced her secret doubts as to the quality of her love. The more her feet burned and her back ached, the better, for this pain whispered in her ear 'How much I must love them if I do all this!' That is the second motive.

_____

_____

_____

We also have to understand that if it is truly better to give than to receive, and we are constantly refusing to be served by those who love us, we are actually keeping them from the joy of service. When we are imbalanced in this way, we can easily become a martyr and hold our needs in while constantly serving others. All the while, we internally complain about how unloved we are, though secretly (sometimes even unbeknown to us) find pleasure in being used because it makes us feel valuable. Outwardly we might say things like "I just don't want to bother anyone…" But inwardly we usually struggle with deep amounts of insecurity and we feel so unworthy of service.

Now let's contrast that with the love of God. Though God doesn't need anything from us, He still receives and delights in our service towards Him. God is like a proud Father who delights in His children's service. He delights in our joy and He understands that true joy comes through serving others out of genuine love and affection. He knows the great value of having your service received with thankfulness, not rejected awkwardly, so He receives our acts of service. Listen to how Paul exemplifies this when he wrote to the Philippian church after they sent him a gift:

> *I rejoiced greatly in the Lord that at last you renewed your concern for me. Indeed, you were concerned, but you had no opportunity to show it. I am not saying this because I am in need, for I have learned to be content whatever the circumstances. I know what it is to be in need, and I know what it is to have plenty. I have learned the secret of being content in any and every situation, whether well fed or hungry, whether living in plenty or in want. I can do all this through him who gives me strength... Not that I desire your gifts; what I desire is that more be credited to your account.* (Philippians 4:10-17)

Paul doesn't refuse their gift out of some self-righteousness, he simply receives their gift and says "thank you." Paul understood that in order to really bless the Philippians, he didn't need to only serve them, but to allow them to learn to serve him as well, out of that same perfect love that he himself had received.

Even though I don't relate as strongly to being imbalanced in commitment love, I still struggle with this. Sometimes I do struggle with a martyr complex, but more often, I struggle with asking for help because I pride myself on being "independent." The reality behind this, is that I have a hard time trusting other people and letting them into my life. I like keeping people at a comfortable distance, and so I don't invite them in to my struggles and my needs. I find it easy to use other people to get what I want, but I reject the vulnerability that comes from asking for help. If we don't wake up to this imbalance, we can quickly destroy one of the greatest blessings in our relationships, which is the gift of mutual service and appreciation.

Have you struggled with receiving love and service from others?_____

_____

One of the most loving things that you can do, is to point people to God, and when 'committed love' gets unbalanced, it can prevent even this. Because this type of love is obsessed with being needed and depended upon, pointing another to God for His strength and stability in their life, often gets missed. In my selfishness, I want to be the rock for everyone in my life so I point them to me and tell them to depend on me. But I am a frail man, if people depended solely on me, they would be miserable and let down constantly. This doesn't excuse me from my responsibilities in my relationships, (God will hold me accountable for the way I love people), but ultimately, the most loving thing I can do for those around me is to point them to their true joy, stability, and salvation in God.

Also, because people-pleasing is a huge problem for those who struggle this way, it will be hard to encourage people to change bad behavior and go after God, which is a part of protective love. It is easier to cover over the mistakes that someone is making instead of holding them accountable and encouraging them, lovingly, to seek forgiveness and change in God. It might seem loving to support and accept people the way they are, but we need to understand that there is a difference between loving and supporting a person, versus supporting a behavior. In this instance, the most loving thing that someone can do is to gently encourage change, as they grow in knowing God's love. We aren't protecting people by enabling them, we are only hurting them, and allowing them to hurt us and others.

I do want to point out the beauty of this kind of love. Remember, it isn't the love that is the problem, it is the imbalance in our hearts that is. Committed love is, unfortunately, very overlooked in our society today. Because of this, most people in our culture have a consumer-type mentality toward their relationships. Meaning that every relationship is ultimately disposable; we tend to pick and choose what we like about a relationship, and if it isn't working we leave. We even do this to God. We pursue God when it is convenient for us, but when it isn't we put Him on the back burner until we feel "ready" to pursue Him again. This selfish attitude takes advantage of grace and doesn't understand the glory and the importance of God in our lives. Committed love is the kind of love that requires focus on others above ourselves, and while an imbalance of this type of love can lead to legalism, at least someone like this understands the gravity of who God is. In the proper balance, this kind of love can elevate us above our selfishness and bring us to an awesome humility and affection towards God and others.

Another tragic thing about this love being out of balance, is that in order to have truly passionate love, there needs to be freedom and vulnerability. The insecure codependent person will put up walls and disguise their true wants and needs out of fear of being vulnerable. We don't want another person to judge us or leave us if they see who we really are. It is only when committed love is functioning in the right balance, that you can experience the loyalty and faithfulness that will make you feel comfortable and safe so that you can open up. When a relationship is on uncertain ground there can also be a constant fear of being inadequate. We can feel the pressure of having to constantly be "enough" for the people around us, or else they might leave us for someone better. As you can see, true passion can't grow in this environment.

This is also the main reason why God tells us to wait until marriage to have sex. Sex is the most physically vulnerable that you can be with another person. And God wants an actual commitment present before we enter into that vulnerable space with someone else. That commitment provides a safety that allows us to open ourselves up to that level of physical intimacy. That intimacy then becomes a symbol of the complete vulnerability and surrender of the entirety of our lives in marriage to our spouse. In our culture we have so devalued this aspect of love that sex, along with the rest of our romantic relationships, have become completely disposable. We even begin dating people with the perspective of, "I'll try this out, but if it doesn't work, there are plenty of fish in the sea." This mentality has actually made our sexuality cheap and common, instead of holy and beautiful the way that God intended. For a marriage to really thrive, I need to know that my wife is in our relationship one hundred percent, and from that safety, there is so much wonderful vulnerability, intimacy, joy and passion. So if you struggle this way, it isn't that you are incredibly wicked, just that you are imbalanced like the rest of us. And in God we have wonderful hope that He can help us find that balance in Him.

Have you seen "committed love" become unbalanced in your life? Can you see how this has made you selfish?

_____

_____

DIFFERENT KINDS OF LOVE

I would like to go through every one of these loves in detail, but for the sake of brevity, I will briefly go over how the other loves can be harmful to you and I encourage you to spend time thinking through these loves and seeing for yourself the ways that these could be damaging when they are out of balance.

Chabad, or protective love is so beautiful in the right balance. This is the love that will enable people to open up honest dialogue with one another in order to encourage and help others. This is also what enables us to look out for one another, and even sacrificially love others in order to protect and care for those we love. But, if we elevate protective love to be out of balance, we can become overprotective in our relationships. This is where jealousy and controlling behavior come from. This kind of love can also cause us to become overly blunt and harsh with people when we try to correct them. Often, we will say things like, "I was just trying to be honest with you…"

Have you seen "protective love" become unbalanced in your life? _____

Racham, or merciful love, is the love that enables people to compromise and forgive when there are problems in a relationship. It is the love that enables people to be gentle and compassionate. It is also the love that gives us the ability to truly empathize with another human being and find genuine joy in the joy and pleasure of others. This is the love that rejoices with those who rejoice, sorrows with those who are sorrowful, and even finds amazing pleasure in sacrificing for someone else's betterment. But, if merciful love becomes our everything, we can become enabling in our relationships. We can allow abusive or harmful behavior to go unchecked because in our pursuit of mercy, we forget about justice. As you can see, this type of love usually goes hand in hand with committed love.

Have you seen "merciful love" become unbalanced in your life? _____

Rea, friendship love, is a really interesting one, in that it's destructive potential is different in certain types of relationships. If it is out of balance in friendships only, it will create hollow friendships because it will lack the balance of protection, commitment, passion, and mercy to make the friendships true and lasting, but it won't be that destructive. If it is out of balance in relationships between parents and children or between spouses, friendship love can be incredibly destructive and dysfunctional.

Many people in America, and even in the church, make the mistake of having our friendships out of balance. We may have tons of friends, either online or in person, where the relationship never gets that deep. These friendships stay on the level of "having fun." And while this is not that destructive, it also can never produce the kind of wonderful, deep, and personal friendships that God would want for us. We won't be able to share pain or confess to one another. Having all of our friendships be at a surface level means we will miss out on the help that comes when Christians bear each other's burdens and encourage one another.

> *You were cleansed from your sins when you obeyed the truth, so now you must show sincere love to each other as brothers and sisters.* <u>*Love each other deeply with all your heart.*</u> (1 Peter 1:22 NLT)

Have you seen your friendships lacking the deep intimacy that Peter is describing here? _____

Where "friendship love" can become really destructive though is when it becomes out of balance in our other relationships. It's good for a parent to have a friendship love with their kids, but when this love overrides the other aspects of love, it prevents the parent from being an actual parent to their children. They won't provide the forgiveness, stability, discipline, or protection that every child needs. While they might have a lot of fun, it will ultimately damage both the child and the parent. This is equally true in romantic relationships. It's good for a couple to have a friendship with one another, but again, if the relationship never goes deeper than that, then you can never have the beautiful intimacy that God intended in romance. Anyone who has ever been in a long term relationship knows that while fun times will happen, they can't be the basis for a marriage. Real marriage requires commitment to get through the hard times and provide stability and security. It needs mercy to provide forgiveness in failures, joy in service, and compromise in disagreement. It needs protection to provide accountability in the relationship, as well as helpful correction for the betterment of our spouse. It finally needs that passion, because without it marriage becomes dull; you become little more than roommates, and it certainly won't show the passionate, beautiful love of God to those who look in at your marriage.

Has unbalanced "friendship love" hurt your other relationships? _____

_____

We started this study with the quote from 1 John 3:16 which says, "By this we <u>know</u> love, because He laid down His life for us. And we also ought to lay down our lives for the brethren."

And the beautiful thing about this study is that we can see how, in Jesus all of these different loves are perfectly balanced. This truth shows itself most predominantly at the cross. In the cross we see wonderful "passionate love," for it was the passionate love of Christ for us that brought Him through the pains of the cross and counted all of it joy for His beloved. It is no mistake that we call the crucifixion "the passion of Christ."

> *Looking unto Jesus, the founder and perfecter of our faith, who for the joy that was set before Him endured the cross, despising the shame...* (Hebrews 12:2)

We also see wonderful committed love, because in dying for us, Jesus was pledging His love for us for all eternity. In His death, He has demonstrated to us that He is committed to us even in our failures, and that His commitment toward us began before the foundation of the world and will continue throughout eternity. And when we understand this, it gives us wonderful freedom and joy in Christ, to know that He is with us and for us because of His commitment to us (and that it's not based on our faithfulness to Him).

What then shall we say to these things? <u>If God is for us, who can be against us? He who did not spare His own Son, but delivered Him up for us all, how shall He not with Him also freely give us all things?</u> Who shall bring a charge against God's elect? It is God who justifies. Who is he who condemns? It is Christ who died, and furthermore is also risen, who is even at the right hand of God, who also makes intercession for us. Who shall separate us from the love of Christ? Shall tribulation, or distress, or persecution, or famine, or nakedness, or peril, or sword? As it is written: 'For your sake we are killed all day long; We are accounted as sheep for the slaughter.' Yet in all these things we are more than conquerors through Him who loved us. For I am persuaded that neither death nor life, nor angels nor principalities nor powers, nor things present nor things to come, nor height nor depth, nor any other created thing, shall be able to separate us <u>from the love of God</u> which is in Christ Jesus our Lord. (Romans 8:31-39)

We also see "protective love" because Jesus was willing to protect us from the consequences of sin and death even if it cost Him His very life.

Surely He has borne our griefs and carried our sorrows; yet we esteemed Him stricken, smitten by God, and afflicted. But He was pierced for our transgressions; He was cursed for our iniquities; upon Him was the chastisement that brought us peace, and <u>with His wounds we are healed</u>. (Isaiah 53:4-5 ESV)

We can see "merciful love" as He fully pardons all of our sins and pays our debt with His own blood, not counting our sins against us any longer.

And you, who once were alienated and hostile in mind, doing evil deeds, He has now reconciled in His body of flesh by His death, in order to present you holy and blameless and above reproach before Him... (Colossians 1:21-22)

And we see "friendship love" in the most stunning display of love that God could show. Like I said, the basis for "friendship love" was equality, having shared goals and experiences. It was thought to be impossible that man could have this kind of relationship with God. How could the all powerful, perfect, eternal, Creator of the entire universe possibly have a true friendship with His frail creation? It is through Jesus that we see that while we could never become like God, God humbled Himself and became like us in the frailty of our life, and the shame of our death.

For it was fitting for Him, for whom are all things and by whom are all things, in bringing many sons to glory, to make the captain of their salvation perfect through sufferings. For both He who sanctifies and those who are being sanctified are all of one, for which reason <u>He is not ashamed to call them brethren</u>... (Hebrews 2:10-11)

John 15:13 says that "Greater love has no one than this, than to lay down one's life for his friends." Can you see how Jesus perfectly balances all of these loves?

In wrapping up, we see that through experiencing this perfect love, we can be filled and set free to care for others above ourselves. We know that while we do not love perfectly right now, as we begin to understand God's love, we will move towards balance in the way that we love others. We are daily being called by our Father to grow in His perfect love for Him and others. As He works in our lives, we will become more and more like Him. The fight against our selfish inclinations will be present for the rest of our lives, but every step forward is another step closer to the joy we have in God, and the freedom we can have from being consumed by our selfishness.

And then Paul says in Philippians 3:12, "I don't mean to say that I have already achieved these things or that I have already reached perfection. But I press on to possess that perfection for which Christ Jesus first possessed me." (NLT)

How Love Changes Us

"For Godly sorrow produces repentance leading to salvation, not to be regretted; but the sorrow of the world produces death. For observe this very thing, that you sorrowed in a godly manner: what diligence it produced in you, what clearing of yourselves, what indignation, what fear, what vehement desire, what zeal, what vindication! In all things you proved yourselves to be clear in this matter." (2 Corinthians 7:10)

A couple of lessons back we talked about how God is not satisfied with mere behavior change, but instead that He wants to change our hearts. Now let's talk about how He practically does this work in us. In the above passage, Paul says that an inner change happened to the Corinthian church; they weren't just changing their behavior, but they were having a profound outward change which was the product of a genuine internal change. Paul points out that they had experienced a genuine sorrow over the wrong things that they had done. They weren't just outwardly performing good deeds, but they had a wonderful excitement and passion in doing good works, pursuing God, and making things right. Their hearts had truly been changed through a process that Paul calls "repentance."

WHAT IS REPENTANCE?

"Repentance" is a tricky word, and one that is really misunderstood in the church. Growing up, I used to think that repentance was like a door—that once you found the right key and opened the door of repentance you would never struggle with an area of sin again. I heard pastors say things like, "I used to struggle with that sin, but then I repented…" or, "If you are struggling with this type of sin, God wants you to repent…" All of this reinforced to me an understanding of repentance meaning that if I had it, my struggles against sin would be over.

Because of this misunderstanding of repentance, I never believed that I had true repentance in my life. I continued to struggle with, and even fall into porn and various other sins. I also thought that when someone repented it meant that they had a really deep emotional experience accompanied by lots of crying. This caused me to constantly try to manufacture repentance through making myself feel bad for what I had done. This didn't work either.

When we study this passage, we can see that both of my ideas about repentance were wrong. First, the way that Paul describes what is happening to the Corinthians is not as though it happened in the past, he is describing it as something that was currently happening in them.

The word "repentance" means a change of direction; a 180 degree turn. It is not simply a one-time change; it is a deep, ongoing change that alters the very course of someone's life. We should understand this, because repentance is what happened to us when we got saved.

REPENTANCE SAVES US—IT DOES NOT PERFECT US!

We were all walking away from God. At some point in our lives, God called us to walk after Him and away from our old lives. We responded to this call by putting our faith in Jesus as our Savior and we began to pursue God in newness of life. This was the repentance that saved us from the consequences of our sins and brought us into a relationship with Jesus, which will ultimately bring us home to heaven. While that repentance saved us, it did not perfect us.

For all of us, there will continue to be areas of our lives in which we struggle with various sins. Whether it is sexual sin, pride, greed, vanity, laziness, gluttony, or some combination therein, we will constantly, in varying degrees and in different areas, walk away from God and toward our sin.

A question that I wrestled with was this: "If I still struggle with sin, does that mean I never truly repented and therefore, I'm not saved?" Of course this is not true. The Bible makes it very clear that even though we are saved, our struggle against sin will continue until we see Him face to face (Galatians 5:17; Philippians 1:6).

When someone realizes that they are sinning in a particular area and repents (by making the decision to turn away from that sin and towards God), that doesn't mean that they will never struggle again. I have repented, genuinely, of pornography use, but stumble at times, as do many of my brothers and sisters in the Lord. We are still saved and loved by God, but because of the propensity to wander (which remains in our flesh), there is a need for consistent repentance. It would be great if we all turned from sin once and for all, and never looked back; but unfortunately we are still fallen, imperfect, and daily in need of a Savior.

Please read and comment on the following passage:

> *For though the righteous fall seven times, they rise again, but the wicked stumble when calamity strikes.* (Proverbs 24:16 NIV)

_____

_____

_____

It amazes me that I never saw this truth earlier in my life—the Scriptures so clearly demonstrate this fact. So many Christians today don't know how to appropriately fight their sin because they believe that once they repent correctly, their struggles will be over.

They don't understand that the Christian life is one of constant struggle against the flesh, and a constant reaching out to God for help. This simplistic view of repentance has shipwrecked the faith of many Christians because when they continue to struggle against sin, they assume that they never repented and they may even doubt their salvation. If one holds to this simplistic understanding, then sin can creep in unrecognized; this Christian can be in denial of their insidious sins and spend their time focusing only on the outward sins that they aren't committing.

THE PHARISEES

The pharisees are prime examples of this. They were so convinced they were perfectly keeping the commands of God that they denied their own sin. A big part of Jesus' earthly ministry was to forcefully correct the pharisees' understanding of sin. That is why in the "Sermon on the Mount" He spends so much time explaining that sin begins in the heart. Whether we physically sin or not, our hearts remain corrupt and wicked before God.

The pharisees rejected Jesus' point and continued to walk in their own self-righteousness as they proudly judged those around them. As a result of their arrogance, they completely missed their Messiah. They were so busy worrying about their own self-righteousness (and other people's sin) they couldn't see their need for a Savior. When we have a wrong view of repentance, we can easily fall into this same trap.

Please read and comment on the following passage:

> *If we say that we have no sin, we deceive ourselves, and the truth is not in us. If we confess our sins, He is faithful and just to forgive us our sins and to cleanse us from all unrighteousness. If we say that we have not sinned, we make Him a liar, and His Word is not in us.* (1 John 1:8-10)

_____

_____

SOME WHO STRUGGLED IN THE SCRIPTURES

When we look through the Bible text, we don't see a bunch of perfect saints who never struggled; we see deeply flawed individuals who consistently reached out to God for the grace to be forgiven, and to change.

A few examples:

• **Abraham** had sex with his maid;
• **Judah** sold his own brother into slavery and had sex with his daughter in-law while thinking she was a prostitute;
• **Noah** struggled with drunkenness
• **David** had major issues with his anger—he committed murder; plundered towns for money; had multiple

wives and concubines even though he was expressly told not to (Deuteronomy 17:17); he failed as a father, even allowing one of his sons to rape one of his daughters without disciplining him at all; he committed adultery with a married woman and then murdered her husband to cover it up; and failed in many other ways;

• **The Apostle Paul** confessed to having an ongoing struggle with covetousness, and when he was speaking of his sinful nature he said that nothing good dwelt in his flesh (Romans 7:18), that he was a wretched man in desperate need of a Savior (Romans 7:24), and that he was the chief of sinners (1 Timothy 1:15-16);

• **The Apostle Peter** consistently failed throughout Jesus' ministry and even after the resurrection he had to be called out by the apostle Paul for being racist towards the Gentiles, and in so doing, he almost subverted the message of the gospel for those who were looking up to him (Galatians 2:11-16).

The list could go on and on, for every person in Scripture (outside of Christ Himself) was in need of a Savior.

IF GOD CAN HELP THEM, HE CAN HELP US!

Even though these men (and plenty of women) had these severe struggles and failures, they didn't shrug their shoulders and say, "Well this is just who I am." They also didn't deny their issues. They owned their sin and sought repentance in God. If we want an example of a perfect man, we have one in Christ, but the reason why the example of these men is so valuable to us is because Jesus can't be an example to us of how to fall and get back up because He never fell. He can't show us how to change because He is always perfect—but these men can show us these things.

When we read through these biblical accounts, we gain encouragement and hope to know that if God can work in men like this and change them, He can do the same for us. While these men and women didn't experience perfection this side of heaven, they did experience life-altering change, and so can we.

PERFECT REPENTANCE?

The concept of perfect repentance this side of heaven is not present in the Bible. What we do in see scripture are men and women who failed time and time again, and needed to consistently confess their sins, cry out to God for help, and seek deep change.

Even in the above Proverb we see that it is the righteous man who falls seven times, but he gets back up. We need to understand that repentance is not about being completely delivered from your struggles. Repentance is a daily turning from sin to pursue God that will result in the complete change of your heart and your actions in time. In Luke 9:23 it says, "Whoever wants to be my disciple must deny themselves and take up their cross daily and follow me."

Repentance is about learning the discipline and perseverance to fail well. It is about receiving the mercy of God, learning from our mistakes, and seeking to do better each and every day.

Because this truth is not talked about very much in church, I grew up in utter hopelessness. I would see (what seemed to me) perfect Christians all around me, and I would have no idea of how to grow and change. It was almost like every Christian was simply telling me, "It's really easy Peter, just stop sinning and be like Jesus." I would feel this weight of despair because I had no idea how to really change. I didn't know how to cry out to God in the midst of failure, how to fall and get back up, or how to implement new strategies in fighting my sin. The hope we have as Christians is that God will change our hearts, but this is a process not a singular action. *Don't miss out on this truth, or you will miss out on the joy of seeing God's daily work in your life.*

Please read and comment on this quote from C.S. Lewis in *Mere Christianity:*

> *"We may, indeed, be sure that perfect chastity—like perfect (love)—will not be attained by any merely human efforts. You must ask for God's help. Even when you have done so, it may seem to you for a long time that no help, or less help than you need, is being given. Never mind. After each failure, ask forgiveness, pick yourself up, and try again. Very often what God first helps us towards is not the virtue itself but just this power of always trying again. For however important chastity (or courage, or truthfulness, or any other virtue) may be, this process trains us in habits of the soul which are more important still. It cures our illusions about ourselves and teaches us to depend on God."*

_____

_____

THE CORINTHIANS HAD PROBLEMS

This truth is also shown to us in the rest of Paul's letter. When you read through both letters of 1st and 2nd Corinthians, you see that the Corinthians were a mess. Yes, Paul was witnessing change in them, but they continued to need a lot more change in their lives, and even in the areas that they had changed they still needed more work. Instead of claiming that the Corinthians had completed their change fully, Paul was encouraging the work that God had already done in order to give them hope for the work that He would continue to do.

A LIFE-CHANGING TRUTH

Repentance will always be growing in us, in some areas more than others, but it will not be perfected in us this side of heaven. This truth was life-changing for me to understand. Remember, when I believed repentance was a one-time action, it meant that if I fell again to an area of sin then I had not truly repented of it at all.

Because of this, whenever I fell I felt as if I was starting all over and that I had made no progress at all. The truth is, just because you fall to sin doesn't mean that you haven't made any progress. *God is working in us.* When we fall, we have to own what we did, learn from our mistakes, get back up, and keep on pursuing Him out of the forgiveness that He has already given us. *Note that the severity of the damage of our sins will help us determine how severe the actions of our repentance will need to be.* But the main point is that we may fall in the process of our repentance from particular sins—but remember, we can always repent again. His mercies are new every morning!

REALIZE: GOD HAS BEEN AND IS WORKING IN YOU...

In addition to the feeling that I had to start all over again, and the guilt that I felt that I somehow had *never truly repented,* I also felt like something was just wrong with me. It seemed to me that everyone else in church had figured this repentance thing out and had all turned from their sin. I couldn't figure out why I couldn't do the same; this made me feel even worse than I did before and more like an outcast that wasn't loved by God. Being overcome by these lies made me miss out on all the work that God had been doing in and through me. I missed the whole point of repentance. The goal of repentance isn't just about not sinning; the true goal of repentance is gaining more of God, Himself (freedom from sin is merely a fruit of a loving relationship with Him).

Have you ever thought that repentance was a one-time thing? How has your understanding of repentance impacted you in your walk with God?

_____

_____

MUST REPENTANCE BE EMOTIONAL?

We also see that repentance is not necessarily an emotional experience, though it will be coupled with an emotional response. Paul says, "Godly sorrow *produces* repentance," not "Godly sorrow *is* repentance." While the change (and perhaps emotional shift) grows out of this sorrow, they are not the same thing.

Paul also says that there is a type of sorrow that produces repentance; and another type of sorrow that produces death. That means that someone can weep and cry uncontrollably out of sorrow for what they have done, and all the while be producing death and not repentance.

IT'S GOD'S LOVE THAT CHANGES US

This leads to my main point: *Ultimately it is God's love that changes us and nothing else.* The main difference between the two types of sorrows mentioned is their directional nature.

The first type of sorrow is directed toward God; it is a sadness born out of our deep regret over sinning against God.

The second type of sorrow is directed toward the world; it is a sadness over hurting people in the world or about having consequences in the world.

While having sorrow over hurting others or the consequences our sin has brought is not in itself bad, if it is our main motivator we are missing the point. Our deep emotions, including sorrow, ultimately point us to what we love. If I love someone deeply and I offend them, I will be really hurt; but if I don't like someone and I offend them, I won't care.

Paul is saying that if I sin and I am only sorry because I got caught, or because it is damaging my marriage, my reputation, my self-respect, my career, my health, my family... that is a worldly sorrow ultimately produced by my self-love (pride). It makes no difference how passionate this sorrow might be, it can only produce death because it is rooted in selfishness. But, if I sin and I am devastated over offending God and sinning against Him, then I have a godly sorrow produced out of my deep love and affection for God, and it is this sorrow that will produce true repentance, leading to life.

I need to come to place where I can say, like David did after he committed adultery with Bathsheba and murdered her husband to cover it up, "Against You, You only, have I sinned, and done this evil in Your sight... (Psalm 51:4). "

David isn't saying that he didn't wrong anyone else through his actions, but instead he is focusing his attention on God and seeing Him as the prime reason for his sorrow and regret.

Please read and comment on this quote from Charles Spurgeon:

> *True repentance has a distinct and constant reference to the Lord, Jesus Christ. If you repent of sin without looking to Christ, away with your repentance! If you are so lamenting your sin as to forget the Savior, you have need to begin all this work over again. Whenever we repent of sin we must have one eye upon sin and another upon the Cross. Or, better still, let us have both eyes upon Christ, seeing our sin punished in Him and by no means let us look at sin except as we look at Jesus. A man may hate sin just as a murderer hates the gallows – but this does not prove repentance. If I hate sin because of the punishment, I have not repented of sin – I merely regret that God is just. But if I can see sin as an offense against Jesus Christ and loathe myself because I have wounded Him, then I have a true brokenness of heart. If I see the Savior and believe that those thorns upon His head were plaited by my sinful words; If I believe that those wounds in His heart were pierced by my heart sins; If I believe that those wounds in His feet were made by my wandering steps and that the wounds in His hands were made by my sinful deeds – then I repent of sin after a right fashion. Only under the Cross can you repent. Repentance elsewhere is remorse which clings to the sin and only dreads the punishment. Let us then seek, under God, to have a hatred of sin caused by a sight of Christ's love.*

_____

_____

_____

Two Questions to Ask Yourself

The two questions we have to ask ourselves are: 1. "Why can't worldly sorrow save us?" and 2. "How do we get Godly sorrow?

The answer to the first question is pretty simple. As we've already have stated: all the sin in our lives is rooted in our pride and selfishness and this is ultimately producing death. It is our pride that is separating us from

God, hurting our relationships, keeping us foolish, and producing all the other sins that we commit every day. Because of this, any sorrow that comes from pride can't save us, but only feeds the same root that has been killing us all along. It is very possible for someone to experience incredible sorrow over hurting a spouse, losing a career, damaging their reputation, or endangering their health—and for that sorrow to be so deep and powerful that *it actually does change their behavior and get them free from a particular area of sin.* But, if this change is coming from selfishness, not only does this change not please God, but it has actually made us more consumed with pride than we were before.

For most of us, however, this kind of sorrow will not be strong enough to permanently change us. It will only be strong enough to change us for a time. Eventually we will slip right back into our familiar bad habits. This constant failure cycle will lead to despair and self-pity, which comes from our inability to change. Fear and pride might be very powerful motivators, but they just aren't strong enough to change us in the way that God desires. Love, on the other hand, is a far more powerful motivator; love can change people in a much more significant way.

For a simple example of this, consider how you drive your car. We determine how to drive our cars based on the law. But this comes from our fear of punishment, not from love or affection. Because of this, I will only obey the law enough to not get in trouble and my obedience will be merely outward. Also, obedience motivated only by adhering to the law puffs me up so that when I am keeping the law it makes me be overly resentful of people who are getting away with speeding or breaking the law in some other way.

Most of us have a relationship with God that is exactly like this. We attempt to obey God out of fear of His justice and because of this we have very little, or no, joy or affection for God. Ultimately living 'purely' with this motivation makes us bitter at God (frustrated at Him for making us live in a different way than we want) and our lustful passion to break His law only grows stronger in our hearts. When this fear fails to set us free from our sin, it causes us, instead, to constantly question our salvation. In addition, this perversion of God's character feeds our fear that we will never get free from sin. Finally, we will harshly judge and even be jealous towards people who aren't trying as hard to keep the law, because we have bred self righteousness within us.

Have you seen this kind of fear based obedience in your relationship with God? _____

_____

On the other hand, I have also seen a lot of people change their behavior and lifestyles out of love. Think for a moment about all that someone has to give up and change in order to get married or raise a child. The change present in genuine loving relationships is unbelievable. This change goes further than anything that can be produced in a fear-based relationship, and it is powerful enough to even change your heart. Someone experiencing this kind of love can find amazing joy in serving and self sacrifice. When considering two fallen people in a relationship of love-based sacrifice like this, it amazes me even more because this is still an imperfect love. How much more can the power of God's love change us when it is perfect in every way and set toward a perfect being?

Have you tried to be free in the past through worldly sorrow instead of love? Do you see why this can't actually set you free? _____

_____

The answer to the second question is a little more complicated. If it is true that genuine sorrow comes out of genuine love, that means that Godly sorrow can't be manufactured. Unfortunately many people in the church think otherwise. I have heard so many sermons aimed at trying to manufacture this kind of sorrow in people. We can go on and on about how wicked a particular sin issue is and how much it hurts those around us and the world as a whole. And I'm not saying that we should never worry about the damage we are doing to other people in our sin, I'm just saying that a supreme focus on worldly consequences is ultimately just worldly sorrow and it can't actually change us. Charles Spurgeon put it this way: It is easy to bring a man to the river of regret, but you cannot make him drink the water of repentance.

Have you tried to manufacture repentance through making yourself feel sorry?_____

When some Christians hear this, they get a little nervous because it sounds to them like in doing this we are excusing our sin and not taking it seriously. But this isn't true, if I am only sorry as I contemplate the depravity of my sin, I will try desperately to change out of regret, despair, and out of fear of God's wrath, but all of my motivations will be centered on my own self-interest. Yes, it is important to understand that God has wrath towards our sins and that our failures are very serious in His eyes. But, it is only through understanding God's deep love and forgiveness for us that surmounts His wrath, that the obstacle of guilt can be removed and we can be sorry simply for offending God and change out of our love for Him and not our desire to assuage our guilty conscience. When we change out of guilt it will also be an attempt to change for God, and not a faith in God to transform us for His glory. As we have already seen, we can't change ourselves, but praise God that He can! Sorrow that is born out of love and not guilt is the only sorrow that is unselfish and powerful enough to change us inside and out.

Please read and comment on the following passage:

> *Or do you despise the riches of His goodness, forbearance, and longsuffering, not knowing that the goodness of God leads you to repentance?* (Romans 2:4)

_____

_____

Please read and comment on the following quote by Oswald Chambers from *My Utmost For His Highest*:

> *The wonders of conviction of sin, forgiveness, and holiness are so interwoven that it is only the forgiven person who is truly holy. He proves he is forgiven by being the opposite of what he was previously, by the grace of God. Repentance always brings a person to the point of saying, "I have sinned." The surest sign that God is at work in his life is when he says that and means it. Anything less is simply sorrow for having made foolish mistakes— a reflex action caused by self-disgust.*

Let's look at a very famous passage in Hebrews 12:1-2 to illustrate this point further:

> *Let us lay aside every weight, and the sin which so easily ensnares us, and let us run with endurance the race that is set before us, looking unto Jesus, the author and finisher of our faith, who for the joy that was set before Him endured the cross, despising the shame, and has sat down at the right hand of the throne of God.*

Notice that in this passage the author is saying that we as Christians should not just throw off sin, but every weight that hinders us in our pursuit of God. When we have a legalistic mindset we tend to think more about what we can get away with, and our attempts to change will be reactive to negative consequences. In other words, someone with this mindset will always ask questions like "Why can't I still do that, it isn't hurting anyone…" or "Is this really sinful?" What we are really asking in these moments, is what is the bare minimum that I can do for God not to get angry at me?

ANALOGY IN THE BOOK OF HEBREWS

The writer of Hebrews combats this type of thinking by using the analogy of running a race. If you were to ask a serious athlete what their goal was in a race, they would never say "my goal is to simply not fall." That would be a ridiculous goal and you would never win the race with that mindset. In the same vein, if I were to ask someone who was about to be married what the goal of the marriage was, and they responded, "My goal is to not get divorced." That would be a relationship that could never withstand all the hardships and the pains of marriage, and would never enjoy all the wonderful fulfillment of marriage either because the goal was centered on avoiding the negative and not pursuing the positive. And yet, so many Christians live their lives with the central goal of simply not sinning, not understanding how weak and useless this mindset really is, and how living like this will never bring you into the supreme joy that is in a loving relationship with God.

In a race, obviously the runner would not want to fall, but the goal would be to win, and in a good marriage, obviously you wouldn't want a divorce, but this wouldn't be the goal. The goal would never be based on how far you could get from the other person before you got a divorce, but instead how close we could get to our spouse and how rich your love can be for one another. One of the fruits of having a rich and vibrant marriage, is that you won't get a divorce, but that isn't the goal. That's the kind of mindset the writer of Hebrews is trying to bring to us in our relationship with God. We as Christians shouldn't want to sin against God, but that should never be our goal, our goal should be running toward the prize in Christ. And this kind of passionate pursuit of God could never be born of legalistic fear, but only out of genuine love.

To drive this point home, the author of Hebrews points us to our ultimate example in Christ. He points us to our loving Savior, who for the joy He had in His bride endured all the sufferings of the cross. Jesus gave up everything for us, He was ultimately free, all-powerful, immune to pain, suffering, weakness, and death, and He gave all this up to be bound in a fragile body, to be subjected to rejection, loss, weakness, betrayal, torture, and finally death all for our sakes. This kind of sacrifice didn't come from obligation or fear, but from a deep love for us that allowed Him to do all of this willingly and even with joy. And if we follow His example, not seeking obedience from fear, but instead from love, we will finally be free to genuinely change from the inside out for God's glory and not our selfishness.

The following is from a song by John Newton (who also wrote, "Amazing Grace"):

How long beneath the law I lay In bondage and distress! I toiled the precept to obey, but toiled without success. Then to abstain from outward sin was more than I could do. Now, if I feel its pow'r within, I feel I hate it too. Then all my servile works were done a righteousness to raise; now, freely chosen in the Son, I freely choose His ways. Our pleasure and our duty, though opposite before, since we have seen His beauty are joined to part no more. To see the law by Christ fulfilled and hear His pardoning voice, transforms a slave into a child, and duty into choice.

Be Passionate in Your Love for God

The Christian who is passionately in love with God and completely convinced of God's love and forgiveness for him, will serve God and sacrifice for Him more, not less. Please read and comment on this quote from Charles Spurgeon:

The true penitent repents of sin against God, and he would do so even if there were no punishment. When he is forgiven, he repents of sin more than ever; for he sees more clearly than ever the wickedness of offending so gracious a God.

_____

_____

The true answer to gaining genuine repentance is found in our previous couple of lessons. We have to see that if true repentance is born out of genuine love for God, then we have to see that this is a gift from God and not anything that we can produce in ourselves.

2 Timothy 2:25 it says, "…in humility correcting those who are in opposition, if God perhaps will grant them repentance, so that they may know the truth…"

God Grants Repentance

Repentance is something that God Himself has to grant to us, it can't be worked for or deserved. As we are seeking this repentance, we need to be constantly asking for God to do a work in our hearts that we might experience and understand His love for us, and that we might grow more and more in our love for Him. It is only our love for God that will slowly grow that "Godly sorrow" that will lead to our true repentance. This also means that we need to constantly be honest with God. If you don't really feel sorry for what you have done, don't try to fake it or manufacture it, but be honest with God about your lack of sorrow. We need to know that because of our pride, our hearts will always be divided, there will be a part of us that is sorry for offending God, and a part of us that is only sorry for selfish reasons, or not sorry at all. None of us can honestly say "I am only sorry because I offended God, there is no worldly sorrow in me..."

I wish I could honestly say that, but it would be a lie. But God will be faithful to grow us in this area, we just have to trust Him to do this work and be consistent in our pursuit of Him.

Please read and comment on this quote from Charles Spurgeon:

> Repentance" is a grace. If, then, God has given you the least repentance—if it is sincere repentance—praise Him for it and expect that repentance will grow deeper and deeper as you go further on! Then this remark, I think, ought to be applied to all Christians—Christian men and women, you feel that you have not deep enough repentance—you feel that you have not large enough faith. What are you to do? Ask for an increase of faith and it will grow! So with repentance! Have you ever tried to get deep repentance? My friends, if you have failed therein, still trust in Jesus and try every day to get a penitential spirit. Do not expect—I say again—to have perfect repentance at first—sincere penitence you must have—and then under divine grace you will go on from strength to strength, until at last you shall hate and abhor sin as a serpent or a viper! And then shall you be near, very near, the perfection of repentance!

WORK OUT YOUR OWN SALVATION?

It is true that Christians must work out our own salvation (Philippians 2:12). We don't work *for* salvation, but *we work hard with what God puts in us* (Philippians 2:13). There are many practical things that I must do in my repentance if I truly want to turn away from my sin, but the foundation for my works has to be my love for God that brings me to have Godly sorrow, which produces in me repentance. But I can never, in my own strength, manufacture genuine love for God. It is impossible to work for repentance and salvation—these must be *received,* and as I begin to *receive* the gift of repentance, I will grow in my love for God. This will create in me increased sorrow over my sins, directed at God and not the consequences. This is something that I need to *constantly grow in through the grace of God and through the practical tools that He has given us to deepen our relationship with Him.*

For the Christian, repentance becomes a self-feeding cycle of growth, because the more you grow in your love for God, the more it will spur you on to do the acts that will cause you to grow in your love of God. It is the more that you seek God; confess your sins; praise Him; study His Word; spend time with His people; learn to love others... that you will grow in your love for God— This will cause you to have even more joy and passion in doing all of these things for Him.

Not that it will *always feel good* to pursue God, because remember, God's love doesn't always *feel* good. So even when we don't feel that "passionate love" for God, if we continue to pursue Him anyway, it will deepen our "committed love" for God and make our passion even richer when it does come.

THE MAIN PROBLEM

The main problem that we have? It is that we have things in the wrong order. We try to do works out of fearful obedience, not understanding, that love should be the motivation for the works. In fact, works that aren't motivated by love are rejected by God.

In Revelation 2:1 we are introduced to the church of Ephesus that had many great works, but notice what Jesus says to them in verse 4-5: "Nevertheless I have this against you, that you have left your first love. Remember therefore from where you have fallen; repent and do the first works, or else I will come to you quickly and remove your lampstand from its place—unless you repent."

The trap that the Ephesians fell into, is the same one that we can fall into: *They thought that God would be pleased through obedience alone, not understanding that God is more interested in the heart behind our actions than He is in the actions themselves.*

It is easy to manufacture works for God, but God wants to change our hearts and this is why we all need to be constantly praying for increased repentance in our lives.

Finally, just because we have the forgiveness of God doesn't mean that we should diminish the pain that we have caused others in our sin. But, in order to truly make things right with another person, we can't be self-focused.

In order to repair damage to a relationship, we have to be willing to put in a lot of time and effort as we demonstrate consistent faithfulness, patience, and sorrow for what we have done. If our change is all about that relationship though, it will be dependent on how that relationship is going and how that person is responding.

HE WILL GROW YOU IN YOUR LOVE FOR HIM

If progress isn't going the way we hoped, we will quickly go back to doing exactly what we were before, saying "What's the point? I tried and they won't forgive me..." But the person who has their eyes on God alone, will be able to continue in repentance whether their works are appreciated by others or not, because God has become the reason why they are doing all things. I am nowhere near to perfection in this, but God has grown me more in my love for Him than I ever thought possible, and I am excited to see His continued work in me, and I hope you are too.

Finish today's lesson by reading and commenting on the following quotes—and I also encourage you to read through Psalm 51 and Psalm 32 to see how David dealt with his failure before God:

Micah 7:8-9: Do not rejoice over me, my enemy; When I fall, I will arise; When I sit in darkness, The LORD will be a light to me. I will bear the indignation of the LORD, Because I have sinned against Him, Until He pleads my case And executes justice for me. He will bring me forth to the light; I will see His righteousness.

1 Corinthians 15:10: "But by the grace of God I am what I am, and His grace toward me was not in vain; but I labored more abundantly than they all, yet not I, but the grace of God which was with me."

Galatians 5:6: "For in Christ Jesus neither circumcision nor uncircumcision counts for anything, but only faith working through love.

Charles Spurgeon:

There is another mistake many poor people make when they are thinking about salvation, and that is that they cannot repent enough. They imagine that were they to repent up to a certain degree, they would be saved... "

Repentance, moreover, is never perfect in any man in this mortal state. We never get perfect faith so as to be entirely free from doubting. And we never get repentance which is free from some hardness of heart. The most sincere penitent that you know will feel himself to be partially impenitent. Repentance is also a continual lifelong act. It will continually grow. I believe a Christian on his deathbed will more bitterly repent than he ever did before. It is a thing to be done all your lifelong. Sinning and repenting— sinning and repenting make up a Christian's life! Repenting and believing in Jesus—repenting and believing in Jesus make up the consummation of his happiness!

Oswald Chambers, "My Utmost for His Highest:"

The entrance into the kingdom of God is through the sharp, sudden pains of repentance colliding with man's respectable "goodness." Then the Holy Spirit, who produces these struggles, begins the formation of the Son of God in the person's life (see Galatians 4:19). This new life will reveal itself in conscious repentance followed by unconscious holiness, never the other way around. The foundation of Christianity is repentance. Strictly speaking, a person cannot repent when he chooses— repentance is a gift of God. The old Puritans used to pray for "the gift of tears." If you ever cease to understand the value of repentance, you allow yourself to remain in sin. Examine yourself to see if you have forgotten how to be truly repentant.

_____

_____

_____

_____

_____

_____

THE DANGER OF LAZINESS

For the last couple of days, we have been focusing on the beautiful love of God, and seeing how it is this love that changes us. And as we learn to abide in this love, understand this love, and practice this love, we are becoming more like Him, less selfish, and more free from all of our sins.

WHAT KEEPS US FROM CHANGING?

Today, we are going to take a look at a very common, yet mostly overlooked sin, which we call "sloth" or "laziness." This may seem odd, but this is the sin that is most responsible for keeping us from changing. In order to understand the danger of this sin, we are going to take a look at three instances where Jesus spoke about laziness. In these stories we are going to see three main sources for our laziness, the consequences for our laziness, and how to overcome our laziness.

1. JESUS' FIRST OF THREE EXAMPLES OF LAZINESS IN SCRIPTURE

Matthew 25:1-13: "Then the kingdom of heaven shall be likened to ten virgins who took their lamps and went out to meet the bridegroom. Now five of them were wise, and five were foolish. Those who were foolish took their lamps and took no oil with them, but the wise took oil in their vessels with their lamps. But while the bridegroom was delayed, they all slumbered and slept. And at midnight a cry was heard: 'Behold, the bridegroom is coming; go out to meet him!' Then all those virgins arose and trimmed their lamps. And the foolish said to the wise, 'Give us some of your oil, for our lamps are going out.' But the wise answered, saying, 'No, lest there should not be enough for us and you; but go rather to those who sell, and buy for yourselves.' And while they went to buy, the bridegroom came, and those who were ready went in with him to the wedding; and the door was shut. Afterward the other virgins came also, saying, 'Lord, Lord, open to us!' But he answered and said, 'Assuredly, I say to you, I do not know you.' Watch therefore, for you know neither the day nor the hour in which the Son of Man is coming."

In the passage above, what did the foolish virgins not bring? _____

Jesus tells us that the foolish virgins brought lamps, *but they didn't bring any oil,* and here we can see the first source of our laziness, not wanting to suffer personal cost. It should have been obvious to the virgins that they would have needed oil for their lamps, yet they didn't prepare because they didn't want to have to sacrifice any of their own oil. These foolish virgins didn't even stay awake to wait for the bridegroom, they chose instead to fall asleep and rely on others to wake them up. Then when the bridegroom finally comes you can see their selfishness and entitlement come out when they demand that the wise virgins sacrifice for their mistake.

I know that I am guilty of doing the exact same thing in many areas of my life, including my relationship with God. I want to have a better relationship with God, I want to change and not go back toward my sin, but am I willing to make the sacrifices necessary to make that happen? I want to grow closer to God and love Him more, but, am I willing to sacrifice my time and spend more of it with Him in studying His Word, or speaking to Him honestly in prayer? Am I willing to take the time to seriously reflect on my issues and ask for help, both from God and from others? Am I willing to spend time with Christian brothers and sisters who can hold me accountable and encourage me towards God? Am I willing to sacrifice my money and my freedom in order to invest practically in my battle against sin, possibly buying online accountability software or even giving up my phone or my computer? Am I willing to sacrifice bad relationships that are hindering my walk with God? Am I willing to work towards repentance in all areas of sin in my life? Am I willing to sacrifice my reputation by coming clean about my issues to people in the church that can hold me accountable and consistently check up on me? These are just a few examples but I hope you see my point.

> *The desire of the lazy man kills him, For his hands refuse to labor.* (Proverbs 21:25)

Simply wanting to change doesn't change us, we have to be willing to count the cost, and put forth consistent effort. Unfortunately, in our culture we have this idea that if you want something bad enough, you will have it. Because of this, many people today lack serious careers and fulfilling relationships because they are unwilling to sacrifice the time and effort necessary to build these things, they expect these things to just fall into their laps.

This was my idea too. I wanted to change so badly, and I thought that if I just wanted it bad enough it would happen magically without effort. I have heard so many men answer me after I ask them how they expect to change by saying something like: "Well I am praying that God would change my heart." Now this is a great prayer, and I never discourage that prayer, but this prayer not coupled with action is useless. James 2:26 tells us: "For as the body without the spirit is dead, so faith without works is dead also."

It is the same thing as the foolish virgins who simply ask for the oil instead of thinking to take it with them for themselves. We tell ourselves that we are trusting in the power of Jesus to deliver us, but Jesus told us in Matthew 7:24-27: "Therefore whoever hears these sayings of Mine, and does them, I will liken him to a wise man who built his house on the rock: and the rain descended, the floods came, and the winds blew and beat on that house; and it did not fall, for it was founded on the rock. But everyone who hears these sayings of Mine, and does not do them, will be like a foolish man who built his house on the sand: and the rain descended, the floods came, and the winds blew and beat on that house; and it fell. And great was its fall."

It is no good to say that you trust Jesus if you aren't willing to do what He has asked of you. The belief that you don't have to sacrifice to follow God is laziness not spirituality. Most Christians today believe that you can just go to church and hear sermons and these will somehow change you just by listening to them. Hearing the Word of God is crucial and important, but it does nothing unless you are willing to obey what you are listening to. Even as a pastor, this still something that I need to grow in today. Even though I teach and study God's word, it can sometimes go beyond my notice to practice what I am teaching. We all need to remember the importance of being doers of the Word, and not merely hearers.

Has your resistance towards personal loss kept you from doing what you know you should in order to follow God? _____

This issue becomes even more complicated when you consider that our struggles against sin won't be over quickly, but we will need to continue to sacrifice throughout our lives in our pursuit of God. It might be easy to sacrifice for a time, but it is the day in day out grind that produces laziness in all of us. Eventually the sacrifice becomes too much, we become too tired and complacent, and we slowly slip back into old, destructive, bad habits. This is especially difficult in the culture that we live in. We live in a society built around instant gratification, and because of this, we have forgotten the wonderful virtues of patience and consistency and we instead just look for what's easy and fun. And because of this, we become like the foolish virgins, who feel entitled to what they want simply because they want it. When we don't change in the way we think we should, or as fast as we think we should we blame God or other people around us and become frustrated.

But when we do this, we forget that the best things in life don't occur in an instance, but they take time and dedication. There is no short term formula for having a fulfilling career, a loving marriage, intimate friendships, a caring family, and so many other wonderful things. These things must be worked for daily and in sometimes overly simple and seemingly bland ways. It is because of this "drudgery" that we lose sight of our goals and give up. Choosing moments of instant gratification followed by great swelling periods of emptiness, instead of choosing to have seasons of drudgery that produce torrents of joy, love, and satisfaction.

> *Let us not become weary in doing good, for at the proper time we will reap a harvest if we do not give up.* (Galatians 6:9 NIV)

Our relationship with God is like any other loving relationship, there are no shortcuts and no formulas to getting closer to Him, just discipline and consistency in doing the good things that we already know to do.

Please read and comment on the following quote from Oswald Chambers in his book *My Utmost For His Highest:*

> *In the matter of drudgery, you have inherited the Divine nature, says Peter (2 Peter 1:4), now screw your attention down and form habits, give diligence, concentrate... No man is born either naturally or supernaturally with character; he has to make character. Nor are we born with habits; we have to form habits on the basis of the new life God has put into us... Drudgery is the touchstone of character. The*

great hindrance in spiritual life is that we will look for big things to do. "Jesus...took a towel,...and began to wash the disciples' feet." (John 13:4-5)

There are times when there is no illumination and no thrill, but just the daily round, the common task. Routine is God's way of saving us between our times of inspiration. Do not expect God always to give you His thrilling minutes, but learn to live in the domain of drudgery by the power of God.

Because this seems so mundane and boring, we can become scornful of the way God is doing things. We don't want to have a daily, intimate, loving relationship with God, where we have to constantly take up our cross and follow Him, we instead want a cosmic genie that we can order to simply deliver us from all our problems and sins. I have seen so many men over the years begin to find victory in their struggles against their sin, experience a time of freedom and simply give up all the wonderful graces that God has given them to pursue Him. They stop confessing their struggles, they fall out of consistent accountability, they begin to reintroduce all sorts of temptations into their lives, They stop putting forth effort in their marriages, they stop pursuing God the way that they had been...

No Graduation

We have to remember that these graces from our Father are meant to be practiced all the time, we don't "graduate" from them just as we don't "graduate" from struggling against our sin. Just because we have experienced a moment of illumination, or a season of victory doesn't mean that our struggle is dead, and if you are in a season of victory like this, I praise God that He has brought you to this place, but don't fall into this trap of laziness, don't stop pressing into God, keep picking up your cross every day.

Our struggle will get better as our relationship with God deepens, but there is no relationship on earth that will ever reach a point where you no longer need to try or put forth consistent effort. Even the strongest relationships in existence can fade over time if we let them. The graces that our Father has given to us are not the graces that deliver us in a moment, but the graces that sustain us and draw us closer to Him in humility.

In her book, *The Scars That Have Shaped Me,* Vaneetha Risner writes:

"You never hear anyone in the Bible complaining about the parting of the Red Sea, everyone loves the grace that delivers us. But the Israelites, like us, were dissatisfied with daily manna. We all complain about the grace that merely sustains us... I have been scornful of this sustaining grace. In waiting for the huge, monumental deliverance—the kind where I can put my issue to bed and never have to pray about it again—I have overlooked the grace that keeps drawing me to Him. The prayers that may appear unanswered, but actually are fulfilled in ways that keep me dependent and needy."

Have you seen yourself become scornful of God's sustaining grace and repetitively slipped back into your old habits? _____

_____

I have to say, just as she did, that in my selfishness I have demanded God to do things the way that I wanted Him to because I was too lazy to continue fighting my sin and to daily invest in my relationship with Him. And in doing this, I didn't realize, that by God demanding for me to consistently sacrifice and wait on Him, He has been training me in the gifts of patience and love. Love isn't a destination, it isn't about making a relationship good enough and then switching into auto-pilot. The beauty of love is that it is a daily pursuit that perpetually grows in depth and intimacy.

What we miss when we complain about "sustaining grace" is that we could never learn about the beauties of patience or love if God was an instant gratification machine who delivered us immediately. We have to understand, that as frustrating as this can be at times, it is far better for our sakes that God makes us wait. This also shows me that my issue is once again in focusing on myself and my own betterment over God's glory.

Since therefore Christ suffered in the flesh, arm yourselves with the same way of thinking, for whoever has suffered in the flesh has ceased from sin, so as to live for the rest of the time in the flesh no longer for human passions but for the will of God. (1 Peter 4:1)

Peter bluntly tells us that in order to fight our flesh, we will suffer, and he even compares this suffering to the suffering of Jesus on the cross. If the only reason why you and I are suffering is to simply not sin, of course we will become lazy and give up. Jesus was able to suffer on the cross for us because He was first of all realistic about the cost, knowing beforehand what He would have to give so He wasn't surprised or upset when He had to pay the price. But He was also realistic about His reward, Jesus counted the cost and determined that it was worth it because of the love that He had for us. If we want to be freed from our laziness we have to do the same thing. We have to be realistic about the cost of following Jesus, but we also must understand the great gain that we have in a relationship with Him. When my focus is on Him, then I can begin to overcome my resistance toward personal loss, I can become consistent and diligent because God is so infinitely worthy, He alone needs to be our treasure and our prize.

Please read and comment on the following passage in Philippians 3:7-8:

But what things were gain to me, these I have counted loss for Christ. Yet indeed I also count all things loss for the excellence of the knowledge of Christ Jesus my Lord, for whom I have suffered the loss of all things, and count them as rubbish, that I may gain Christ...

_____

_____

_____

2. JESUS' SECOND EXAMPLE OF LAZINESS IN SCRIPTURE

Matthew 25:14-30: "For the kingdom of heaven is like a man traveling to a far country, who called his own servants and delivered his goods to them. And to one he gave five talents, to another two, and to another one, to each according to his own ability; and immediately he went on a journey. Then he who had received the five talents went and traded with them, and made another five talents. And likewise he who had received two gained two more also. But he who had received one went and dug in the ground, and hid his lord's money. After a long time the lord of those servants came and settled accounts with them. So he who had received five talents came and brought five other talents, saying, 'Lord, you delivered to me five talents; look, I have gained five more talents besides them.' His lord said to him, 'Well done, good and faithful servant; you were faithful over a few things, I will make you ruler over many things. Enter into the joy of your lord.' He also who had received two talents came and said, 'Lord, you delivered to me two talents; look, I have gained two more talents besides them.' "His lord said to him, 'Well done, good and faithful servant; you have been faithful over a few things, I will make you ruler over many things. Enter into the joy of your lord.' Then he who had received the one talent came and said, 'Lord, I knew you to be a hard man, reaping where you have not sown, and gathering where you have not scattered seed. And I was afraid, and went and hid your talent in the ground. Look, there you have what is yours.' But his lord answered and said to him, 'You wicked and lazy servant, you knew that I reap where I have not sown, and gather where I have not scattered seed. So you ought to have deposited my money with the bankers, and at my coming I would have received back my own with interest. Therefore take the talent from him, and give it to him who has ten talents. For to everyone who has, more will be given, and he will have abundance; but from him who does not have, even what he has will be taken away.' And cast the unprofitable servant into the outer darkness. There will be weeping and gnashing of teeth."

According to this passage, why did the lazy servant bury the talent? _____

_____

Another major source for our laziness can be our fear of failure. This servant told his master that he didn't invest his talent because he knew what a savvy businessman the master was. Because of this, the servant got the idea that he would never be able to measure up to his master's expectations, so he gave up and buried the talent without even trying to make a profit. For countless people, the fear of failure and not measuring up has consistently prevented them from positive growth and change in many areas of their lives.

This particular source of laziness reminds me of a talk given by a psychologist named Guy Winch entitled "How To Practice Emotional First Aid." In this talk, he mentions a time when he was sitting in a waiting room at a doctor's office. While he was there he saw three children playing with a toy that had a red tab where if you slid it, a cute doggy would pop out and you could play with it. The first kid looked at the toy, tried to pull a lever on the box, and when it didn't work, he started crying and gave up. The second kid watched the first boy try to make the toy work, and when he failed, she burst into tears and gave up without even trying. The third kid wasn't deterred by the failure of the kids around her, or her own initial failures, instead she kept trying until she made the dog come out and she squealed with delight over her accomplishment.

HANDLING FAILURE

The reason why the other two children failed wasn't because they were incapable of sliding a lever, the reason why they failed was because they didn't know how to handle failure. When their fears and frustrations overcame their rationale, they gave up on something that they could have easily succeeded at, and they sank down into self-pity and despair. While commenting on this story, he said this:

Are you aware of how your mind reacts to failure? You need to be. Because if your mind tries to convince you you're incapable of something, and you believe it, then like those two toddlers, you'll begin to feel helpless and you'll stop trying too soon, or you won't even try at all. And then you'll be even more convinced you can't succeed. You see, that's why so many people function below their actual potential. Because somewhere along the way, sometimes a single failure convinced them that they couldn't succeed, and they believed it.

NEVER QUIT!

For so many of us, the reason why we aren't moving forward in certain areas, and the reason why we feel helpless in certain things isn't because we are incapable, but because we are so afraid of failing we quit too soon or we don't even try. I also believe that fear of failure has become far worse in our current society as a result of social media. What we have taught ourselves to do in social media, is to hide our real struggles and failures from the world so that we can present our lives as we would want them to be.

Because people hide their failures, we can't see what it looks like to fail *well*. We don't have any *good examples* of people *who fall, get back up, and persevere;* and what this has done, is convince many of us that really important things like romantic relationships, finances, school, work, raising children, our relationship with God, and many other things, should come natural to us and that success should not be difficult.

Because of this we try to teach ourselves how to do these things through books and YouTube so we don't have to admit ignorance, and when we begin to have issues in any of these areas, we can think that there is something wrong with us and we will be too embarrassed to ask for help. When we do this, we aren't seeing the truth that no one is naturally successful at any of the important things in life. All of us have to learn through trial and error, and all of us need help and advice.

FAILURE CAN TEACH MORE THAN SUCCESS!

What we need to understand is that *failure can actually teach us more than success,* and if we can train ourselves to overcome our perfectionist tendencies, and push past our fears and our initial failures and setbacks, we can learn from our mistakes and become better in every area, over time. The alternative is to be like that lazy servant, who was so paralyzed by his own fears that he buried his talent and didn't even make an effort.

Now, there are certain things in our lives that would be foolish and even dangerous to try, and sometimes failure can rightly teach us that some endeavors should be abandoned. But if we never search our hearts and scrutinize our goals and actions we won't be able to see if we are giving up out of wisdom, or fear. We have to renew our minds and see failure not as something to fear, but as something to learn from. If we grow in our humility we will be able to review our mistakes, see where we went wrong, ask for help and advice, and do better next time.

How do you handle failure in your life? _____

_____

As terrifying as failure can be in most areas of our lives, we can feel far more scared of failing in our relationship with God. We serve an absolutely perfect and holy God, and the thought that everything is laid naked and bear before Him, and we must give an account to Him for how we live, is a terrifying one to say the least.

For much of my life I lived in fear of my God, knowing that I could never possibly measure up to His standards, and because of this I constantly felt judged, and at times even hated by Him. And every flaw in my character and fall to sin affirmed to me my belief that I was worthless and that I would never be able to change.

God Is NOT Done with You!

After falling repetitively into sin, it can be daunting to get back up and keep trying. This is true especially when you look around the church culture and feel like you are the *only one struggling* to find success, while everyone around you is living the Christian life free from failure. Because of this, we get false ideas of God, we can feel like He is sitting up in heaven saying "I don't understand why you can't just figure this out, my Son lived a life free from sin and you can't go one day without messing up, I'm done with you." *God does not think that!*

When we have this negative view of God and of ourselves, it can be far easier to just give up and stop trying altogether. Most of us do this, we have fought valiantly for a long time, but we keep falling in many different areas and so we lose heart and become lazy and stop trying because we think it's better to never try, than to try and then fail. But notice what the master's response was to the servant: "So you ought to have deposited my money with the bankers, and at my coming I would have received back my own with interest." The master wasn't mad at the servant for failing, but for not trying at all, he said if the servant would have done something as small as invested the money in the bank, he would have been happy.

Has fear of failure kept you from persevering in your pursuit of God? _____

_____

Replace Your False View of God

If we want to have any hope of not succumbing to laziness in our walks with God, we have to renew our minds and replace our false image of God with His true character and nature. God is not some disappointed Father figure in the sky who is constantly ashamed of you.

He is an unbelievably loving Father who cares for you and wants what all loving fathers want for their children, for you to grow and do better, especially after failure.

Hosea 11:3-4: "I taught Ephraim to walk, taking them by their arms; but they did not know that I healed them. I drew them with gentle cords, with bands of love, and I was to them as those who take the yoke from their neck."

This passage has saved my life in so many ways. Notice first of all that God describes Himself as a Father teaching His child how to walk. What kind of a loving parent would get angry at His child for falling down when they attempted to walk? If a father had a son who never tried to walk and spent the rest of their life crawling on all fours, then he would have some disappointment, but every parent knows that when children are learning to walk the more they try, the more they will fall.

This amazed me! It showed me that all of us are in this boat, learning to walk under the guidance of our loving Father, and no one us is free from falling. We always have to remember, God isn't our Father because of how amazing we are, He is our Father because of His grace towards us.

John 1:12-13: "But as many as received Him, to them He gave the right to become children of God, to those who believe in His name: who were born, not of blood, nor of the will of the flesh, nor of the will of man, but of God."

It's Not About Works!

If your relationship with God is founded on your works, then you will see Him as an overbearing boss, and eventually you will be too discouraged to keep fighting your sin. But...if you can keep in mind that *you are His beloved child by grace through faith,* then you will have a solid foundation that will enable you to try to walk after Him not to earn love, but because you have already received it.

Everyone Fails At Times...He Will Catch Us!

None of us can walk without falling, but we are all growing and getting better as long as we continue to try. Our Father doesn't have unrealistic expectations for us, He doesn't think that we are never going to fall, but He is there to catch us and encourage us on.

Notice also, that God says that He is the One that heals us and takes the yoke from our neck. God is not dependent on us to get free from sin, He alone has the power to do that work in us. He isn't our boss who is impatiently waiting for us to put forth a product, as if He needed anything from us. The master didn't give the servants talents because he was broke and needed them to make him money, but instead, he wanted them to enter into his joy and be partakers in his kingdom. Fathers don't teach their children to walk for their own sakes, but for the joy and betterment of their children. And our Father in heaven is no different. He isn't training us in righteousness because He needs something from us, but He is doing this so that we might have supreme joy in our relationship with Him. This passage tells us that God draws us with gentle cords of love, not with carrots and sticks, and when we understand this, we can begin to overcome our laziness that is produced by our fear of failure.

Can you see that we don't have to be afraid of failure in our relationship with God? _____

_____

This truth becomes doubly important when we take into account the power of regret. For some of us, the reason why the fear of failure has crippled us is because we are currently wallowing in the fallout of our personal failures and we have lost hope that true change and restoration is possible for us.

Has regret and shame convinced you that you can't change?_____

_____

> *So I will restore to you the years that the swarming locust has eaten, The crawling locust, The consuming locust, And the chewing locust, My great army which I sent among you. You shall eat in plenty and be satisfied, And praise the name of the LORD your God, Who has dealt wondrously with you; And My people shall never be put to shame.* (Joel 2:25-26)

BEEN THERE, DONE THAT

I personally underwent a time like this when I came back from my second deployment. At that time in my life, I looked at all I had become and all that I had accomplished in my life, and all I could feel in response was intense amounts of regret and shame. My life wasn't at all what I wanted it to be, and I knew that I only had myself to blame. In that season of hopelessness, and at the verge of giving up altogether trying to change, this verse became life to me *and it remains a firm foundation of hope.*

GOD'S PEOPLE HAVE EXPERIENCED FAILURE

This section of Scripture was given to the people of Israel after a time of tremendous failure. A time of backsliding that was so severe, that God had to rain down on His own people a horrible plague of locust to get their attention. These locusts came in and devoured the crops of Israel and brought the nation to the brink of collapse. In this moment, God doesn't sugar coat the cause of their issues, but He tells them that He allowed this destruction into their lives as a consequence for turning against Him.

When we read through this section, we can see a powerful metaphor for the tragedy in our own lives. God points His people to look at the fields that were once their source of hope and life, and shows them how they are now empty and desolate, completely consumed by the consequences of their actions. Maybe you are going through a divorce, or you have lost your health, your career, your family, or your reputation... as a result of your sin. Whatever your loss might be, the things in your life that were once such a source of strength and vitality are now lying desolate and empty and there is little to no hope of ever having these things back. In times like this, we can become so down on ourselves that we can believe every nasty thing that is said about us, and become self-destructive, believing that we are not worthy of forgiveness or restoration.

In the midst of this hopeless situation, God makes them a very strange, but powerful promise. He promises them that He would restore to them the years that the locust had eaten. *Notice, God does not promise that He will restore to them the crops that the locust had taken, but instead the years.*

God never promised us that He will give us back what we have lost. Sometimes He does and I could share many stories of people that I have seen that had no hope of restoring their marriage, their families, their careers.. But through miraculous circumstances, these things were restored to them. But I could also share many stories where in spite of the truly sincere efforts of the one who did the wrong, what they lost was never restored to them. You might never get back the things that you have lost to your sin, but that doesn't mean all hope is lost. God's promise to us is instead that He will restore to us, not things, but time. I used to look back on all the time that I wasted in sin, and I felt all this regret, like I had completely wasted my life and I would never get that time back.

Now, when I look back on my past, while I do regret what I have done, I see, woven throughout my failures, the grace and love that God had for me even in my most severe failures—*I see so clearly how God used, even my failures, to draw me to Himself.*

Loss Does Not Mean God Has Given Up On You

Maybe you are in a season of intense loss, but do NOT take this as a sign that God has given up on you, take it as *God calling you to understand His grace and love in a deeper way...and as Him calling you out of your sin.* \

> *And you have forgotten the exhortation which speaks to you as to sons: "My son, do not despise the chastening of the LORD, Nor be discouraged when you are rebuked by Him; For whom the LORD loves He chastens, And scourges every son whom He receives." If you endure chastening, God deals with you as with sons; for what son is there whom a father does not chasten?* (Hebrews 12:5-7)

Just like the Israelites, we are very hard-headed, and as much as God would love to get our attention through gentleness, sometimes we need a much firmer approach. God will literally let your entire life burn if it means getting through to you. "...For it is more profitable for you that one of your members perish, than for your whole body to be cast into hell (Matthew 5:29)."

Even in the wake of your failure, your Father still loves you and desires to save you. But if you let your shame and regret consume you, and you believe the depressed thoughts of your damaged heart, then you will never get back up and you will never see the fruit of repentance.

Believing that God is for you in a season like this is a matter of faith, all evidence can be to the contrary. But if you can accept these truths, even in the darkest pit of despair, God can take this season of regret in your life and turn it into a season of hope. He can redeem all of your past failures and turn them into examples of the supreme grace and love that He has for fallen sinners, both to us, and to all those who look at our lives.

For me, while I do still regret so much falling into pornography, I know for a fact that I would never have learned the truth of God's undeserved grace for me, become a part of the ministry of running light, or be in the church that I am a part of, (which is consequently where I met my wife) if it wasn't for my failing in this particular area and God restoring me. I want to be clear that I am not condoning sin, or saying that God is ever for us sinning, it's just that our God is so good that He can actually work out His good plan and purpose for our lives even through our failures. It is always better to not fall at all, God would much more prefer to work through our successes rather than our failures, but God saves us as we are, and then brings us to where He wants us to be. When you look back on your deepest regrets, through the eyes of faith, trust that your good Father in heaven has plans for you that will redeem your moments of greatest failure. Otherwise your deep shame, which we can so easily mistake for holiness, will keep you from ever changing. But this all comes back to our trust in the nature and power of our great God. Without this trust, you will never be able to overcome your laziness that is produced by your shame and your regret. I have a question for you:

Do you believe that the love of God is great enough to forgive you for what you have done, and that He is powerful enough to redeem your life and change you for His glory?

_____

_____

3. JESUS' THIRD EXAMPLE OF LAZINESS IN SCRIPTURE

Let's take a look at one more scripture dealing with laziness:

And when Jesus saw great multitudes about Him, He gave a command to depart to the other side. Then a certain scribe came and said to Him, "Teacher, I will follow You wherever You go." And Jesus said to him, "Foxes have holes and birds of the air have nests, but the Son of Man has nowhere to lay His head." Then another of His disciples said to Him, "Lord, let me first go and bury my father." But Jesus said to him, "Follow Me, and let the dead bury their own dead." (Matthew 8:18-22)

ANOTHER SOURCE FOR LAZINESS: PROCRASTINATION

Here is one more major source for our laziness, procrastination. This is someone who isn't daunted by personal sacrifice and isn't consumed by fear of failure, but someone that is willing to serve God. But Jesus still has a correction for him because he has an excuse to procrastinate and not follow Jesus just yet. This section may sound harsh to us, but it is very possible, and likely, that this man's father wasn't even dead yet. It wasn't like his dad had just passed away, and Jesus is telling him that he can't have a proper burial for his own father, but this man was actually saying that he couldn't follow Jesus until after his dad had passed away and he had received the inheritance.

This is another very easy mistake to make. Unfortunately we live in a culture that is saturated with distractions and reasons to procrastinate. This is definitely one of Satan's favorite tools to use on people, because it is difficult to get people to oppose God, but it is so easy to get people to procrastinate with God. If Satan can get us to put God off for long enough, we will never come to Him. So many people never get saved because they keep putting it off. And so many Christians start out strong in their walks with God, and they have every intention of keeping it up, but over time, other things come up and they slowly drift away. Or, they know that they have a problem in a particular area of sin, but instead of dealing with it now, they put it off until a more convenient time and they never get around to it. If you find in your language a lot of different excuses for why you can't do a particular thing, examine yourself. See if these excuses are legitimate, or just another form of your laziness and resistance to change.

Have you seen procrastination get in the way of your walk with God? _____

_____

It is also important to understand that while some of our excuses will lead to procrastination, other excuses will prevent us from doing anything. This is also a very easy trap to fall into because you won't even know that you are being lazy, instead you will have convinced yourself by your own justification. For instance, when I read in the Bible, or heard sermons that encouraged me to confess my struggles to other believers I would say, "That won't do anything, my sin is before God alone so I need to deal with it before Him…." Or when I read passages like Matthew 5:29-30 where Jesus tells us that we need to completely amputate the things in our lives that cause us to sin, and I knew that unfiltered Internet access was a major stumbling block to me I would say, "Well the real problem is in my heart, so amputation won't do anything." Or when I knew I had to have an uncomfortable confrontation with someone I would say, "They won't listen to me, so why bother." Or when I grew tired of fighting my sin, or following God I would say, "I've tried my hardest, I guess I'm just never going to get it right so why bother."

I used all of these excuses to convince myself that I wasn't lazy, but instead was acting in wisdom. But I had deceived myself and was actually completely stagnant in many areas of my life because of my laziness. Some of our excuses are legitimate, but what I found for myself, is that many of them weren't. They were obstacles that I was too lazy to try to overcome, and so these obstacles had overcome me. It is important to take special care when it comes to excuses and evaluate them. See if they are legitimate, or just your flesh justifying your own laziness or masking your fear.

Do you have any excuses that are holding you back from doing what you know to be right? If you do, take some time to write them down and think through them. Then take some time to talk through them with an accountability partner._____

_____

2 Corinthians 6:2 says, "Behold, now is the accepted time; behold, now is the day of salvation."

When we struggle in this way, we need to pray and seek God to train us in discipline and commitment. This might be the hardest form of laziness to combat because, unlike the other two, it is completely unconscious and unintentional, we don't even realize that we are doing it. When we struggle in this way, one of the most important things that we can do is get with people that can hold you accountable to the things you need to do. And don't put this off, this is something that you need to make a plan to do as soon as possible, we can't just say, "I'll get to this later…" Because later will probably never happen.

In Hebrews 3:13 we are told: "But exhort one another daily, while it is called 'Today,' lest any of you be hardened through the deceitfulness of sin."

Notice that this passage tells us to exhort one another daily, otherwise we can be hardened by the deceitfulness of sin. It is the constant encouragement of our fellow brothers and sisters that keep us from falling into this trap of laziness, but we have to be willing to invite people into these areas of our lives and hold us accountable. And these have to be people that we will see often, because it can be really easy to become distracted and stop contacting these people as often as we need. We need people that we see at least once a week that can be a constant source of encouragement in our walks with God.

Do you have people in your life that you see often and who hold you accountable? If you don't, make a list of potential people that can help you do this:

_____

_____

_____

_____

I hope you can now see the dangers of laziness. It may not be the most obvious sin in our lives, but it can be one of the more deadly because it can single handedly keep us from the change that God has in store for us. Spend some time and read and reflect on the following passages :

Proverbs 19:24: "A lazy man buries his hand in the bowl, And will not so much as bring it to his mouth again."

Proverbs 6:6-11: "Go to the ant, you sluggard! Consider her ways and be wise, Which, having no captain, Overseer or ruler, Provides her supplies in the summer, And gathers her food in the harvest. How long will you slumber, O sluggard? When will you rise from your sleep? A little sleep, a little slumber, A little folding of the hands to sleep— So shall your poverty come on you like a prowler, And your need like an armed man."

Proverbs 13:4: "The soul of a lazy man desires, and has nothing; But the soul of the diligent shall be made rich."

Colossians 3:23-24: "Whatever you do, work heartily, as for the Lord and not for men, knowing that from the Lord you will receive the inheritance as your reward. You are serving the Lord Christ."

ENVY

A sound heart is life to the body, But envy is rottenness to the bones. (Proverbs 14:30)

Today we are going to take a look at the sin of envy, (sometimes called *covetousness* or *lust.*) The simple definition for this sin, is *an intense craving for the forbidden*, but there is a deeper way to understand it. If you take a look at this sin in relation to God, we can define envy like this: envy is the selfish craving for our own happiness apart from God, that is propelled by dissatisfaction. That is why the above Proverb says that envy rots our bones. In our envy we are constantly unhappy with what we have, and so we are constantly craving what we had, or what we could have, or what someone else has. All the while thinking, "If only I had that, then I would be happy."

We also need to understand that envy is a broad sin that has different categories within it. For instance, if you have passionate cravings in your sexuality, always looking to find pleasure and satisfaction in porn, sex, relationships…, we would call this sin "sexual lust." If I am craving pleasure and fulfillment in my career, money, power, and control, we call that "greed." If you find your comfort and peace in food, we call that gluttony. If you crave satisfaction in your appearance or in the approval and praise of others, we call that vanity. All of these sins are specific areas of envy, but envy is the central issue. And, no matter what area of envy you are struggling with, the deepest problem with envy is that it can never provide what it promises. In our envy we crave wealth, sex, relationships, beauty… All the while thinking that our pleasure and satisfaction will be found in these things, but ultimately we will be let down.

The biblical authors liked to use the metaphor of "fire" to describe envy (Proverbs 30:15-16). The reason is because no matter how much you feed a fire, it is *never* satisfied—it simply grows in size and consumes more and more fuel, never knowing when to stop or say "enough."

Lust works in the same way. When you feed your lust, it will burn hot and bright in passion for a time, and then it will fade and need more and more "fuel" to keep burning. In the grips of envy, you will believe the lie that there is some amount of beauty, success, money, fame, or sex that you can obtain that will finally silence your cravings, then causing you to be content.

Destructive Like A Fire

Just like a fire, no matter how much you feed your envy, it will never say "enough." The wealthiest and most successful people on earth are still consumed with greed. The prettiest and most famous people are still insecure and consumed by vanity. Also, the most sexually active people still crave more sex. *You can never satisfy your lust by feeding it.* Your appetite will only grow and leave you more empty.

Just like fire, the more envy grows, the more destructive it will become. As we have mentioned before, the central desire of humanity is for love, so most people will see their strongest amounts of envy towards love and relationships.

We have already talked alot about the damage that we do to ourselves and others as we seek to love, and be loved, out of our need.—but we also need to see how our envy for other things damages our relationships. For instance, maybe you struggle with vanity, and because you are constantly concerned with your self-image, you have a tendency to push people away and isolate yourself when you are feeling unattractive or undesirable.

Comparing Yourself with Others

Or maybe you struggle with comparing yourself to those around you—because of this you are constantly unhappy with the way you look, and with what you have. This perpetual unhappiness, insecurity, and need to compete with those around you drives people away.

Relationships and Approval

You might also struggle with intense amounts of anxiety about what people think about you, what you look like, what you dress like, what kind of car you drive, who you are dating, what kind of job you have… And you tend to pour that stress out on those who are closest to you. Or maybe you put an unfair weight on those around you to constantly validate you and this puts strain on your relationships as you become frustrated with people for not giving you enough attention. In turn, your friends and family become frustrated with you and how attention hungry you can be at times.

Relationship Struggles: Or…

Or maybe you struggle with sexual lust. Because of that, you struggle with committing in romantic relationships because the second you find a flaw in your partner, you think that you can do better and so you sabotage the relationship and move on.

Or, maybe you are so desperate for attention, that you will date someone who doesn't share your values, or someone who might even be mean or abusive, but you put up with it because you fear being alone more than you fear compromising your values or being treated badly. Or maybe you struggle with putting up healthy boundaries in your relationships and so you have a pattern of moving way too fast in your romantic relationships, and you may even struggle with having premarital sex even though you are trying to wait for marriage.

Or...maybe you are married or in a very committed relationship, but you can't help comparing your partner to other people and wishing that they either looked, or acted like these other people around you. Or maybe you struggle with fidelity in your relationships, and so you view pornography and fantasize about other people.

Or...maybe you go as far as to be flirtatious with other people and maybe even commit adultery.

Or...maybe you have a secret sin that you are ashamed of, and so you break trust with those closest to you by lying to them all to keep your secret safe.

Or...maybe your sin takes priority over your friends and family and you choose to indulge your behavior even when you know that this will hurt those closest to you.

Or...maybe you struggle with greed, and so even though you have a family who loves you very much, you neglect them for the sake of your work.

Or...maybe you are stingy and you hoard your money and struggle with giving your money to help others in need.

Or...maybe you spend large amounts of time and money in an attempt to live like the people you idolize.

Or...maybe, because you are envious for power, you have a deep need to be in control in every relationship. And because of this, you push people away when you become too controlling and opinionated in the relationship. You also might lack the ability to be vulnerable or to truly trust another person and so you keep people at arms length due to your fear of letting anyone in and risking being hurt.

Or...you might lack the ability to take correction or change because it is so important for you to be "the strong one" that you can't admit failure or mistakes, because of this you constantly push away everyone who is trying to help you.

Or...maybe you struggle with holding down a job, because no matter how amazing a job might be, eventually you get sick of it, thinking the pay is too little, or you aren't making enough of a difference, or you resent being told what to do... and so you quit thinking that a perfect job is out there waiting for you.

Envy Is Devastating to Relationships

There are many more examples I could give, but I hope you see that no matter what type of envy you struggle with, they are all devastating to our relationships. Take some time and write down the types of envy you most struggle with, and how these sins are damaging your relationships: _____

_____

_____

We also need to understand, that for most of us, envy will only damage your relationships with others, but for some of us, our envy will completely destroy our relationships. You see, most people find the vast majority of their satisfaction in their relationships, so while they may struggle with things like greed, vanity, gluttony, or sexual lust, ultimately they will seek to put their relationships first, and they will have varying degrees of success with protecting their relationships from the damage of their envy.

ADDICTIVE BEHAVIOR TYPES

There is a small group of people who, for a variety of reasons, (like being abused, not fitting in at school, being bullied, a narcissist, obsessed with one particular area of lust, or many other factors), turn primarily to other things for comfort and satisfaction...*and not to relationships.* It is people like this that are at a very high risk for exemplifying what some would call "addictive behaviors." This is the difference between the average person who struggles with greed, and the person who will sacrifice their morals and every relationship just to get ahead in business—it is also the difference between the average person who struggles with sexual lust, and the person who spends hours viewing porn every day, or the person who is constantly seeking casual sex with numerous different partners regardless of whether or not they are already in a relationship or if they have had severe consequences like unplanned pregnancies or STDs. There is also the average person who struggles with portion control, compared to the person who is morbidly obese to the point that their health is rapidly fading. And then there is the person who struggles with body image, versus the person who literally starves themselves to attain a certain weight.

LABELED "ADDICT"

When people struggle at this level, even though I wouldn't, some people would label these people "addicts" in these areas because their behavior has become just as compulsive and destructive as someone who is addicted to alcohol or drugs.

In their cravings, they have become incredibly self-destructive, but are so consumed by their desire that they can't stop and may have even become numb to the damage that they are doing to themselves and others.

It is important for us to understand that just because someone struggles in an area of lust, *that doesn't necessarily mean that they will go to extremes like this.*

DON'T LABEL PEOPLE

This is the major issue that we can fall into when we label people "addicts." When someone is labeled this way they can assume that they will fall into these dangerous levels of lust, when that might not be true. We are all different in our struggles and so we have to evaluate our issues on an individual level—this is why I try to avoid using labels and generalizations.

TAKING STEPS IN CHRIST THAT HELP

Depending on the level that you struggle in a particular area, you may need to take far more severe steps in your fight against your sin, and so I encourage you to talk to a spiritually mature accountability partner about the specifics of your struggle to get guidance and to help you understand the steps that you will need to take to better pursue God.

The hope here is that no matter what area or level you struggle with in lust, you are not alone—everyone struggles with lust. And there is wonderful hope for all of us in finding tremendous amounts of healing and repentance in Christ.

Can you see the damage that your envy is doing to you? Can you see that everyone struggles with lust, and we all have the same hope in Christ? _____

_____

Man In Misery

David Foster Wallace was an author who committed suicide a few years back, and right before he died he gave a speech that expressed a lot of his inner anguish related to envy:

> *...Here's something else that's weird but true: in the day-to day trenches of adult life, there is actually no such thing as atheism. There is no such thing as not worshiping. Everybody worships. The only choice we get is what to worship. And the compelling reason for maybe choosing some sort of god or spiritual-type thing to worship—be it JC or Allah, be it YAHWEH or the Wiccan Mother Goddess, or the Four Noble Truths, or some inviolable set of ethical principles—is that pretty much anything else you worship will eat you alive. If you worship money and things, if they are where you tap real meaning in life, then you will never have enough, never feel you have enough. It's the truth. Worship your body and beauty and sexual allure and you will always feel ugly. And when time and age start showing, you will die a million deaths before they finally grieve you...Worship power, you will end up feeling weak and afraid, and you will need ever more power over others to numb you to your own fear. Worship your intellect, being seen as smart, you will end up feeling stupid, a fraud, always on the verge of being found out.*

Even though he was an atheist, David Foster Wallace saw the misery of this continuous, unfulfilled longing for happiness. The deep well of his depression centered in his realization that there was nothing on this earth that could actually fulfill this longing, nothing that would truly satisfy his soul. The irony that he saw was that the greatest source of our satisfaction, also becomes the greatest source of our insecurity and fears.

Look to Your Dreams and Your Anxieties

That is why the best way to see your areas of your greatest envy, is to look at your dreams, what you most long after and fantasize about. Also, look at your deepest insecurities, and the areas you most complain about and are the most picky about, complaining is the language of our envy.

In our vanity, we will be consumed by thoughts of our own ugliness and worthlessness, and we will have paranoid illusions of others hating us. And we will try to silence our insecurities by pursuing greater amounts of beauty and fame, whether it is through our looks, our accomplishments, or through people pleasing and good deeds. We will find ourselves complaining about our looks and our relationships—always longing for a better body, more beauty, a greater sex appeal, a better personality, or more friends.

In our greed, we will complain about our house, our car, our clothes, our paychecks. In our sexual lust we will complain about our spouse, our relationship, our sex life, or our singleness—or we will be filled with thoughts of loneliness—our thoughts will be saturated with sexual fantasy and desire for romance and intimacy, always wanting more and more of what *we think we deserve*.

WATCH YOUR MOTIVES

This can even bleed it's way into your relationship with God. For many of us, we will struggle with envy in our righteousness. We will be looking for validation through our good deeds and we will find ourselves praying, reading our Bibles, giving money to charity, sharing our faith, and doing many other truly beautiful *works*—all for the praise of others, or for our own self-respect. Because of this, we will struggle with constant insecurity about whether or not we are doing enough for God.

We will also become very judgmental of other Christians who aren't doing as much as we are. We can also start judging our own church with this type of picky and shallow heart—complaining about the teachings, the worship, the people... That can then cause us to go from church-to-church looking for that "perfect fellowship that will meet all of our needs," never thinking about how we can invest in and better those around us. In all areas of our envy, we will be incredibly picky, self-centered, and insecure as we complain about what we do have, and we fantasize about what we don't have.

What things do you have the *most* envy towards? _____

_____

I can personally see the destruction and unhappiness that my own envy causes me in many different areas. I am constantly longing for more in my life to satisfy my emptiness, but I never feel like I quite find what I was looking for no matter where I try to find it.

I can find a momentary passion and pleasure in my pursuits, but eventually this dies out and I am left feeling more empty than before. This lust also drives me to do things that I know aren't right before God, I know I shouldn't fantasize about other women, view porn, lose my temper, or find my value in my job, my income, my accomplishments, or my relationships—but I find in myself a twisted part of my heart that is constantly craving things I know to be wrong.

At one level, I know that these things are wrong, and I even know why they are wrong and what they are doing to me, but in moments of craving I forget all of this and I fall to my lust. In that moment, I fall for that foolish lie "that maybe this time, I will find my pleasure, satisfaction, and peace in my lust," but I never do.

On the contrary, the more I fall to my sin, the more my craving grows right along with my guilt and shame. What I think will bring me peace, ends up bringing me greater pain, and more dissatisfaction—this fuels my cycle of self destruction because the more dissatisfied I feel, the more I will crave satisfaction in these broken things that can never satisfy me.

C.S. Lewis also felt this truth and in *Mere Christianity* he wrote:

> *The longings which arise in us when we first fall in love, or first think of some foreign country, or first take up some subject that excites us, are longings which no marriage, no travel, no learning, can really satisfy. I am not now speaking of what would be ordinarily called unsuccessful marriages, or holidays, or learned careers. I am speaking of the best possible ones. There was something we grasped at, in that first moment of longing, which just fades away in the reality.*

TEMPORARY SATISFACTION

When we first begin to look for pleasure in something, whether it be a new relationship, career, place, hobby… we find a powerful passion and longing that brings great pleasure and fulfillment for a time. But after a while, that feeling will fade, and that is why most of us are always moving from thing-to-thing, person-to-person, place-to-place, job-to-job, video-to-video, or image-to-image....

We are always looking for *that initial fire that has since burned out.* You see, instead of seeing envy as an internal problem, we deal with our discontentment by *blaming what we are chasing.* We think that the reason why we are so dissatisfied is because we just haven't gotten it right yet. That there is a level of beauty, fame, success, power, sex…that will finally satisfy us and make us OK. Hence, we are forever pursuing genuine happiness and fulfillment, but never quite finding it.

This constant disillusionment is so painful and causes so many bad decisions, that many of us have completely given up in our pursuit—we just throw our hands in the air and we tell ourselves that *true satisfaction and peace don't exist,* and we try to learn how to be somewhat happy in our unhappiness.

While it is true that people who make this decision tend to be more content than those who are always pursuing true satisfaction to no avail—no matter what you do, this burning envy will always be a problem for you.

Please read and comment on the following passage:

Proverbs 27:20: "Hell and Destruction are never full; So the eyes of man are never satisfied."

_____

_____

But why is it that we are all so eaten up by this envy?

The answer to this goes back to our first couple of studies. In the "fall of man," we doubted the goodness of our God and we began to pursue our pleasure in the creation instead of relationship with our Creator.

What we failed to see was that we were designed by God to find our ultimate fulfillment in Him alone. There is no pleasure outside of God that will ever satisfy the longing of the human heart. The philosopher Blaise Pascal on page 75 of his book, *Blaise Pascal's Pensees* (New York; Penguin Books, 1966)] put it this way:

> *What else does this craving, and this helplessness, proclaim but that there was once in man a true happiness, of which all that now remains is the empty print and trace? This he tries in vain to fill with everything around him, seeking in things that are not there the help he cannot find in those that are, though none can help, since this infinite abyss can be filled only with an infinite and immutable object; in other words by God himself"*

Because we have rejected our true fulfillment in God, this has left us in our state of constant burning envy, always chasing satisfaction in this world, but never truly finding it.

This is a side thought, but whenever I counsel a couple suffering in the wake of infidelity, this is one truth that I will always bring them back to. The reason that I do this is because whenever a spouse discovers that their partner has been secretly viewing porn, or has been romantically chatting with other people, or has had a full on affair with another person, this is a thought that can haunt them: "Maybe the reason why they strayed is because I am not enough for them…"

They might think that if only they were more attractive, more interesting, more sexually active or spontaneous… then they could have kept their spouse faithful. Unfortunately this can work both ways as the person who did fall in these areas might blame their lust on their partner's faults.

Esther Perel is a marriage counselor; she is not a Christian but she sees the same truth that the Bible purports. She deals primarily with the topic of infidelity, and in a talk she gave entitled "Why Happy Couples Cheat" she said this:

> *The logic goes like this: If you have everything you need at home, then there is no need to go looking elsewhere, assuming that there is such a thing as a perfect marriage that will inoculate us against wanderlust. But what if passion has a finite shelf life? What if there are things that even a good relationship can never provide? If even happy people cheat, what is it about?*

GOD MUST BE THE CENTER OF OUR SATISFACTION

The reason why people lust and stray in their marriage has little to do with the marriage itself. Even if someone were married to the most attractive, sexually active, caring, supportive spouse on earth, they would still find a dissatisfaction in their hearts towards their marriage. If God is not the center of our satisfaction, nothing on this earth, including your marriage, can fully satisfy you. While there are always ways that both parties need to recognize failure and seek betterment in Christ.

We can't move forward the way that we need to unless we see that our marriage is not the solution to our lust. Unless I am seeking my fulfillment in God supremely, I can never love my spouse unconditionally, show grace and patience towards their shortcomings, or find the satisfaction in my marriage that I am looking for. *As with every other area of lust, your marriage isn't your problem, your heart is.*

If you are married, take some time and reflect on how lust has impacted your own marriage.

_____

_____

We also need to see that it's not that the creation is bad, (1 Timothy 4:4), it's just that it is insufficient to fully satisfy the human soul. It was supposed to be out of the fullness of our relationship with God, that we would be able to enjoy His wonderful creation as a sort of a dessert, while our relationship with Him was supposed to be the main course.

Read how God puts this in Isaiah 55:1-2:

Come, all you who are thirsty, come to the waters; and you who have no money, come, buy and eat! Come buy wine and milk without money and without cost. Why spend money on what is not bread, and your labor on what does not satisfy? Listen, listen to me, and eat what is good, and your soul will delight in the richest of fare.

If you look in the above passage you will see that God is upset with us, but not because we long for satisfaction, but that we are looking for our fulfillment in wrong places. Just like with food, dessert is amazingly enjoyable after a hardy meal, but if you tried to live off of only dessert it wouldn't satisfy your hunger. Instead it would make you worse off than you were before and actually intensify your craving. While you ate your dessert you would feel pretty good, but when you were done, you would find that your energy would run out quickly and, over time, this diet would actually be deadly to you.

This is what God is telling us is happening in all areas of our lives. Notice what He says to us, "Why spend money on what is not bread, and your labor on what does not satisfy? (Isaiah 55:2)"

We are spending all of our time and money, laboring endlessly for satisfaction apart from God, but it doesn't exist and so we remain unsatisfied.

Please read and comment on the following quote from Martin Luther:

"God created everything to be used as a means of enjoying and loving him, but in sin we make them ends in themselves, placing a weight upon them they were not created to sustain."

_____

_____

COMMANDMENTS FROM A LOVING FATHER

In our distrust of God, we doubt His commandments on how to properly use His good creation. Instead of seeing these commandments as being from a loving Father who is trying to help us, we see His commandments as hindrances keeping us from real joy. When someone buys a car, they don't look at the owner's manual with contempt, thinking that the designers of the car are putting restrictions on the buyer that will keep them from really enjoying the vehicle. No, we read the owner's manual knowing that the only people who really know how to use the car to its full potential are the creators.

God is our Creator. When He gives us commands it isn't to steal joy from us, but it is to give His children a perfect guide to honor Him and enjoy His creation to their full potential. In our doubt, we don't trust that He knows what is best for us, and we rebel against His good commandments, thinking that this will bring us happiness—instead all we ultimately find is regret.

Please read and comment on the following passage:

> *And the LORD commanded us to do all these statutes, to fear the LORD our God, for our good always, that He might preserve us alive, as we are this day.* (Deuteronomy 6:24)

———————————————————————————————

———————————————————————————————

FIRST SEEK SATISFACTION IN GOD

Enjoying the creation isn't sin, God longs for us to enjoy His creation to its fullest, but the only way that we can fully enjoy the creation is to seek to be fully satisfied in God first. Then we need to trust and obey His commands that teach us the proper contexts for enjoying the creation. Then our enjoyment of the creation is brought to its full potential as it brings us into greater intimacy with our God and Savior.

If we are in sin, we put things out of their proper order—we are trying to be satisfied first in the creation. Most of the time we are even treating our relationship with God as a means to enjoy the world more, instead of the world being the means that we enjoy God supremely. That is why we can begin to resent God when we suffer materially, and why we forget about God altogether when we are prospering.

GET IT IN PERSPECTIVE

To put this in perspective, imagine for a second that you are a very wealthy person and you are going to marry someone who is very poor. Because you love this person, you would love to bless them with your finances, but only if this person loved you first and was only thankful for your wealth, not demanding of it.

If, on the other hand, this person only wanted a relationship with you when they were in need, and if you refused to give them exactly what they wanted they would resent you. If you gave them money they would leave you to enjoy the money without you. You would most certainly feel used and unloved.

This is exactly how we are treating God. God loves us and so He wants for us to enjoy His creation. But in our envy, we are constantly dissatisfied with our lives, and so we complain about what we do have and selfishly demand from God to give us more and more. When He doesn't give us what we want, we sin and walk away from Him in frustration, and most of the time, we try to find pleasure in our own way that is against His commands. When He answers our prayers, we stop pursuing Him because we got what we really wanted.

Please read and comment on the following passage.

James 4:2-3: "You lust and do not have. You murder and covet and cannot obtain. You fight and war. Yet you do not have because you do not ask. You ask and do not receive because you ask amiss, that you may spend it on your pleasures."

_____

_____

The greatest irony in all of this, is that we are selfishly pursuing our pleasure apart from God and we never actually find it. All the while, God is longing to give us the very satisfaction and pleasure that we are laboring for in a loving relationship with Him.

Look In the Right Place

God's not offended because we are looking for too much pleasure, He's offended that we aren't looking for it in the right place.

I didn't understand this growing up, and I used to think that the Christian life was one of abstinence and suffering—that we should live our lives without pleasure and seek to serve God out of religious duty. I thought I had to choose between having a satisfying life, and having a life that pleased God.

We will talk more about this in the next lesson. Denying our envy will never make it go away. The only way to fight our envy is to begin to find a greater joy and a better pleasure in God. God wants us to be joyful and content, to experience intense, all-satisfying pleasure, but this can never be found apart from Him, _it can only be found in Him_. And when we seek that joy and pleasure in Him alone, we aren't being selfish, but we are instead giving great glory to our God who alone can satisfy.

Pastor John Piper has a great illustration for this point. He says that if he told his wife today "Honey, I love you so much, and I just want to spend all of today with you because of how much joy and pleasure our relationship gives me."

She would never say, "I can't believe how selfish you are, seeking satisfaction and fulfillment in our relationship and wanting to spend time with me because of how much you love me…"

The reason she wouldn't say that, is because by him expressing that he finds pleasure and fulfillment in their relationship he "gives glory" to her—she is the source of his satisfaction.

In the same way, God wants and even commands that His children come to Him and find satisfaction, because, as John Piper puts it, "God is most glorified in you when you are most satisfied in Him."

This is why Jesus tells us in John 7:37 "…If anyone thirsts, let him come to Me and drink. He who believes in

Me, as the Scripture has said, out of his heart will flow rivers of living water."

Can you see your own emptiness, and your need to pursue your joy in God? _____

_____

GETTING FREE FOR GOD?

This was such a beautiful truth to realize, I had always thought that I was getting free from porn for God, and I even believed that my sexuality and desire for pleasure were offensive to God. But now I see that the only way to be set free is to first be filled by the greater pleasure of God. Going back to the food metaphor, if you took someone who lived off of only junk food for years and put them on a clean diet, it would take a long time for their body to adjust and be properly filled and satisfied with healthy food. Even after they got healthy, the cravings for junk food would never fully go away. What will act as a deterrent from going back to junk food will hopefully be the richer and fuller joy of feeling healthy, as opposed to the momentary satisfaction of junk food that is followed by feeling miserable.

In the same way, because we are fallen, we are naturally geared towards looking to the world for satisfaction, and not turning to God. Because of this, we will spend the rest of our lives fighting our cravings for pleasure in the world. We need to be daily praying for God to give us right desires and longings for Him as we seek deeper intimacy and satisfaction in our relationship with Him.

Keep in mind that our lust toward our flesh won't go away. Just like cravings for food, our cravings for sinful things will come and go, sometimes they will be really strong, and sometimes they will be weak and easily resisted. The more we experience the richer and fuller joy and satisfaction in God, the more we will be able to resist the cravings for the passing pleasures of sin when they come because we have found something infinitely greater than this world.

In the next lesson we will take an in depth look at the joy that we have in God, but let's finish today's lesson by reflecting on a couple quotes:

Charles Spufford, *What Sin Really Is:*

> *...You glimpse an unflattering vision of yourself as a being whose wants make no sense, don't harmonize: whose desires, deep down, are discordantly arranged, so that you truly want to possess and you truly want not to, at the very same time. You're equipped, you realize, for farce (or even tragedy) more than you are for happy endings.*

C.S. Lewis, *Mere Christianity:*

> *If I find in myself a desire which no experience in this world can satisfy, the most probable explanation is that I was made for another world. If none of the earthly pleasures satisfy it (our longing for fulfillment), that does not prove that the universe is a fraud. Probably the earthly pleasures were never meant to satisfy it, but only to arouse it, to suggest the real thing. If that is so, I must take care, on the one hand,*

never to despise, or be unthankful for, these earthly blessings, and on the other, never to mistake them for the something else of which they are only a kind of copy, or echo, or mirage. I must keep alive in myself the desire for my true country, which I shall not find till after death; I must never let it get snowed under or turned aside; I must make it the main object of life to press on to that other country and to help others do the same.

C.S. Lewis, in *Weight Of Glory:*

Indeed, if we consider the unblushing promises of reward and the staggering nature of the rewards promised in the Gospels, it would seem that Our Lord finds our desires not too strong, but too weak. We are half-hearted creatures, fooling about with drink and sex and ambition when infinite joy is offered us, like an ignorant child who wants to go on making mud pies in a slum because he cannot imagine what is meant by the offer of a holiday at the sea. We are far too easily pleased...

These things—the beauty, the memory of our own past—are good images of what we really desire; but if they are mistaken for the thing itself, they turn into dumb idols, breaking the hearts of their worshipers. For they are not the thing itself; they are only the scent of a flower we have not found, the echo of a tune we have not heard, news from a country we have never yet visited.

JOY

Thus says the LORD: "Cursed is the man who trusts in man and makes flesh his strength, whose heart departs from the LORD. For he shall be like a shrub in the desert, And shall not see when good comes, But shall inhabit the parched places in the wilderness, In a salt land which is not inhabited. Blessed is the man who trusts in the LORD, And whose hope is the LORD. For he shall be like a tree planted by the waters, Which spreads out its roots by the river, And will not fear when heat comes; But its leaf will be green, And will not be anxious in the year of drought, Nor will cease from yielding fruit. (Jeremiah 17:5-8)

In today's lesson we are going to take an in depth look at one of the most glorious aspects of our lives with Christ: JOY.

Joy is another one of those much used Christian terms that is very rarely defined. The above passage sheds a lot of much needed light on this topic with a really interesting metaphor to help us understand the intricacies of true joy. In this metaphor, joy is pictured as a plant that is rooted in the ground and produces the fruit of happiness. So unlike happiness, which is just an emotion that comes and goes, our joy is a peace and contentment that is rooted in something greater than itself and that grows up into happiness. And the better the source that our joy is rooted in, the more intense our happiness will be, and the more immovable our peace and contentment will be. So, for instance, if you have a deep amount of joy rooted in your family, things at your job might be going terrible, but as long as you are able to provide for your family and spend time with them, you will still have peace, contentment, and even happiness in the midst of your struggles.

This understanding is something that is sorely missing from our culture today. We tend to think that the end goal of life is to find happiness, not understanding that true happiness is simply a fruit of deep-rooted joy. What this means is that instead of investing in things and attempting to sink our roots down deep into the joy-filled things of life, we instead give in to our envy and pursue quick amounts of happiness wherever we can find it. But, as we talked about in the previous lesson, *this is not the way to genuine happiness or satisfaction.*

The "cursed" man of Jeremiah 17 had fallen into that trap—he put his trust in foolish things and therefore had nothing constant to sink his roots into. Because of this, he was dependent on inconsistent rain; therefore he shrivels up in the desert and never "sees when good comes."

Anyone who has ever had a successful career, loving marriage, intimate friendship, or has been a parent knows that if your goal in any of those endeavors is simply to feel happy, you will never be able to properly invest in these things and push through the hard times to develop deeper roots. Instead you will give up on these things and by pursuing ease and happiness, you will deny yourself all true joy and satisfaction. Having true joy doesn't mean that you won't ever experience sorrow, it is just that your joy will serve as an anchor for your soul and get you through the tough times and deliver you into the wonderful bliss that is on the other side. Pursuing joy may be much more difficult than pursuing happiness, but it is also far more fulfilling and pleasurable in the long run.

THE MILLENNIAL CONCEPT

In the generation of millennials, this is one of the hardest concepts to accept. We have been sold a bill of goods. We've been told that "when you find what you were meant for, everything should fall into place with ease." Because of this, we don't know how to commit and press on in relationships—we firmly believe that if we find "the one," the relationship will be problem-free and instantly awesome. We hold off on getting married out of fear that we will commit to the "wrong person" and miss out on meeting "the one" for us. If we have any relationship problems, we will assume that "this must not be the right relationship for me." Even when we do get married, most of us will hold off on having children for years, or even permanently, because we understand that having kids is challenging and we don't want any added stress.

We don't know how to deal with issues in the workplace either because we have been told that when you find what you are meant to do, everything will be easy—you will get the exact pay that you want, and you will enjoy every facet of your job. It is hard for us to stay with a job for very long because whenever issues at work come up, we assume that *we just haven't found the right job yet* and so we move on.

When you add religion to the mix, things actually get worse, not better. Because now we have found a way to spiritualize our laziness and our envy. When we are breaking up with someone we say things like, "I don't think that you are the one that God has for me…" Or, when we struggle at work we will say, "I feel like God is calling me somewhere else…" Or "I don't think that I have been gifted in this way…" Even when we have issues at church we will say "This just isn't the church that God has for me…"

JOY IN WHAT WE DO FOR OTHERS

All these things sound very spiritual, but it is just a mask for our flesh whether we admit it or not, and the great tragedy is that this is what is keeping us from being truly joyous. God wants us not to simply look for something that fits our needs, but to instead invest in our relationships, our jobs, and our communities. He does not want us to seek what these things can do for us, but what we can do for others. It is from this type of investment, as we root our joy deep into Christ, that we will find true joy in all of areas of our lives.

Have you noticed this problem of commitment and investment in your life? _____

Ultimate Joy In God Alone

We also need to remember that the Bible tells us that this "cursed" man could have tried to sink his roots in the most satisfying and blissful things in this world and still shriveled away in his lust. What we as Christians need to understand is that while we should have joy in other areas of our lives, our ultimate joy has to be rooted in God alone. Only God is constant enough, and worthy enough to satisfy our souls and bring us joy in any circumstance. That is why it says of the blessed man, that his hope is the LORD. Not just that he hopes in God, but that all of his hope and joy are rooted in God alone. That is why this man can go through "the year of drought" without being anxious and continue to be fruitful. The apostle Paul experienced this blessedness in his own life and said it this way: 2 Corinthians 6:10 ...As sorrowful, yet always rejoicing... Even though Paul was full of sorrow, he certainly had a tough life that was full of pain and disappointment, this did not stop him from rejoicing because his ultimate joy was rooted in the unchanging character and pleasure of God, not the shifting dynamics of his life. We as Christians should be the most joyful people on this earth, we are literally called and commanded to pursue the most pleasurable and wonderful being in existence. And it is from our supreme joy in the Creator of all things, that we can enjoy His creation in peace instead of being burdened by it. So, if this is the case, why aren't more Christians overcome with this joy? And why do we spend so much of our lives trying to be satisfied in this world that can't satisfy us, instead of pursuing God who can?

I've spent a lot of time reflecting on these questions in my own life, and I have boiled down the answer to a couple big reasons. As I go over each main reason I will have a list of Bible passages that have helped me renew my mind in God's truth and break down the lies that have kept me from pursuing joy in God.

The first big one would be my view of God's character. For various reasons, other than my fallen nature, I have always had a mental image of God as being a very boring and judgmental person that was always out to put a damper on my fun. A big reason why I felt this way was because of my experience around other Christians. As a kid, I never really enjoyed hanging out with other Christian kids, I more gravitated towards friends that weren't interested in God. I never really saw Christians as being super happy, or fun people. And when I became a teenager and I started watching porn, I found that I really enjoyed what I was doing so I always felt condemned when I went to church. I had much more fun hanging out with my friends who also viewed porn and didn't seem to judge me for the things that I was doing. Subconsciously I put that image on God and assumed that if Christians were like that, God must be even more intense, and since He knew what I was doing, He must have been very disappointed in me. So think about this, if I saw God this way, do you think that I would ever think that spending time with God would be pleasurable?

Do you have trouble seeing God as being pleasurable or enjoyable? _____

_____

Please read through and comment on the following passages:

Psalm 45:7: "You (Jesus) love righteousness and hate wickedness; therefore God, Your God, has anointed You with the oil of gladness more than Your companions."

113

Psalm 149:4: "For the LORD takes pleasure in His people; He will beautify the humble with salvation."

Zephaniah 3:17: "The LORD your God in your midst, the Mighty One, will save; He will rejoice over you with gladness, He will quiet you with His love, He will rejoice over you with singing."

Hebrews 12:2: "Looking unto Jesus, the author and finisher of our faith, who for the joy that was set before Him endured the cross, despising the shame."

As I read through passages like this, it started to change my perspective on God. As you can see, the Bible never depicts God as a bummer, it actually says in Psalm 45 that Jesus was anointed with gladness more than anyone else. Meaning that Jesus was literally the happiest person who ever lived. And we are told in John 1:18 No one has seen God at any time. The only begotten Son, who is in the bosom of the Father, He has declared Him. Meaning that in Jesus we have the most complete understanding of the true nature and character of God, so it isn't just Jesus who is "anointed with gladness," but God Himself is supremely joyous above all other beings. This was a crazy concept for me, I never thought of God as being happy or pleased, but you can see through the other quotes that God is constantly pleased and filled with pleasure in what He does. And what does God find a lot of His pleasure in? It is in His people and in what He does for us. God is certainly unhappy with a lot of the things that we do, but just as a loving parent will be very upset with a lot of the actions of their children, they still love and adore their kids. This perspective change was huge for me, I was starting to look at God in a whole new light and see Him as someone who is enjoyable to be with. Having my heart change in this area freed me up to see this next truth, that God is not only said to be a joyful God, but that intimacy with Him is our greatest pleasure and joy.

Please read and comment on the following passages:

Psalm 5:11: "But let all those rejoice who put their trust in You; Let them ever shout for joy, because You defend them; Let those also who love Your name Be joyful in You."

Psalm 16:11: "You will show me the path of life; In Your presence is fullness of joy; At Your right hand are pleasures forevermore."

Psalm 36:8: "They are abundantly satisfied with the fullness of Your house, and You give them drink from the river of Your pleasures."

Notice the language of these psalmists, they aren't saying that following God is better than going to Hell, or that God is kind of pleasurable. They literally describe God's joy as rivers of pleasure, they say that the fullness of joy is with Him, and eternal pleasures are in His right hand. Once again, this was a revelation for me, I followed God out of fear of consequences, it never occurred to me that the joy of God was actually better than what I was experiencing in the world. That far from God telling me to give up my pleasure to pursue Him, He was literally leading me away from pleasure that could never ultimately satisfy me, to bring me into His presence where I could find the fullness of my joy in Him. And while there is still a long way I need to go still before I can see God as my ultimate joy and pleasure, every day is a new opportunity to experience joy in Him.

Have you struggled to believe that the pleasure of God was better than the pleasure of this world?

_____

This all may be true, but doesn't Jesus call us to take up our crosses and die to ourselves? Doesn't all this talk about pursuing pleasure in God seem selfish? We did already touch on this point in the previous lesson, but the simple answer is no. Yes Jesus calls us to take up our crosses in Matthew 16:24, but listen closely to all that He says:

> *Then Jesus said to His disciples, "If anyone desires to come after Me, let him deny himself, and take up his cross, and follow Me. "For whoever desires to save his life will lose it, but whoever loses his life for My sake will find it.* (Matthew 16:24-25)

Christians are to take up their crosses and deny themselves, but we don't do this just for the sake of loss, but for gain. Notice that He tells us to do this in order to follow Him, and that by doing this, we will find our life because it was in Him all along. God desires for us to find pleasure in Him because God loves us. Anyone who has ever been in love understands that genuine love has to include joy in the beloved. If my wife served me and stayed with me simply because divorce is tough and she needs me to provide for her, that wouldn't be love. I want my wife to delight in our relationship and find amazing pleasure with me. In fact, in Deuteronomy 28, Moses prophecies to the people of Israel that they would fall into captivity in the future, and in verse 47 he gives the main reason why God would allow this to happen. It says, "Because you did not serve the LORD your God with joy and gladness of heart, for the abundance of everything…"

Notice, it wasn't that they weren't serving God, it was that they didn't serve Him with joy. God doesn't want our cold, legalistic service of Him, God wants His children to delight in Him with joy and gladness. In fact, far from making me selfish, I have found that the more I delight in God and praise Him, the less self-focused I am. But the more I complain and follow God out of obligation and legalism, the more self-centered and proud I become.

Can you see why God rejects passionless service and demands joy in Him? _____

_____

Please read and comment on the following passages:

Isaiah 55:2: "Why do you spend money for what is not bread, And your wages for what does not satisfy? Listen carefully to Me, and eat what is good, And let your soul delight itself in abundance."

Jeremiah 2:11-13: Has a nation changed its gods, Which are not gods? But My people have changed their Glory for what does not profit. Be astonished, O heavens, at this, And be horribly afraid; Be very desolate," says the LORD. "For My people have committed two evils: They have forsaken Me, the fountain of living waters, And hewn themselves cisterns—broken cisterns that can hold no water."

John 15:11: "These things I have spoken to you, that My joy may remain in you, and that your joy may be full.

John 16:22: "Therefore you now have sorrow; but I will see you again and your heart will rejoice, and your joy no one will take from you."

John 16:24: "Until now you have asked nothing in My name. Ask, and you will receive, that your joy may be full."

John 17:13: "But now I come to You, and these things I speak in the world, that they may have My joy fulfilled in themselves."

_____

_____

_____

I can struggle to ask God to fill me joy, thinking that by doing this I am being selfish. But, in these passages, God is saying that He literally longs for us to have joy in Him, and Jesus even says that He is teaching His disciples things so that their "joy may be full." Because of these truths, the saints in the Bible regularly prayed and asked God to give them joy in Him because they knew that they couldn't produce it in themselves. And the apostles were so sure of the joy that was in God, that everything they did was for the purpose of spreading this joy to other people.

Please read and comment on the following passages:

Psalm 90:14: "Satisfy us in the morning with Your steadfast love, that we may rejoice and be glad all our days".

Romans 15:13: "Now may the God of hope fill you with all joy and peace in believing, that you may abound in hope by the power of the Holy Spirit."

2 Corinthians 1:24: "Not that we have dominion over your faith, but are fellow workers for your joy; for by faith you stand."

Philippians 1:25: "And being confident of this, I know that I shall remain and continue with you all for your progress and joy of faith..."

1 John 1:4: "And these things we write to you that your joy may be full."

_____

_____

Have you ever asked God to fill you with joy? _____

I know that this can be a difficult thing to do, especially after you fall to sin, but the more you study the character of God, and the joy that is in Him, the more you will boldly pursue joy in Him knowing that this greatly pleases and glorifies God. Not only that, but it is only when we are armed with this joy, that we have the power to fight against the false pleasures of sin, without it we are helpless against our lusts. As Nehemiah 8:10 says: ...Do not sorrow, for the joy of the LORD is your strength."

This is also why David, in Psalm 51:12, had the boldness to pray this after his horrible fall to sin in sleeping with a married woman and then murdering her husband, "Restore to me the joy of Your salvation, And uphold me by Your generous Spirit."

It can seem offensive to us that David had the boldness to ask for joy after he failed in such a horrible way. But David here is recognizing his need for the joy of God. He knew that guilt and fear wouldn't be enough to change him, he needed to refocus his life and root himself even deeper in the supreme joy of God so that he wouldn't go back to the false pleasures of this world. And what happens to us as we become more and more filled with this joy? Our pickiness and our complaining will begin to fade away and be replaced with wonderful praise. You see, if complaining is the language of envy, praise is most certainly the language of joy. Because those who are filled with joy can't help but express it, even in the most horrible of circumstances, joy will still flow out because the joy of God can never be taken away.

> _Though the fig tree may not blossom, Nor fruit be on the vines; Though the labor of the olive may fail, And the fields yield no food; Though the flock may be cut off from the fold, And there be no herd in the stalls— Yet I will rejoice in the LORD, I will joy in the God of my salvation._ (Habakkuk 3:17-18)

Habakkuk saw that even if all of his worldly pleasures were taken from him, there was always cause to rejoice in God. This is the polar opposite of envy. In envy we look past all of the good that we are experiencing in order to complain about what we currently have. But God in His supreme joy looks past what is bad in us in order to love us and rejoice over us. And the person who is filled with joy in God will be able to do the same thing, they will be able to see the bad, and even sorrow in their trials, yet still be filled with joy and praise. In times like this, we aren't rejoicing about our circumstances, but we are rejoicing in our amazing God who never ceases to be worthy of praise and who can work all things together for our good and His glory.

We have to understand that the fullness of joy for us is not found in experiencing material blessing, it is found in glorifying God because that is our ultimate purpose and fulfillment in life. If you are experiencing blessing in your life, know that enjoying God in the midst of prosperity is awesome but difficult to do because we can make the mistake of praising the gifts and not the giver. The encouragement that I can give you is that when you appropriately praise God for what He has done, you can bring Him great glory and you can experience an unshakable happiness free from envy because your joy is rooted in God and not this world. But, if you are in the midst of suffering know, that when you enjoy and praise God in the midst of suffering, you glorify God supremely. When you do that, you are showing that God Himself is all satisfying, not the gifts that He gives, but His presence alone is all that you need. When you do this you honor and glorify God more than any other time of your life. This is the lesson that Job teaches us when after he lost everything he said this:

> *Then Job arose, tore his robe, and shaved his head; and he fell to the ground and worshiped. And he said: "Naked I came from my mother's womb, And naked shall I return there. The LORD gave, and the LORD has taken away; Blessed be the name of the LORD."* (Job 1:20-21)

These were the sweetest words of praise that Job ever spoke. Even though he tears his robe and shaves his head, signifying that he was in intense amounts of grief and mourning, he still expresses praise and faith towards God showing us that the joy of God is so supreme, that even when everything falls away, God is still worthy. Our praise of God should not be contingent on blessing, but it should be founded in the unchanging, all satisfying, eternal beauty of God Himself.

Please read and comment on the following passages:

Ephesians 5:18-21: "And do not be drunk with wine, in which is dissipation; but be filled with the Spirit, speaking to one another in psalms and hymns and spiritual songs, singing and making melody in your heart to the Lord, giving thanks always for all things to God the Father in the name of our Lord Jesus Christ, submitting to one another in the fear of God."

Philippians 4:4: "Rejoice in the Lord always. Again I will say, rejoice!"

Psalm 132:9: "Let Your priests be clothed with righteousness, And let Your saints shout for joy."

_____

_____

_____

Passages like this not only showed me that I should have boldness to ask God for joy, but they also changed my perspective on thankfulness and praise. Because I am such a naturally cynical and lustful person, it has always been hard for me to praise, but it is really easy for me to complain. And so, I have always struggled with praising God, and I was even resentful of God for demanding that I praise Him. It seemed wrong and selfish to me that God would demand that His people sing praises to Him. But what I didn't understand is that as you experience the pleasure and the joy that is in God, it naturally leads you to praise Him, not because you have to, genuine praise can't be forced, but because you want to. C.S. Lewis in his book on the Psalms helped me to understand this really well, please read and comment on his quote:

C.S. Lewis, *Reflections On The Psalms:*

I had not noticed how the humblest, and at the same time most balanced and content, praised the most, while the cranks, misfits and unhappy praised least...

I have never noticed that all enjoyment spontaneously overflows into praise... The world rings with praise—lovers praising their mistresses, readers their favorite poet, walkers praising the countryside...

I think we delight to praise what we enjoy because the praise not merely expresses but completes the enjoyment; it is its appointed consummation... The worthier the object, the more intense this delight would be. If it were possible for a created soul fully to "appreciate," that is to love and delight in, the worthiest object of all, and simultaneously at every moment to give this delight perfect expression, than that soul would be in supreme beatitude..."

_____

_____

_____

All these new perspectives have softened my hard heart and brought me into the understanding that God is truly the greatest pleasure that there is, and that by calling us to trust, obey, praise, and love Him, He is really calling us into the deepest joy and pleasure that there is. The Christian life is all about pursuing joy, and for us, the best is always yet to come because in heaven what we only understand at a distance will be brought near, and the joy that we have been searching for all of our lives will be fulfilled in His eternal presence. Please spend some time reflecting on these last couple quotes:

Finally, my brethren, rejoice in the Lord. For me to write the same things to you is not tedious, but for you it is safe. Beware of dogs, beware of evil workers, beware of the mutilation! For we are the circumcision, who worship God in the Spirit, rejoice in Christ Jesus, and have no confidence in the flesh, though I also might have confidence in the flesh. If anyone else thinks he may have confidence in the flesh, I more so: circumcised the eighth day, of the stock of Israel, of the tribe of Benjamin, a Hebrew of the Hebrews; concerning the law, a Pharisee; concerning zeal, persecuting the church; concerning the righteousness which is in the law, blameless. But what things were gain to me, these I have counted loss for Christ. Yet indeed I also count all things loss for the excellence of the knowledge of Christ Jesus my Lord, for whom I have suffered the loss of all things, and count them as rubbish, that I may gain Christ and be found in Him, not having my own righteousness, which is from the law, but that which is through faith in Christ, the righteousness which is from God by faith; that I may know Him and the power of His resurrection, and the fellowship of His sufferings, being conformed to His death, if, by any means, I may attain to the resurrection from the dead. (Philippians 3:1-11)

C.S. Lewis, in *Reflections On The Psalms:*

I want to stress what I think that we (or at least I) need more; the joy and delight in God which meets us in the Psalms... These poets knew far less reasons than we for loving God. They did not know that

He offered them eternal joy; still less that He would die to win it for them. Yet they express a longing for Him, for His mere presence, which comes only to the best Christians or to Christians in their best moments. These saints long to live all their days in the temple so that they may constantly see "the fair beauty of the Lord." Their longing to go up to Jerusalem and "appear before the presence of God" is like a physical thirst... Lacking that encounter with Him, their souls are parched like a waterless countryside. They crave to be "satisfied with the pleasures" of His house. Only there can they be at ease, like a bird in the nest. One day of those "pleasures" is better than a lifetime spent elsewhere.

SELF-CONTROL

But the fruit of the Spirit is love, joy, peace, longsuffering, kindness, goodness, faithfulness, gentleness, self-control. Against such there is no law. And those who are Christ's have crucified the flesh with its passions and desires. (Galatians 5:22-24)

As we have been studying sin, we have been using a metaphor that sin is like a tree that is rooted deep in our hearts that produces all sorts of horrible fruits. And from this we understand that the "major" sins that we commit every day, are mere symptoms of our problem and not the actual problem. That is why it is also important to keep in mind that God Himself has rooted a different tree in our hearts that is producing good fruit. It is this fruit that grows up in the life of a Christian that combats the fruit of sin and will eventually destroy the tree of sin from the roots up. We are called not just to stop sinning, but to be a new creation, zealous for good works in God. And what is most interesting about the above passage that tells us about these Godly attributes is that it says that the fruit of the Spirit is… not that the fruits of the Spirit are… Meaning that there really is only one fruit of the Spirit, and that is love. But from God's love, we see that all these other attributes are growing up in our lives simultaneously, and we have already talked about quite a few of these. In today's lesson we are going to talk about the final attribute listed here, self-control.

As we learn about the beauty of God's love, and the wonderful joy that we can have in Him, we can make a fatal mistake and believe that the Christian life is easy. That the pleasure and joy of God are so good and glorious that we won't struggle with our flesh anymore. But if this were true, we would have no reason for self-control. Self-control is only a useful attribute if you have desires and thoughts that need to be controlled. Self-control carries the very unpopular idea that we will have to constantly resist temptations and struggle against our cravings and emotions, when we would much rather just have God take away all of these things and make life easy for us. Also, in order for me, or any other teacher of the Word to talk about the merits of self-control, we would first have to admit that there are a lot of impulses, desires, and thoughts that we have that we need to control within ourselves. This is awkward to admit, I would rather tell people that I always want to do the right thing, and that if you follow God, your heart will change and you won't struggle with sin anymore.

I do believe that this is one of the greatest weaknesses in the church today. When I was growing up in the church, I didn't really have many good examples of self-control. I heard a lot of eloquent and convicting sermons about what God commands of us and what we shouldn't be doing, but I never really heard sermons that explained to me how to go from being trapped in sin to being free. So as a teenager, I knew that I shouldn't be proud, or vain, or view porn, or get angry at my parents…, but even though I knew I shouldn't, that didn't change the fact that I constantly craved these things, and fell to them regularly. You see, because no one really explained self-control to me, I thought that there was something really wrong with me as a Christian. I thought I was the only one who craved these wrong things, and because no one really opened up to me about their own struggles against sin, I never learned how to control these cravings, or how to practically fight temptations. I was only taught about how I should be, I was never told how to change from where I was to how I should be. Because of that, I thought that I was a lost cause, and sometimes I even believed that I wasn't saved at all.

Can you relate to this? _____

> *For though we walk in the flesh, we do not war according to the flesh. For the weapons of our warfare are not carnal but mighty in God for pulling down strongholds, casting down arguments and every high thing that exalts itself against the knowledge of God, bringing every thought into captivity to the obedience of Christ, and being ready to punish all disobedience when your obedience is fulfilled.* (2 Corinthians 10:3-6)

Galatians 5:17 says, "For the flesh lusts against the Spirit, and the Spirit against the flesh; and these are contrary to one another, so that you do not do the things that you wish." These passages are just a few of many Scriptures in the Bible that describe the Christian walk as one of warfare, which was far different than the picture of ease that was painted for me in church settings. These passages show that we as Christians have a kind of dual nature. One, is our sinful nature of the flesh that we inherited by birth in this fallen world, and our other nature is made by the Spirit of God and we inherited that when we were born again into the kingdom of God. These two natures are in constant conflict with one another, and we will continuously feel the pull of these two opposing sides, where on one hand we will want to do the right thing, and on the other you will want to do the wrong thing.

Can you relate to this feeling of warfare within you? _____

Some Christians may agree with this in principle, but they would say, "Yes this is true for new believers, but the struggle will fade for mature Christians."

But lest we think this way, even the apostle Paul, in Romans 7:15-23, wrote this about himself: "I don't really understand myself, for I want to do what is right, but I don't do it. Instead, I do what I hate. But if I know that what I am doing is wrong, this shows that I agree that the law is good. So I am not the one doing wrong; it is sin living in me that does it. And I know that nothing good lives in me, that is, in my sinful nature. I want to do what is right, but I can't. I want to do what is good, but I don't. I don't want to do what is wrong, but I do it anyway. But if I do what I don't want to do, I am not really the one doing wrong; it is sin living in me that does it. I have discovered this principle of life—that when I want to do what is right, I inevitably do what is wrong. I love God's law with all my heart. But there is another power within me that is at war with my mind. This power makes me a slave to the sin that is still within me. (NLT)

Paul wrote this passage all in the present tense. At no point does he say, "this is how my life used to look until I got saved…" This was the current state of affairs for his life. We must always remember that we live in a fallen world, and in this world we can have partial intimacy with God, but never the fullness that we will have in heaven. Because of this, all of us will struggle against our fallen nature until we see Christ face to face. Far from what we tend to think in church, experiencing this warfare is proof that you are saved, the unsaved person will never experience this type of warfare in their lives. Meaning, that during my time walking away from God, I didn't experience this warfare anymore. If I wanted to view porn or masturbate, I did it, and I didn't feel bad about it at all. It was only after I started going back towards God that this warfare picked up again because I found that there was a part of me that still wanted to view porn and another part of me that wanted to please God and resist these urges. It is reassuring to know that if you struggle with this kind of internal warfare, you are not weird or unsaved, this is actually proof that you are saved. Because it is only the regenerate Christian that will fight against his flesh. The unsaved person will never experience this warfare because they don't have a new nature.

Even Jesus?

Remember also, that even our Lord and Savior struggled against temptation, yet without sin. Jesus was so pressed by temptation, that in the Garden of Gethsemane, before His crucifixion, He sweat blood as He resisted His temptation to not go to the cross for us. This demonstrates to us first that being tempted to do something isn't sin, it is pursuing these temptations that is sin. And second, it shows us that if our Lord had to exercise self-control, so will we. But, it is in Jesus that we begin to see the hope that we have in self-control. As we listen to this seemingly bleak picture of the life of constant warfare, some will say, "This doesn't sound like a very hopeful or joyous existence if this is true…" But when we think this way, we are being influenced by our instant gratification culture, not by the Word of God or reality. As we talked about yesterday in our topic of joy, it is a fallacy to believe that our pursuit of joy is something that will always feel good. The Bible tells us in Psalm 126:5 that "Those who sow in tears shall reap in joy…"

One of the reasons why we are so unhappy in our culture, is that we believe joy and love are things that are easy and without pain. But, Jesus was the happiest and most loving person who has ever lived, and yet He practiced self-control even to the bitter end of His life. Jesus' life teaches us that our desires are not always good and need to be resisted at times.

I remember that when I was a little kid, I used to hate that my parents wouldn't let me eat junk food for dinner. I made a promise to myself that when I was old enough, I would eat whatever I wanted whenever I wanted because I believed that living like this would make me happy. But here I am as an adult, and I still don't eat junk food for dinner. It's not that I no longer crave to eat like this, but it is because I have discovered that the way to maximize my pleasure with dessert, is to exercise self-control and eat a small portion of sweets after I have eaten a healthy meal.

You see, by suffering for a small amount of time and resisting the urge to eat cookies for dinner, I gain the far greater joy and pleasure of not getting a stomach ache and being in better shape. In regards to food, my self-control is a pathway towards greater joy, not an absence from it. Why wouldn't this principle stand up in all areas of my life? What the Bible tells us is that if we learn to control all of our desires in this same way, we will have far greater joy, not less of it.

Unfortunately, we don't understand this in our current culture. It reminds me of the biosphere experiment that began a couple decades ago. The biosphere was an attempt to create a man-made ecosystem; but when it first began there were a myriad of issues. One of the biggest issues was that they found that the trees had no stability and would tip over randomly. What they discovered with time, is that they planted these huge trees in an enclosed environment without any wind and with a daily watering system. The reason why this ruined the trees was because in nature, it is the wind and the lack of water that forces a tree to grow its roots deep into the ground. Without these natural "trials" the trees had no reason to anchor their roots down deep and they became unstable and collapsed under their own weight. You see it is actually our trials and our temptations that cause the Christian to push their roots deeper and deeper into Christ and find their true joy and pleasure in Him.

How does the following passage relate to our topic: Romans 5:3-5 says, "And not only that, but we also glory in tribulations, knowing that tribulation produces perseverance; and perseverance, character; and character, hope. Now hope does not disappoint, because the love of God has been poured out in our hearts by the Holy Spirit who was given to us."

_____

_____

_____

In our impatience, we have become just like the trees in our unstableness. We don't understand that genuine love and joy don't occur from following your heart and doing whatever is easiest. If we seek to be this way, we will become very shallow in every area of our lives. Yes, self-control is not an easy path and trials aren't very fun, but they lead to far deeper and more meaningful joy and satisfaction, that is why God encourages us in this way and why He doesn't take away all resistance from our lives.

Hebrews 12:11: "No discipline seems pleasant at the time, but painful. Later on, however, it produces a harvest of righteousness and peace for those who have been trained by it (NIV)."

THE EXAMPLE...LOVE

Let's take a look at love for a powerful example of this truth. All genuine loving relationships will have their share of heartache and difficulty. But if we jump ship whenever things get difficult or when the passion begins to fade, we would never develop our love for others and grow our roots down deep. Instead we would remain shallow and unhappy in all of our relationships.

Please read the following quotes from C.S. Lewis and a marital counselor named Esther Perel on the topic of love. Then comment on what they are saying and explain how it relates to our topic today.

C.S. Lewis in *Mere Christianity* says:

What we call 'being in love' is a glorious state, and, in several ways, good for us. It helps to make us generous and courageous, it opens our eyes not only to the beauty of the beloved but to all beauty, and it (controls) (especially at first) our merely animal sexuality; in that sense, love is the great conqueror of lust... Being in love is a good thing, but it is not the best thing... You cannot make it the basis of a whole life. It is a noble feeling, but it is still a feeling. Now no feeling can be relied on to last its full intensity, or even to last at all..

Love, as distinct from 'being in love'—is not merely a feeling. It is a deep unity, maintained by the will and deliberately strengthened by habit; reinforced by (in Christian marriages) the grace which both partners ask, and receive, from God...

Esther Perel in *The Secret Of Desire:*

(Passionate) couples also understand that passion waxes and wanes. It's pretty much like the moon. It has intermittent eclipses. But what they know is they know how to resurrect it. They know how to bring it back. And they know how to bring it back because they have demystified one big myth, which is the myth of spontaneity, which is that it's just going to fall from heaven while you're folding the laundry like a deus ex machina, and in fact they understood that whatever is going to just happen in a long-term relationship, already has. Committed (passion) is premeditated (passion. It's willful. It's intentional. It's focus and presence.

_____

_____

_____

_____

So how do you grow in self-control? There is no simple answer here, self-control is grown through habit and commitment. But we first must be grown through self reflection and honesty. Meaning that in order to resist something, you have to acknowledge that it's there. So many Christians refuse to admit a struggle because they are embarrassed by it. This is an aside, and for more information on these topics please refer to our pamphlets and podcasts on these issues, but that is also why so few Christians know how to deal with things like homosexuality. In our culture we have been told a lie that your attractions are what define you. So if you have same sex attraction, you must be gay. But what this lesson should show you, is that every single one of us have attractions that go against God's word, but we aren't defined by our attractions, but by our faith in God's identity for us. One of the most powerful passages that shows us this is 1 Corinthians 6:9-11 Do you not know that the unrighteous will not inherit the kingdom of God? Do not be deceived. Neither fornicators, nor idolaters, nor adulterers, nor homosexuals, nor sodomites, nor thieves, nor covetous, nor drunkards, nor revilers, nor extortioners will inherit the kingdom of God. And such were some of you. But you were washed, but you were sanctified, but you were justified in the name of the Lord Jesus and by the Spirit of our God.

This is one of the most beautiful passages in the whole Bible. That although the Corinthians were struggling with every sin in that list, Paul says that these struggle didn't define them anymore. Because as believers our identity is based on God's finished work, not on our struggles and failures. And when you embrace this new identity, it gives you the freedom to, not deny, but to accept the struggles that you have, and resist them in self-control. When we refuse to admit our struggles, our struggles will dominate us and confuse us. But when we admit them, we will understand them with greater clarity and we can grow in learning how to resist them instead of just denying them. This will also help us understand what we can and can't handle, and what is beneficial for our struggle. For instance, for me, when I was able to admit my craving for porn, I was able to set up filters on my computers because I know that having unrestricted access to Internet is a stumbling block for me and my struggle. I have also realized that when I hang out with men who talk about women in a lustful way, it impacts my view of women and makes me more lustful and increases my craving for porn. So, I need to have friends that encourage me in my purity, who I can be honest with in my struggles and encourage me in the areas that I have amputated avenues of temptation.

Hebrews 10:24-25: "And let us consider one another in order to stir up love and good works, not forsaking the assembling of ourselves together, as is the manner of some, but exhorting one another, and so much the more as you see the Day approaching."

I can never oversell the importance of constant accountability in the life of the Christian. Because as we develop in our self-control, we will need other believers to help keep us accountable to the things that we have purposed to do. These people will also be invaluable in showing us aspects of our struggle that we might be blinded to and encouraging us in our walks with God.

Take time to write down your specific areas of struggle in sin. Then think of practical things you can start doing to help you in your struggle. _____

_____

_____

_____

_____

I also need to remember that I need self-control in my relationships. I can't just go into cruise control in my marriage and expect it to thrive. I need to take time to think about ways to make it better. I need to carve out time to spend with my wife, to develop our communication, and to learn how to love her better. I need to spend time and see the areas that we have trouble in, knowing that these "little things" will turn into major issues over time if I let them.

Song of Solomon 2:15: "Catch all the foxes, those little foxes, before they ruin the vineyard of love, for the grapevines are blossoming!"

If I don't do this, I know how easy it is for me to fall into my selfish habits and for my love to grow cold. This goes double for my walk with God. I need to spend time seeking after God. I need to plan time every day to read His Word, and spend time in prayer with Him. If I don't specifically plan time for God, I know I will get busy and never get around to being with Him. I need to go to church and cultivate relationships with other believers who will help me in my walk and who I can confess to regularly so that they can keep me on guard for those areas of sin that I have become calloused to. Always remember however that this self-control is a means to help you love God more, it is not an end unto itself. Sometimes we can slip into legalism and think that our works are what are saving us and making us better. So instead of reading the Word and praying to get closer to God, it becomes an intellectual exercise that makes us feel superior to others. And instead of fighting sin to draw closer to God, we are doing it because of our own selfish desire to be free, not to glorify Him. Always remember that self-control is an attribute of love, it can't stand on its own, but when it comes out of love, it is one of the most important attributes. Without self-control, all the other attributes of love will fade, self-control is the glue that holds the fruit of the Spirit together. It is what we need to combat our sin and pursue God daily.

Please take some time to reflect on these last couple quotes:

Proverbs 25:28: "Whoever has no rule over his own spirit is like a city broken down, without walls."

Galatians 6:7-9: "Do not be deceived, God is not mocked; for whatever a man sows, that he will also reap. For he who sows to his flesh will of the flesh reap corruption, but he who sows to the Spirit will of the Spirit reap everlasting life. And let us not grow weary while doing good, for in due season we shall reap if we do not lose heart."

2 Peter 1:5-8: "But also for this very reason, giving all diligence, add to your faith virtue, to virtue knowledge, to knowledge self-control, to self-control perseverance, to perseverance godliness, to godliness brotherly kindness, and to brotherly kindness love. For if these things are yours and abound, you will be neither barren nor unfruitful in the knowledge of our Lord Jesus Christ."

DECEPTION

Proverbs 6:16-19 teaches us: "There are six things that the Lord hates, seven that are an abomination to him: haughty eyes, a lying tongue, and hands that shed innocent blood, a heart that devises wicked plans, feet that make haste to run to evil, a false witness who breathes out lies, and one who sows discord among brothers."

For the next couple lessons we will be focusing on the sin of deception. Deception is unlike the other sins that we have been studying because it isn't an end unto itself, it is a means to an end. Meaning, that no one lies simply to lie, they lie in order to get something else, which makes deception a sort of tool that we use for the sake of something greater. So for instance, if I am lying for the sake of my sexual lust, I will be telling lies in order to satisfy my sexual lust. So this lying might be in order to get someone to have sex with me, lying to make me seem more attractive, or lying in order to flirt with someone I'm attracted to… If I lie for the sake of vanity, I might lie to hide secret sins that I am embarrassed about, I might lie to make myself seem better than I really am (social media is filled with this kind of lying), or I might lie to make someone else look worse (gossip), or might make up stories in order to get attention… Because of this, the areas where we will be most deceptive are going to be the areas of sin that we struggle most with. It's also important to understand that you can lie by breaking promises as well. So for instance, if you tell someone that you will be somewhere and you don't show up, this is a form of deception. Or even more seriously, if you cheat on your spouse, this is also deception because you broke your vows to them. There is no doubt that all of us lie, what is different about us is how much we lie, and the reasons why we lie.

What are the areas that you feel you are most deceptive? _____

_____

Dan Ariely is an author and the Professor of Psychology and Behavioral Economics at Duke University, and he has spent a lot of time studying the topic of lying. One of his most famous social experiments that he does, is he has centers all over the world that offer testing for cash. So you would come into one of these centers and take a random test, and for every answer you get right, you get some amount of money. The trick is, that after people finish taking the tests, the procurator will ask the people to mentally tally up how many questions that they got right, shred the test without showing anyone your answers, and then verbally tell the employees there how many questions they got right. Little did the people know that the paper shredders were rigged to only shred the sides of the paper, leaving the center portion in tact, which would give these centers the ability to see how much people lied. What they found, is that pretty much everyone lied a little bit, usually only exaggerating the truth by one or two answers, but there was a very small portion of people who lied a lot and swindled them out of a lot of money.

In order to understand why most people only seem to lie a little, they changed the experiment several times to see if they could find out what the cause of this was. The first thing that they did, was they changed the amount of money that you got for correct answers. And they found that when they raised the amount of money per answer, lying actually went down, not up. This really surprised them because they assumed that people would certainly lie more if there was more money at stake. So they changed the experiment one more time, this time they left the payment the same, but they told the test takers that for every dollar that they earned, the center would donate a dollar to a charity. This made cheating skyrocket and proved a very important point that Dan Ariely put this way:

> The amount we lie correlates most to how much we can rationalize the lie. We want to be able to look ourselves in the mirror and say we are honest and good people, that we are doing the right thing.

Meaning this, we all want to lie and do the wrong thing, but we all want to think of ourselves as good people. So, we are looking for an excuse to do the wrong thing so that we can sin without having a guilty conscience. This is why lying went down when the amount of money went up, it is easy to justify stealing one or two dollars, but most people couldn't call themselves honest if they stole 40 or 50 dollars. And when they were told that the answers that they got right would also benefit others, this made it much easier for them to lie and say, "Well I am really doing this to help the less fortunate." So what is the difference between people who lie a lot, versus those who lie just a little? Justification. If we had a good enough justification, we would lie about anything.

And the more selfish we are, the less of a good excuse we will need for deceiving others. That is why in the extreme example of a sociopath, they are able to tell huge lies all the time without much of a reason behind their deception. But, even though most of us don't fall under that category, we all have many "good" excuses for the lies we do tell. It reminds me of the series "Pirates of The Caribbean" by Disney. In the first movie you meet Captain Jack Sparrow who is an unrepentant pirate who lies, cheats, and kills all to get money and save his own skin. Then you are introduced to Will Turner and Elizabeth Swan who are supposed to be the heroes of the series. But as the films go along, and the stakes get higher and higher, you see both Will and Elizabeth become more cutthroat and deceptive than Jack Sparrow ever was. And by the time you get to the third film, Jack Sparrow is now the hero and Will and Elizabeth are full fledged pirates. As an audience you might ask yourself how you got to the place where you are rooting for a self proclaimed selfish pirate, while being disgusted by the so called "heroes." Jack Sparrow gives us the answer to this question in the first film: "I'm dishonest, and you can always trust a dishonest man to be dishonest. Honestly, it's the honest ones you have to look out for because you never know when they are going to do something incredibly stupid."

You see his point? Everyone is deceptive at heart, and the worst people on the planet are the ones who are so deceptive that they have actually tricked themselves into thinking that they are completely honest and good human beings. For every one of us, there is something that we are willing to be dishonest for.

Why is this so important? One reason is that the more you lie to get what you want, even if you have the best motives, the easier it becomes to lie the next time. That is why Paul says in 2 Timothy 4:2 ."..speaking lies in hypocrisy, having their own conscience seared with a hot iron..."

This passage doesn't just refer to lying either, it also refers to breaking promises. The more you lie and break promises, the easier, and less personal deception can become for you. I can see this crystal clear in my walk with God. When I first started falling to porn, every time I viewed it I felt terrible for sinning against God. I would also get very nervous about being caught by those around me, and it was nerve racking to lie in order to cover my tracks, but I justified it by thinking "I don't want to burden others with my struggles..." But over time of repeatedly falling to the same sin and repeatedly lying to cover up my faults, I started to become less and less concerned with how my actions were impacting my relationship with God and others, and my bad behavior became easier and easier to fall into. It is amazing how quickly deception can sear your conscience.

Have you seen your own conscience be seared by deception?_____

The next reason comes from the Proverbs 6 passage at the top, and many other passages throughout the Bible that talk about God's hatred for lying. God hates lying and broken promises and wants for all of us to walk in honesty just as He does. The big issue with this is that almost none of us are willing to admit that we are liars, because we have justifications for almost all of our deceptive behavior. This is incredibly dangerous because, for one thing, you can't repent of something that you are unaware that you do, and you can't understand fully the damage you have done to others unless you understand the depth of your own deception.

Psalm 101:7 says, "No one who practices deceit shall dwell in my house; no one who utters lies shall continue before my eyes."

So why is it that God hates lying so much? The simple answer is that God created us to enjoy wonderful community with Him and with one another. Going back to Adam and Eve in the garden, remember that they were naked and unashamed. Meaning that they didn't have any defenses up and were able to be completely vulnerable with one another without any fear of being betrayed. But after Adam and Eve broke their promise to God and ate of the fruit, trust was violated. Not just between us and God, but also between each other. That is why the first thing that Adam and Eve did was put on clothing to cover their shame. When trust is broken, community is broken with it, and now it is almost impossible for us to have true vulnerability with another person or to genuinely trust those around us. We all, just like Adam and Eve cover ourselves up and try to keep people at arms length because we are terrified of being betrayed. This also broke our trust with God, not because God ever lied to us, but when we lied to God, we projected our own dishonesty on Him and doubted His Word. But without trust, love can't grow, trust is the foundation for both love and community.

This is really unfortunate, because as a pastor , I see so many couples that have experienced the pain of infidelity.

And one of the most apparent things to me, is that as traumatizing as the actual adultery was, the deception cuts far deeper. Nothing makes someone feel quite as violated as having their trust broken by another person who they were vulnerable with. Esther Perel is a marriage counselor who deals with the topic of infidelity a lot, and this is what she says about the effects of this type of betrayal:

> *We have a romantic ideal in which we turn to one person to fulfill an endless list of needs: to be my greatest lover, my best friend, the best parent, my trusted confidant, my emotional companion, my intellectual equal. And I am it: I'm chosen, I'm unique, I'm indispensable, I'm irreplaceable, I'm the one. And infidelity tells me I'm not. It is the ultimate betrayal. Infidelity shatters the grand ambition of love. But if throughout history, infidelity has always been painful, today it is often traumatic, because it threatens our sense of self.*

> *So my patient Fernando, he's plagued. He goes on: "I thought I knew my life. I thought I knew who you were, who we were as a couple, who I was. Now, I question everything." Infidelity —a violation of trust, a crisis of identity. "Can I ever trust you again?" He asks. "Can I ever trust anyone again?"*

For those of you who are in a marriage that has been shaken by infidelity and broken trust, I want these words to sink in for you. After something like this, it is rare for a marriage to even survive this level of betrayal, and even the marriages that do survive, it takes a long time for any amount of trust to be restored in the relationship. And so, if you have failed in this way and have committed adultery, know that the mercy of God is just as applicable to your sin as it is to anyone else's. But also know, you need to really start praying for patience and understanding for your marriage. Don't expect healing to be quick, but know that it is possible if you are willing to demonstrate genuine remorse over what you have done, consistent faithfulness towards the one you have hurt, and constant patience and understanding towards the healing process that your spouse will be in. And if you haven't already done it, begin biblical counseling with your spouse to work through your issues.

And even though I am using adultery in a marriage as an example, this applies to every relationship. I have also seen the trauma caused to children when they have parents that constantly break promises to them, or friendships that are ruined through gossip, or a spouse who finds a hidden sin, and countless other examples. An even more serious example that most people wouldn't label as deception, would be abuse. In all relationships, there is an unspoken promise of common courtesy and care that abuse breaks. That is why when someone is abused, whether it is emotionally, physically, or sexually, the wounds that they carry are not merely physical. There will, more often than not, be deep wounds in their heart that can express themselves in severe trust issues and fear of intimacy. Broken trust has hurt all of us, and our own personal hurt can help us understand what we have done to others in our own deception.

Have you ever had anyone violate your trust? How did it impact you? _____

_____

_____

It's so important for this point to sink in, because we need to understand the importance of honesty in our relationships. And even though we might have a variety of justifications for our deception such as: "Telling them would just hurt their feelings… It was just one time… They broke my trust first… It's not that big of a deal… It was an accident so I shouldn't have to tell them…" It doesn't change the fact that we were deceptive, and it certainly doesn't take away the pain or the damage that our lies will do. We need to own what we have done, and understand that all the justifications in the world can't make up for the trust that we have shattered. We also need to take seriously the fact that we can't take back what we have done, but we can, with patience rebuild trust. When trust is broken there are no shortcuts, there has to be consistent faithfulness demonstrated in order to build it back.

Proverbs 18:19: "A brother wronged is more unyielding than a fortified city; disputes are like the barred gates of a citadel."

Can you see the severity of the lies that you have told? _____

And because of how deception has seared our conscience, it will also take a lot of time to build up honesty in ourselves. One of the main reasons why I recommend constant accountability is because this is a habit that can help you develop honesty in your life even when it is uncomfortable. This will also help you develop gentleness and understanding in your honesty. Meaning, that some of us can pride ourselves on being honest, and while we are being honest, we are also being abrasive and blunt with the way that we share truth. So, maybe a husband is finally walking in honesty with his wife after a betrayal, but now instead of failing on the side of deception, now he bluntly tells his wife all the horrid details of what he did and what he thinks of her without understanding that he is damaging her just as much in his honesty as he did in his deception. When we have accountability with mature believers, we can learn how to tell the truth in love, how to build healthy boundaries of what details to share, and what details to leave out, and we can ask our accountability partners for help in how to word things to the ones that we have hurt so we don't become overly blunt and cruel in our efforts to be honest.

This will also help repair the damage to the church itself. The fall of man has hurt the unity of every community on earth, and the church is no exception. There is so much deception in the church because, just like our ancestors, we are covering up our shame in front of others because of our fear judgment and betrayal. That is why, even in the church, there is so much deception and hypocrisy. We fear judgment in the church and so we lie hiding our struggles from others and we pretend that we are far more righteous than we really are. I have seen this even in counseling and accountability groups, people will still hold on to their deception and try to dress up their sins to make themselves look better than they really are. So, someone might sit down in a counseling session with me and admit that they fought with their spouse, but they will conveniently forget that they started the fight and screamed hurtful obscenities at their partner. Or they will listen to counsel that was given to them, and they tell this counsel to their spouse, but leave out all of the counsel that was about their issues, and twist the rest of the counsel to condemn their spouse for things that they have a problem with. Or someone might confess to struggling with lust, but they will leave out the fact that they viewed pornography multiple times that week, or that they visited a strip club, or that they were flirtatiously talking to an ex, or that they actually committed adultery again… Accountability is only as useful as we allow it to be. If we want healing from our deception, partial honesty won't cut it, there has to be genuine transparency with those that we have hurt and those who are helping us in our issues.

The parts of our hearts that are calloused towards deception will be healed when we learn the beauty of honesty. That even though honesty is difficult, and sometimes even shameful, it is far better than hiding in the dark. We need to know and believe that because of what Jesus has done for us, we no longer have to hide behind our false identities that we have built. We can be vulnerable knowing that our identity in Christ is firm and that He is pleased in our honesty. And as we confess in the peace of our identity in God, we will also be able to accept correction. Knowing that this honesty isn't just for the purpose of "getting things off of my chest" or pursuing emotional validation, but to help build the community of the church and grow us closer to God no matter what it takes. If this isn't your motive and perspective, then even your honesty will be twisted by your selfishness and pride.

Please read and comment on the following quote from Dietrich Bonhoeffer:

Dietrich Bonhoeffer: *Life Together:*

> *Sin demands to have a man by himself. It withdraws him from the community. The more isolated a person is, the more destructive will be the power of sin over him, and the more deeply he becomes involved in it, the more disastrous is his isolation. Sin wants to remain unknown. It shuns the light. In the darkness of the unexpressed it poisons the whole being of a person. This can happen even in the midst of a pious community. In confession the light of the gospel breaks into the darkness and seclusion of the heart. The sin must be brought into the light. The unexpressed must be openly spoken and acknowledged. All that is secret and hidden is made manifest. It is a hard struggle until the sin is openly admitted. But God breaks gates of brass and bars of iron (Ps. 107:16).*

> *Since the confession of sin is made in the presence of a Christian brother, the last stronghold of self justification is abandoned. The sinner surrenders; he gives up all his evil. He gives his heart to God and he finds the forgiveness of all his sin in the fellowship of Jesus Christ and his brother. The expressed, acknowledged sin has lost all its power. It has been revealed and judged as sin. It can no longer tear the fellowship asunder. Now the fellowship bears the sin of the brother. He is no longer alone with his evil for he has cast off his sin in confession and handed it over to God. It has been taken away from him. Now he stands in the fellowship of sinners who live by the grace of God in the cross of Jesus Christ. Now he can be a sinner and still enjoy the grace of God. He can confess his sins and in this very act find fellowship for the first time. The sin concealed separated him from the fellowship, made all his apparent fellowship a sham; the sin confessed has helped him to find true fellowship with the brethren in Jesus Christ.*

_____

_____

_____

And the part of our hearts that has been so hurt by the deception of others will be healed here as well. When we have been hurt by deception, we naturally want to protect ourselves from being hurt. So we put walls up and refuse to trust others in order to keep other people from ever getting close enough to hurt us. So by protecting ourselves, we are really isolating ourselves and preventing any amount of love to enter our lives. As we grow close in this type of mutual confession, we can find safety to be vulnerable again. That is why whenever I counsel someone who has been hurt by deception, I always encourage them to seek out support and accountability. I often hear people rebel against this advise and say something like "But I'm not the one with the problem, they are…" When they say this they are missing the point. The purpose of their accountability is first and foremost to help them grow in their healing and their restoration after they have been hurt. Their accountability partners can help them by listening to their hurt, praying for them, and pointing them to God.

These people can also help you set up healthy boundaries for honesty as well. Over and over again I have seen people who have been hurt by deception begin to do something called "pain shopping." This is where the hurt party will barrage the person who hurt them with damaging questions that will only deepen their wound and cause them more anguish. So for instance, a wife who caught their husband cheating might ask questions like this "Do you find her more attractive than me… Were they better in bed than I am… How many times did you sleep together... " Or a wife who finds out that their husband has been viewing porn, in an attempt to "help" their husband they might demand to have total accountability with their husband. And so they ask for all the details about what kind of porn they watch, which women they have lusted after, or even to know every time that they struggle and to hear all the details of their struggle…

Having renewed honesty is a very important thing, and there is a level where you should be allowed into the struggle of the person who hurt you, but part of restoring trust is to trust that the person who hurt you is seeking help with the kinds of people who can hear all these details without being crushed. If they aren't seeking help, than that is a different story, but if they are, you might need to take a step back and pray for the faith to trust in God's power to work in their lives. When we are betrayed like this, we usually feel out of control and helpless, and so while it might help you feel more in control to ask questions like this, be diligent to examine yourself and see if you aren't just putting yourself through hell out of fear and an attempt to be strong. Having these accountability partners can help you see the level you should be involved in this other person's struggles, and to examine the truth of your heart and help you to let go of control and trust in the work of your heavenly Father.

These accountability partners can also help you see the areas of sin that you struggle with. When someone is the victim of betrayal, it is so common for that person to assume that all of the problems in the relationship fall squarely on the shoulders of the person who deceived them. In a weird way, this "victim status" can be appealing to some people because it gives them excuse to never work on themselves and to it gives them so much sympathy and understanding from others. So whenever a fight happens or a problem arises, the hurt party can throw their pain right back in the face of the person who hurt them and completely get out of any personal responsibility for issues in the relationship. This kind of mentality will kill any relationship. Obviously there is a huge responsibility placed on the one who deceived because they are the one who did the most damage. But unless the person who was deceived can look at the relationship and say: "Yes you hurt me and you need to bear the responsibility for what you did, but I also recognize that I am not guiltless in this relationship and I too need to commit myself to change and betterment in Christ." The relationship will never heal. And since it will be almost impossible in the beginning to hear correction from the person who wronged you, it is useful to have accountability partners who can gently show you your errors and help you in your own process of repentance.

Proverbs 20:9: "Who can say, 'I have made my heart clean, I am pure from my sin'?"

The accountability is also to help you not slip into the dark abyss of bitterness. For so many couples, even though they outwardly want to work on their issues, no progress is made because the hurt party holds onto their bitterness and refuses to forgive or trust their partner ever again. Because of this, even if the person who did the wrong is making huge amounts of progress and they are constantly reaching out to the person that they hurt, no progress is being made, and none of their loving acts are received. Trust is absolutely necessary for love to grow, without trust relationships are doomed from the beginning. Once again, it is understandable for someone who has had their trust broken to never want to put themselves through that again. But, unless they can trust again, they will sabotage and destroy all of their relationships.

We need to understand that we are not called to be naive and be completely vulnerable with everyone all the time. There is a level of discretion that is good in new relationships and in relationships that are being restored, but as the relationship grows and develops and as you see faithfulness demonstrated, you need to be able to slowly open yourself up again or else the relationship will die. As you pray, think through this, and seek counsel from your accountability partners, you will learn how to be more wise in being balanced so that you aren't completely shut down so that you never trust anyone no matter what. But you also aren't foolishly naive and overly exposed, and you definitely shouldn't put your faith back into a person who hasn't demonstrated faithfulness yet. We also need to remember that, unfortunately there is no such thing as someone who is totally honest and trustworthy. And so as we build community and let our guards down, over time and with discretion, we will be able to do this knowing that the ultimate honest person, Jesus, has made promises to us that He will never break. And in the comfort of His protection, you will be able to experience that safety that will enable you to be vulnerable and trust other people even though you will know that they might break your trust again. And you will do this knowing that God alone will protect your heart and preserve you even if you are deceived again.

Psalm 73:26: "My flesh and my heart fail; but God is the strength of my heart and my portion forever."

So much of our identity and value are found in our relationships, and that is why deception and betrayal can crush our very identity and sense of self. If Jesus is to be the protector of our heart though, He has to become the source of our value and identity. As this happens, while deception and betrayal will still hurt us, they can't crush us because the strength of our heart and our treasure are in Christ alone.

2 Corinthians 4:7-9: "But we have this treasure in earthen vessels, that the excellence of the power may be of God and not of us. We are hard-pressed on every side, yet not crushed; we are perplexed, but not in despair; persecuted, but not forsaken; struck down, but not destroyed—"

Do you struggle with being vulnerable? Do you see how keeping your walls up will destroy your relationships?

_____

_____

_____

The ultimate point to all of this, is that whether you are being honest, or being vulnerable in trusting others, there is a cost to honesty and that is why we choose deception. But, even though there is a cost to honesty, the cost of deception is far greater. Deception can be a comfortable mask that we wear to protect us from shame, and it can be a tool that we use to get what we want, but ultimately it will alienate us from God and others.

Proverbs 20:17 teaches us that, "Bread gained by deceit is sweet to a man, but afterward his mouth will be full of gravel."

It is always better to have love and community, even if those people can hurt you, than it is to be "safe" behind our deception and our walls all alone. Jesus gives us a wonderful example for us to trust in. Even though we were the ones that broke our promise to God, in order to keep His promise to us, Jesus died on our behalf. Not only this, but Jesus was vulnerable with us, fully knowing that by being vulnerable with us, He would ultimately be killed by the ones He came to save. But it says in Hebrews 12:2 that He did all of this for "the joy set before Him." Jesus counted the cost of faithfulness and saw that it was worth it. He loved us so much that He saw even His shameful death on the cross as a worthy price to pay. And as we study His example and ask for increased faith in Him and healing from our past, we can gain more and more of the courage and the self-control necessary to build honesty in our own lives. Knowing that there is no cost that is too high to pay if it means intimacy with God, and expressing His love to others.

Self-Deception

Obadiah 1:3 tells us all: "The pride of your heart has deceived you…"

Yesterday, we started looking at the sin of deception, and we talked about how outward deception towards others can damage our relationships. In today's lesson we are going to look at the most dangerous form our deception can take: self-deception. The reason why this is so deadly is because when we deceive ourselves it makes it impossible to be able to see what we are doing wrong, or even understand our own bad behaviors. In short, our self-deception will stunt growth in every area of our lives and blind us to our own sin. This was something that I never really thought about until a couple years ago. I was never a very trusting person, but the one thing that I always trusted was my own mind. Because of this, it never occurred to me that my pride had been deceiving me all along. As we talked about in our study on pride, our pride can either be arrogant, thinking too much of ourselves, or depressive, thinking too low of ourselves. So in my arrogant pride I was justifying and denying sin that was destroying me, I was suppressing the truth of God so that I didn't have to deal with my own guilt over the many sins that I was committing, and I was suppressing memories and emotions that were secretly controlling me in order to convince myself that I was strong and in control of my own life... And in my depressive pride, I was believing in my own worthlessness, thinking that I had no hope to grow or change, thinking that I was worse than everyone around me and that I was unloved by God and others.

Jeremiah 17:9: "The heart is deceitful above all things, and desperately sick; who can understand it? (ESV)"

And it wasn't until God began to reveal to me my own self-deception that I was finally able to begin to grow in these areas. So what we are going to do in today's lesson is focus on some common areas of self-deception and talk about how to start getting free from this.

Cortney Warren is a psychologist and author who has studied self-deception in some amazing detail. So we are going to look over some quotes from her, and line these up with some biblical truths to get more clarity on our own self-deception. But as we go through these things, it is important to know that because it is our own hearts that are deceiving us, it really does take a work of God's Spirit in us to reveal the truth. Without Him, we are doomed to stumble around in the dark.

Proverbs 4:18-19: "But the path of the just is like the shining sin, that shines ever brighter unto perfect day. The way of the wicked is like darkness; they do not know what makes them stumble."

This Proverb tells us that in our wickedness and self-deception, we won't be able to understand why we are falling. So many of us are like this, and even though we can see all sorts of bad behavior in our own lives, we have no idea where this behavior is coming from or how to change it. But the beauty is that when we walk towards God, He gives clarity to our path and helps us understand what is making us fall which will in turn help us change our behavior. It is in the darkness of our pride that we isolate ourselves from God and others, because, if we can't be honest with ourselves, it makes it impossible to be honest with other people, including God. By doing this, we are doomed to get worse and worse as we become more blind to our issues. But, God can change us, and in drawing closer to Him, He can show us our issues and this will change us and bring us into deeper fellowship with Him and others.

Please read and comment on the following quote by Cortney Warren:

> *Understanding our self-deception is the most effective way to live a fulfilling life. For when we admit who we really are, we have the opportunity to change.*

_____

_____

_____

The first type of self-deception that we are going to look at is, deceiving ourselves in order to live up to ideals.

Cortney Warren says:

> *We lie to ourselves about the smallest details, such as how much we really ate today, and why we didn't list our actual height and weight on our driver's license. We lie to reflect our aspirational goals: 'I'll only have one glass of wine tonight,'— when I know I'm drinking at least three. We lie to uphold social ideals: 'I never have sexual thoughts with anyone except my spouse,' because that wouldn't be acceptable. We lie about our most important life choices, such as why we married who we did, or chose our given career path.*

When we engage in this type of self-deception, it is because we have a goal, or standard that we are trying to live up to. And when we realize that we aren't quite measuring up, our subconscious mind begins to trick us into thinking that we actually have met our goal. This can also come out in what we call denial.

Cortney Warren, "Denial:"

> *Refusing to believe that something is true, even though it is. "I don't have a problem with alcohol," — even though I drink everyday. "I'm not jealous," — even though I secretly check my partner's email.*

I do this all the time. When it comes to working out, I'll tell myself, "I'm tired right now, but I'll work out later." Even though I secretly know that "later" will never come. While I'm on the Internet I will see myself going towards lustful material but I'll say, "I'm not actually going to look at that stuff, I'm just curious about something else…" I trick myself into thinking that I have "conquered" sin in various areas. For instance, I like to believe that I am no longer bitter, so when I have a bitter thought I'll say something like "I'm not being bitter, I'm being honest…" Or, I might trick myself to believe that I am far more spiritual than I really am. And so when I hear sermons that convict me of being greedy, selfish, arrogant… I'll say, "Yeah I used to struggle like that, but thank God I'm not like that anymore." Or I might trick myself into thinking that my life is far more problem free than it really is. So even if there are obvious signs that my marriage isn't doing great, or my struggle against sin is getting far worse, or my relationship with God is cold and dead… I convince myself that everything is going great even when everything is falling apart.

Proverbs 14:8: "The wisdom of the prudent is to discern his way, but the folly of fools is deceiving."

The issue here is that by deceiving ourselves, we may think that we are good internally, but outwardly we are bad and getting worse. It is only when we are able to admit that we are falling short, that God can help us to get better.

Psalm 139:23-24: "Search me, O God, and know my heart; try me, and know my anxieties; And see if there is any wicked way in me, And lead me in the way everlasting."

Psalm 51:6: "Behold, You desire truth in the inward parts, and in the hidden part You will make me to know wisdom."

Do you see this kind of self-deception in your life? _____

Another type of self-deception is repressing pain and trauma.

Cortney Warren says:

> *As adults, we will most want to lie about how psychologically painful realities experienced as children affected who we are today…As an adult, when someone points out your imperfections, you feel tremendous anxiety but deny where it comes from. Perhaps you felt ugly as a child because you were teased for your appearance. You learned to eat in response to emotional pain. As an adult, you struggle to maintain a stable weight, because your eating has very little to do with hunger. Perhaps you watched your parents fight. You learned to avoid conflict. Now, you struggle to admit even feeling negative emotion. Although each of our specific childhood learnings will be unique, what we learned will be exemplified in the lies we tell ourselves as adults.*

This is a very common form for self-deception because of how painful these realities can be. It is so hard to admit deep trauma and pain like this, just thinking about memories like this can make us feel physically sick, or push us into depression or an anxiety attack. It is far easier to just repress these memories and pretend like they don't bother us, then to experience the pain that we have been running from. The issue is that just because we say that things don't bother us, doesn't make it true. It was so disconcerting for me to realize that even though I thought I was strong and that things didn't bother me, so many of my painful memories have controlled my behavior. For instance, I grew up as the youngest of four from two very smart and successful parents. All of my siblings got straight A's throughout school and excelled in ways that I never could. So even though my parents never verbally told me that I was worse than them, slowly but surely I developed a massive inferiority complex.

I truly believed that I was nothing special and wasn't good at anything. This also made me feel as though I could never earn the approval or love of anyone. So I retreated into a shell as a teenager and told myself that I didn't care what anyone thought of me. Even though God has given me tremendous growth in this area, this inferiority complex is still alive and well in me to this day. I am constantly questioning my worth and believing that I am worse than other people and ultimately useless. I find that I have tendencies to shut people out and use sarcasm, anger, and apathy as masks for my deep insecurities. I have even found that some of my most negative habits are sometimes coping mechanisms for my pain and regret that are rooted in my past.

Cortney Warren says:

> *Self-deception leads to massive amounts of pain and regret. To avoid being honest, we frequently make choices with harmful consequences to ourselves and others — we may use drugs, alcohol, eat, shop, gamble, steal, lie, leave people or pass our emotional baggage down to those we love the most. Or, we may choose not to change even when we are miserable or causing profound harm to those around us.*

You see, I thought I was strong by not thinking about these things, and I thought I was tough to not need anyone else. But deep down I was an insecure mess hiding behind walls I put up for my own protection. But all these walls could do was keep me alone and cold towards everyone, even God. Unfortunately, our egos are so fragile in our pride, that if we begin to search our hearts for these painful memories, it might do more damage than good, but God gives us a better solution. Throughout the Bible, you see the saints of old crying out to God and they lay out their trauma before Him. As they do this, God begins to heal the damage done to them and draw them closer to Him. It is no mistake that Jesus is called our wonderful counselor in Isaiah 9:6; and as we learn to be honest with God and ask Him for honesty in ourselves, it will grow your intimacy with God and He will begin to heal the hurts in you.

1 Peter 5:6-7 tells us: "Therefore humble yourselves under the mighty hand of God, that He may exalt you in due time, casting all your care upon Him, for He cares for you."

Do you deceive yourself in order to cover up past pains? _____

We can also deceive ourselves to deal with our guilt by justifying our bad behavior.

Cortney Warren:

> *Rationalization: Creating a reason to excuse ourselves. "I wouldn't have yelled at you if you hadn't treated me so unfairly," thereby justifying my yelling. "I know that smoking isn't good for my health, but it helps me relax," thereby justifying my smoking.*

Here she gives two types of rationalization. The first is blame-shifting. So even though I did something wrong, I blame my bad behavior on an experience or on someone else. So for me, when I see myself being overly judgmental, or unsympathetic, or angry... I tell myself "Well, I wouldn't be this way if I didn't go through two combat deployments..." So, in these moments I am, justifying my behavior by blaming my experience in the marines. Or, just like in her example, I will blame the person I wronged by saying that they "started it," or I'll blame my upbringing, or my education... All the while I see myself as the hero and everyone else as the villain. Really common examples that I hear as a counselor in the area of marriage are "If my spouse were more caring than I wouldn't have done this..." "If they would be more sexual this wouldn't be a problem..." "They aren't pulling their weight in this marriage so why should I?..." And so on.

This blame shifting can also express itself through what we call "projecting."

Cortney Warren says this about projection:

> *Taking an undesirable aspect of ourselves and ascribing it to someone else. "I'm not like that. You're like that. When dating someone you've lost interest in, you say things like, "You're not ready for this relationship," when, in fact, you're not ready for this relationship and never will be.*

When we think like this, we are in so much denial about what we are doing, and we are so desperately trying to justify our behavior, that we actually project onto others our own insecurities and bad behaviors. We can also project the behavior of a past relationship on a current one. For instance, if a couple gets into a fight, one spouse might conjure up negative memories from their past relationships, or even from fights with their parents, and project that unresolved fight into the present. This will give justification to continue to act in an unwarranted and petty way.

The other type of rationalization that she mentions is self justification. This is when you know that you were wrong, but you give some reason as to why your behavior is actually OK. So if I lose my temper on someone I say "I was just being indignant at sin..." This allows me to spiritualize my bad behavior and actually see myself as being the Godly one even in the midst of my sin. I've seen this type of self-deception become so bad that even when someone is in the midst of some truly heinous sin, they will actually think that they are being righteous. I have heard people who are in the midst of divorcing their spouse for unbiblical reasons, cohabitating with their boyfriend or girlfriend, being controlling and manipulative towards their children... say things like "I have never felt closer to God..." The truth is that God is not in any of their decisions, but they have deceived themselves into believing this reality because they don't want to face the guilt of what they are doing.

This might sound like a good solution for a guilty conscience, but unfortunately it isn't. For one thing, this method is almost never fully successful, and so even with all of these justifications, we still feel guilty and full of shame. So we compensate through doing good works and comparing ourselves to others. But, even if we are completely successful in this, and we really don't feel guilty at all. Our self justification will drive everyone around us crazy because we can never admit when we are wrong. And worst of all, it will completely separate us from God. It reminds me of the Christians at Laodicea:

> *And to the angel of the church of the Laodiceans write, "These things says the Amen, the Faithful*

and True Witness, the Beginning of the creation of God: I know your works, that you are neither cold nor hot. I could wish you were cold or hot. So then, because you are lukewarm, and neither cold nor hot, I will vomit you out of My mouth. Because you say, 'I am rich, have become wealthy, and have need of nothing'—and do not know that you are wretched, miserable, poor, blind, and naked—" (Revelation 3:15-17)

These people were so successful at self justification, that they really thought that they were good apart from the grace of God. This literally sickened God and He said that He didn't want anything to do with them. The way that we are supposed to deal with our guilt is before God. The reason why we feel guilty is because we have sinned against God and need His forgiveness. No amount of self justification will appease God, only through the blood of His Son are we forgiven. So few Christians know the blessing of admitting your failure to God and experiencing His forgiveness that comes from His grace and love, freely given to us through His finished work on the cross, and not earned through our own works or self justification.

DAVID'S JOY IN FORGIVENESS

In Psalm 32, David was struggling with a guilty conscience from sin, and he expresses his joy in God's forgiveness like this:

Psalm 32:2-5 Blessed is the man to whom the LORD does not impute iniquity, And in whose spirit there is no deceit. When I kept silent, my bones grew old Through my groaning all the day long. For day and night Your hand was heavy upon me; My vitality was turned into the drought of summer. Selah

I acknowledged my sin to You, And my iniquity I have not hidden. I said, "I will confess my transgressions to the LORD," And You forgave the iniquity of my sin.

Can you see self justification, projecting, and blame shifting in your life? _____

_____

There are many more examples that we could go through, but for the sake of time, we will go through one more: emotional reasoning.

Cortney Warren says this about emotional reasoning:

Thinking that our feelings accurately reflect reality. "I feel hurt; so you must have done something bad to me." "I feel stupid; consequently I am stupid."

This form of self-deception is incredibly dangerous in our culture today because of our emphasis on our emotions. We are taught from a very young age to trust our instincts and to listen to our heart. This belief system is so prevalent in our society, that it has even permeated the church. For most people in the church today, if you were to ask them how to recognize a move of the Spirit, they will almost always describe some sort of an emotional experience. For instance, if I asked a believer how they know that God is calling them to something they will say "I felt peace about it..." The feeling of peace is just that, a feeling. Our feelings aren't inherently good or bad, they are just feelings. Sometimes our feelings are in line with truth and they should be listened to, but sometimes our emotions can be way off. The apostle Paul gives us this piece of wisdom:

1 Thessalonians 5:19-21 Do not quench the Spirit. Do not despise prophecies. Test all things; hold fast what is good.

We shouldn't quench the Spirit by denying emotions altogether, but we need to be able to test all things to see their value. If you don't test your emotional experiences, then you will be led by your emotions into many disastrous situations. Timothy Keller is a pastor out in New York who wrote a book on prayer and in this book he gives an extreme example to drive this point home.

Please read and comment on the following:

From Timothy Keller's book *Prayer:*

> *If we leave the Bible out, we may plumb our impressions and feelings and imagine God saying various things to us, but how can we be sure we are not self-deceived? The eighteenth-century Anglican clergyman George Whitefield was one of the spearheads of the Great Awakening, a period of massive renewal of interest in Christianity across Western societies and a time of significant church growth. Whitefield was a riveting orator and is considered one of the greatest preachers in church history. In late 1743 his first child, a son, was born to he and his wife, Elizabeth. Whitefield had a strong impression that God was telling him the child would grow up to also be a "preacher of the everlasting Gospel." In view of this divine assurance, he gave his son the name John, after John the Baptist, whose mother was also named Elizabeth. When John Whitefield was born, George baptized his son before a large crowd and preached a sermon on the great works that God would do through his son. He knew that cynics were sneering at his prophecies, but he ignored them.*

> *Then, at just four months old, his son died suddenly of a seizure. The Whitefields were of course grief-stricken, but George was particularly convicted about how wrong he had been to count his inward impulses and intuitions as being essentially equal to God's Word. He realized he had led his congregation into the same disillusioning mistake. Whitefield had interpreted his own feelings—his understandable and powerful fatherly pride and joy in his son, and his hopes for him—as God speaking to his heart. Not long afterward, he wrote a wrenching prayer for himself, that God would "render this mistaken parent more cautious, more sober-minded, more experienced in Satan's devices, and consequently more useful in his future labors to the church of God. The lesson here is not that God never guides our thoughts or prompts us to choose wise courses of action, but that we cannot be sure he is speaking to us unless we read it in the Scripture.*

_____

_____

_____

I believe that this is one of the biggest issues in the church today. I hear so many Christians claiming that they are hearing directly from God on major life decisions. And it isn't that I don't believe that God can speak to individuals, I know that He can, it's just that most of these "revelations" are emotional experiences that didn't actually come from God. But because they have made their emotions their God, they can't be convinced that they are wrong, or even consider testing their apparent revelation. After all, how can you be wrong if you are obeying the personal commands that God has given you? Because of this, they remain blinded in their pride as they convince themselves that they are following God's direct commands when in reality they are following their own wants and desires and not God.

In our next three lessons we will talk about emotional sin in depth, but for now, let's focus on this, if we don't test our emotions, we will seek to conform reality to our emotions and not the other way around. For instance, let's say that I feel insecure today and I feel as though my wife doesn't love me. If I don't test that emotion, I will begin to project my negative emotions onto my wife and treat her as if she is unloving, even though that might not be true. You see, I am deceiving myself into thinking that my emotions are ultimately true no matter what facts come my way. And if I deceive myself enough, I can actually justify myself in treating my wife badly, and even feel as if she owes me an apology even though it was my emotions that led me to believe that, not her actions. Cortney Warren shares a personal example of this:

> I knew that I didn't feel safe, but I believed it was my boyfriend's fault — if he just called me more, told me he loved me more, then I would feel safe. The truth was there was nothing he could do to make me feel safe, because my feelings had nothing to do with him. The reason I didn't feel safe is that I learned as a child that people would always leave me, and I lived my life making choices consistent with that belief. When we don't take full responsibility for who we are, we hurt ourselves and everyone around us.

This can play out in a myriad of different ways, from feeling so intensely proud that you convince yourself that you are always right and so you don't listen to others. To feeling so intensely worthless or stupid, that you completely write yourself off and convince yourself that no one loves you or cares about you even though that isn't true. For me, it was when I felt hopeless, and began to believe that emotion, that I gave up in so many areas of my life, and even began to have suicidal thoughts. No matter how you look at this issue, it is incredibly destructive to put your emotions in the place of God.

Proverbs 14:12 clearly tells us: "There is a way that seems right to a man, but its end is the way of death."

Can you see this type of emotional reasoning happening in your life? _____

_____

_____

So what is the solution for us in our struggles with self-deception? Unfortunately, like our other struggles, there is no easy way out of this one, it takes time, patience, and dependence on God. The first thing that we have to start doing is praying and asking God to reveal these struggles to us. But, it is so important to know that prayer was never intended by God to be a passive activity. Meaning that prayer isn't just a time where we speak our peace to God and then forget about what we asked. When you look through the Psalms you see that while these men were pouring their hearts out to God they were also contemplating deep things of their own hearts. It is so important to evaluate yourself:

Proverbs 4:26 tells us to, "Ponder the path of your feet, and let all your ways be established."

The Bible is constantly encouraging us to think, to reason, to evaluate, not just to shut our minds off and expect God to miraculously deliver us from everything. When you read through the Proverbs you see that we should be pursuing and seeking wisdom in God, and the miracle is that God is going to give it to us.

James 1:5 teaches to ask for the wisdom: "If any of you lacks wisdom, let him ask of God, who gives to all liberally and without reproach, and it will be given to him."

But James doesn't mean that we just ask God for an answer to a particular problem and He will just tell us the answer. What he means is that by consistently pursuing God and thinking through our issues, God will begin to give you insight and understanding to what your problems are and why you are struggling with them. It is a powerful and miraculous thing that He does for His children, but because it isn't instantaneous and easy, we don't like it.

So as you are struggling with strong emotions, think. Ask yourself, "Why am I having this strong of an emotion? Is there some hidden trauma, fear, sorrow, disappointment, insecurity, or resentment that I am suppressing and not dealing with?" When you catch yourself sinning, ask yourself, "Why am I falling in this way? What led to this sin? Could I have done something to protect me better?" This constant self assessment is what the Proverbs mean by telling us to "ponder the path of your feet." For some, it really helps to write these things down and journal about your struggles and your issues. To go over your deepest emotions with God and as you do this, pray over what you are thinking about, and as you pray and seek Him, He will grant you wisdom. Maybe not all at once, but over time as you pray to Him and think these things through, God will begin to lead you into understanding. And while God is doing that, you also need to renew your mind in the truth and comfort of His Word. For me, as I evaluate myself and I start to become discouraged by my failures and my issues, I think on passages of God's love for me. I remember that even when I was a sinner Christ died for me. That God loves me so much that He was even willing to give His own Son so that I might be forgiven. And as I think through amazing truths like this I continue to think through my problems, and God's word becomes a shield for me that allows me to go through my issues with God without being crushed by regret, trauma, and guilt.

It is also through this prayer and confession before God, that He will begin to heal you and draw you closer to Him. In the last couple years that I have been growing in this, I have seen so much growth in my love for God. When I kept God at a distance and didn't open myself up to Him in really honest and vulnerable talks, I was never able to experience genuine intimacy with Him. But as I grow in my honesty with God, not only does He lead me into wisdom that helps me in my struggles against my sins, but He also deepens my relationship with Him, which is the main goal of everything that we are doing. There is a lot more that I have to work on, but

God is with me every step of the way and He will be faithful to complete in me the good work that He began.

It is also important to talk these things through with an accountability partner. Because my main issue comes from my own heart, it is incredibly helpful to have someone else hear what I have to say, and correct me as I need it.

Proverbs 18:1-2 tells us, "A man who isolates himself seeks his own desire; he rages against all wise judgment. A fool has no delight in understanding, But in expressing his own heart."

My pride is what isolates me and convinces me that no one else has anything to offer me in the way of wisdom. But this is foolishness and believing this lie can only make me worse. As I talk through things with those believers that I have come to trust and confide in, they are able to help me see things that I am blind to, and I am able to help them as well. So as we fight this sin of self-deception, as hard as it is, know that while you are fighting this sin, not only will it make you more free from sins and issues in your life, but more importantly it will draw you closer to God and to those around you.

Proverbs 12:1 also teaches us, "Whoever loves instruction loves knowledge, but he who hates correction is stupid."

1 John 1:5-7 tells us, "This is the message which we have heard from Him and declare to you, that God is light and in Him is no darkness at all. If we say that we have fellowship with Him, and walk in darkness, we lie and do not practice the truth. But if we walk in the light as He is in the light, we have fellowship with one another, and the blood of Jesus Christ His Son cleanses us from all sin."

2 Thessalonians 2:10 also teaches us: "And with all wicked deception for those who are perishing, because they refused to love the truth and so be saved."

Isaiah 44:20 even has said, "He feeds on ashes; a deceived heart has turned him aside; and he cannot deliver his soul, nor say, 'Is there not a lie in my right hand?'"

CYNICISM

In our last lesson we talked about the sin of self-deception and how it affects us. While going through that sin, we took a quick look at how our emotions can be responsible for deceiving us and leading us down some harmful paths. For the next 3 lessons we will be talking about the emotional sins of cynicism, anxiety, and wrath. Before we get into today's study on cynicism, I wanted to take some time to point out a flaw that Christians can have in regards to our emotions. For some Christians, we look at emotions, almost as being our key to hearing from God. Because of this, when we have strong emotions of peace, joy, fear, anger, or sorrow, we can falsely believe that this is God speaking to us. As we talked about yesterday, I'm not saying that God can never talk to you through emotions, but I am saying that because of the inconsistency of our emotions, they are a really shaky foundation to plant your faith. Emotions can be good to supplement our belief in something, but they are really terrible sources for belief. When it comes to emotions, we need to exercise caution and self-control.

Proverbs 28:26 He who trusts in his own heart is a fool, But whoever walks wisely will be delivered.

Do you find yourself trusting your emotions too much? _____

_____

But on the other end, some Christians believe that emotions are inherently bad. I used to think this way, and because of this I used to spend all my time trying to purge myself of all emotions thinking that this was holy. I had seen how wrong and powerful my emotions could be, and so I thought that the best and most profitable way I could live was free from my manipulative emotions. I was also convinced that God was a being who never felt emotions either. But this is incredibly false. In previous lessons we have already seen that God feels deep, passionate love and that it is from this love that God experiences all other emotions. Love is kind of like white light in that white light contains all the other colors within it but you can only see this truth when you shine it through a prism and then it reveals all of these other colors. Love works in much the same way. It is from love that all other emotions have their life, without love there is no emotion. For instance, when we feel an emotion like happiness, it comes when something that you care deeply about is prospering or doing well. So, if a parent sees their child, who they love, succeed at sports, or do well in school, the emotion of happiness wells up inside of them. But if a parent can watch their child do well and be completely apathetic, that would be directly reflective of that parent's care for their child. Or with sorrow, if my mom died today and I felt absolutely no sorrow and was completely unmoved by the experience, it would show that I don't really have much love for my mom.

Because God's love is more pure, passionate, and powerful than any love that we are capable of, God actually experiences emotions in a much deeper way than we do, yet without sin. Throughout the Bible you see God experience feelings of wrath in judgment, joy and happiness in His people, and even deep sorrow over the sorrow and misery of people. This is very clearly demonstrated for us in the life of Christ. At the funeral of Lazarus in John 11:35, Jesus actually feels such sorrow that He weeps. He also laments over the judgment that Israel would endure after His death, and mourns that they wouldn't receive life through Him in Matthew 23:37-39. Right before the cross Jesus experiences worry about His coming death, and feels such intense stress that He sweats blood in Luke 22:44. Finally, Jesus experienced wrath in Matthew 21:12-13 when He drove out the money changers from the temple; and in Revelation 19:11-21 there is a frightening description of Jesus coming to the earth to judge the wicked in His wrath towards sin. Since it is clear that Jesus never sinned, (Hebrews 4:15), Jesus having these emotions proves that emotions aren't sinful in themselves.

So, us having emotions is actually a direct result of being made in the image and likeness of God, and linked to our capacity to love, there is nothing inherently bad about emotions. But because of the fall, our emotions have been spoiled to a certain extent, and therefore must be evaluated, and at times controlled. So, before we get into today's study, I want to make sure that I am being as clear as possible on this issue: Experiencing emotions is not sinful, but when we obey these emotions and allow them to shape our reality, that is where we have fallen into sin. These emotions are also bad because of our issues with love. Unfortunately, because pride is so rooted in all of our hearts, the person that we all love the most is ourselves. And so our emotions are, most of the time inflected inwards and directed at our own selfishness. This is why, when we fall into extreme emotions of sorrow, anxiety, and anger, we usually isolate and spend time over-thinking our lives and making our emotional states even worse. We can even get to the place where our emotions feed on themselves until you are most anxious that you are anxious, most depressed that you are depressed, and most angry that you are angry. And so you try to suppress these emotions, but the more you try to hold them down, the more they come out. So with each one of these emotions, we are going to see the good purpose each emotion serves, how they can go bad, and how we can control them, and even use them to glorify God and to draw us closer to Him and His people.

Have you thought of your emotions as being bad? _____

_____

Lamentations 3:15-20 says, "He has filled me with bitterness and given me a bitter cup of sorrow to drink. He has made me chew on gravel. He has rolled me in the dust. Peace has been stripped away, and I have forgotten what prosperity is. I cry out, 'My splendor is gone! Everything I had hoped for from the LORD is lost!' The thought of my suffering and homelessness is bitter beyond words. I will never forget this awful time, as I grieve over my loss (NLT)."

The first emotion that we are going to take a look at is cynicism. But, in order to understand cynicism, we first have to understand the difference between sorrow, grief, and depression. Sorrow is a very important emotion that comes from experiencing loss and disappointment. So if I were striving for something and fell short, I would feel sad. Or if someone, or something was taken away from me, I would naturally experience sorrow in response to that loss. And far from it being bad, it is good because it was our love and care for these things and people that resulted in us experiencing this emotion. Andrew Solomon is an author who speaks on depression, and he says this about sadness:

> *Depression is the flaw in love. If you were married to someone and thought, "Well, if my wife dies, I'll find another one," it wouldn't be love as we know it. There's no such thing as love without the anticipation of loss, and that specter of despair can be the engine of intimacy.*

You can't truly care about someone or something and then feel nothing when you lose it. It is a result of God's deep love for His creation that moves Him to sorrow over our pain and suffering and we can't learn to love like Him, unless we are willing to experience grief and sorrow. As bad as sorrow can feel, there is nothing wrong or sinful about it, it is a necessary aspect of loving in this world where loss and disappointment are constant possibilities.

1 Corinthians 13:4: "Love suffers long and is kind…"

However, grief and depression are a little different from sorrow. As someone who struggles with depression, I do believe that the biblical definition of it is the best. In order to express what grief and depression are like the Bible uses the phrase "broken spirit." The Word "spirit" in the Hebrew is the Word "ruach" and it can refer to wind or power. When it talks about the human spirit, it is referring to our emotional vitality and strength, and so to have a broken spirit, is to have all our vitality and emotional strength taken away.

Proverbs 18:14 The spirit of a man will sustain him in sickness, But who can bear a broken spirit?

For most people, you will experience a broken spirit from some sort of trauma or ongoing problem. After a while of experiencing a powerful, negative emotion like anxiety or deep sorrow, your heart can naturally shut down and put up walls to protect itself. So for instance, if you are going through an incredibly stressful time of your life, you might experience intermittent periods of emotional shut down. Times where you really do feel like just lying down and never getting up again. Or if you experience severe trauma after losing someone close to you, or getting fired from a job, or going through a bad breakup or divorce, or experiencing intense guilt and regret from making a horrible mistake, or many other different causes, you can go through a period of grief where your emotional vitality dries up and steals all your will and passion in life. But, if it is truly grief, over time, the grief will get better and you will begin to recover. The reason why depression is so dangerous, is because it doesn't always have a cause, it can just appear in people. And because of that, it doesn't always get better with time. For a truly depressed person, depression becomes the veil that surrounds their life and through which everything is processed, and it sometimes lasts for months or even years. I feel like Andrew Solomon expresses this in a really powerful way when he describes his own depression:

I found myself losing interest in almost everything. I didn't want to do any of the things I had previously wanted to do, and I didn't know why. The opposite of depression is not happiness, but vitality. And it was vitality that seemed to seep away from me in that moment. Everything there was to do seemed like too much work. I would come home and I would see the red light flashing on my answering machine, and instead of being thrilled to hear from my friends, I would think, "What a lot of people that is to have to call back." Or I would decide I should have lunch, and then I would think, but I'd have to get the food out and put it on a plate and cut it up and chew it and swallow it, and it felt to me like the Stations of the Cross.

Have you ever experienced a broken spirit before? _____

_____

I never really understood this growing up, and so even though I have been struggling with depression since I was a teenager, I never knew that I was. I used to think that depression was being sad all the time, and I viewed it as an emotional weakness. Also, I had such a good life that I didn't understand why I felt the way I did, I thought I was being childish and weak and so I sought to suppress my emotions and get rid of them. Little did I know, that I wasn't helping my depression, I was actually making it much worse. The more I shut down my emotions, the more I became cold and dead on the inside. It increased my selfishness and made my heart impenetrable.

During my time in the marine corps, my problem became much worse. Most people who are trained in the infantry are taught to shut down their emotions because emotions can be a liability in combat. So by the time that I got out, I was about as cold and emotionally dead as someone could be. I found myself not really caring about anything. I was constantly sarcastic and cutting to those around me. I never really hoped for anything, I always assumed the worst in every situation and I kept myself at a comfortable emotional distance from everyone around me, unable to truly trust another human being. This is what the sin of cynicism is all about. It isn't sinful to experience sorrow, grief or depression, the quote from Lamentations at the top is a true expression of depression, and there was nothing sinful about it. The sin comes when you begin to feed, and believe that negative emotional state.

I was never sinning by experiencing depression, but when I was constantly feeding my depression, not just feeling hopeless, but actively shooting down all hope in my life, then I was being sinful. Beyond that, I truly believed my own depression. So if I felt that my life had no meaning, or that no one loved me, or that no one could relate to me, or that God was disappointed in me, or that everyone would be better off if I were dead… I really believed that I was right for thinking this way, I was completely self deceived by my own emotions and I didn't even realize it. This sin of cynicism will steal all your emotional vitality and leave you completely empty and isolated from everyone else.

Have you ever experienced cynicism? _____

_____

So what is it that causes us to go towards cynicism? One reason is the power of emotions. I know for myself, that when I am in a depressed state, my emotions are so strong that it can be almost impossible to not listen to them. For most people, when you experience strong emotions, you can experience a kind of narrowing of focus that is so powerful that you forget all that you know to be true. A simple example that most people can relate to is when you are in traffic and someone cuts you off. Before that happens, you know deep down that something like being cut off in traffic is ultimately trivial, it doesn't really amount to much and won't really cost you that much time. You also know that getting angry at the car who did that and yelling at them will do nothing to improve the situation. But in the moment, you forget all of that, your anger takes over and your focus narrows to that one single event, and excludes everything else in your life. But, for most people that narrowing of focus only lasts for a short amount of time, and then after a minute or two, all that anger will dissipate and you can go about your life. Imagine for a second that your focus never widened again, that you would live in that narrowed focus for days, weeks, or even months. That your entire reality was being filtered through that powerful and sustaining negative emotion and no matter what you did it never went away. That is the reality of someone who has depression, anxiety, or severe rage.

I can speak from experience with depression that I will sometimes go weeks or even months in that narrowed focus, unable to lift my emotions over that depression. For me, it isn't usually a constant thing, but for that season that I am depressed I will get hit with random waves of depression over and over again throughout the day. It doesn't seem to matter what I am doing, or who I am with, I will suddenly feel empty and hollow, as if I am just going through the motions and all that I am or could possibly accomplish is nothing. I also feel utterly alone and isolated, as if no one can ever understand me or help me, and that ultimately I will die alone. Elijah the prophet expressed his depression in this way when he was fleeing for his life in 1st Kings 19:

1 Kings 19:4 tells us, "But he himself went a day's journey into the wilderness, and came and sat down under a broom tree. And he prayed that he might die, and said, 'It is enough! Now, LORD, take my life, for I am no better than my fathers!'"

When you are experiencing these extreme emotions, it can be impossible to keep functioning. This depression presses down on you until you are ready to collapse and then you can end up like Elijah, lying down on the ground and literally praying for death. So cynicism can enter into our lives as a sort of surrender to your emotions, just getting so tired of trying to be happy in the midst of pain that it becomes easier to give in to what you are feeling and forfeit up all hope.

Have you ever experienced extreme emotions like this? _____

_____

Another reason why we slip into depression is because sometimes, feeling nothing is better than feeling pain. If you struggle with extreme anxiety, regret, shame, or even anger, you can become so sick of dealing with these emotions, that you long to be numb and to not care. So maybe you struggle with anxiety, or you have gone through a bad breakup, or you are dealing with the memories of a traumatic childhood, or you just got fired... And you are feeling these deep and painful emotions all welling up inside you and you have this thought "It would be so much easier to just not care about anything." So you close yourself off and use cynicism as a shield to guard you from pain. Or, maybe you are going through a season like Job, where it isn't just one thing, but many tragedies are happening one after the other and as they bear down on your soul you will feel as if life itself is a burden and you will long for emotional numbness or even death.

In Job 3:20-26, he says, "Oh, why give light to those in misery, and life to those who are bitter? They long for death, and it won't come. They search for death, more eagerly than for hidden treasure. They're filled with joy when they finally die, and rejoice when they find the grave. Why is life given to those with no future, those God has surrounded with difficulties? I cannot eat for sighing; my groans pour out like water. What I always feared has happened to me. What I dreaded has come true. I have no peace, no quietness. I have no rest; only trouble comes (NLT)."

I fell into this trap as well. From a young age, I have always struggled with tons of insecurities and feelings of inferiority. I always felt desperate for approval that I thought I wasn't getting. And no matter how many compliments I did receive it never quite filled the hole of inferiority that was burned into me from a young age. I also found that I was socially awkward and didn't really fit in at school which added to my feelings of isolation and worthlessness. These things combined with other issues that I have, and slowly the pain of feeling constantly rejected and unimportant welled up in me until it was unbearable. When you mix that with the fact that I already struggled with depression, I found that shutting off my emotions and not caring were very attractive coping mechanisms. So I told myself that I didn't care about anything or anyone and that I was fine on my own, and slowly, I began to believe it. This put an icy shell around my heart that I thought was making me strong, but instead, all it did was isolate me from everyone who cared about me, including God.

It is also important to understand that we can also turn to substances and distractions to help numb us to our own reality. It makes me think of Ephesians 5:18 "Do not be drunk with wine, in which is dissipation; but be filled with the Holy Spirit."

Paul is using drunkenness as an example for us, that when we turn to alcohol, sex, drugs, or even neutral things like social media, television, video games... In order to distract us from our pain, these things will ultimately dissipate. Meaning that they will soon evaporate and leave us, and when we sober up, or get tired of our distractions we will find that everything is still exactly as it was before we started trying to numb ourselves. Right when we finish with our distractions, our problems are right there waiting for us and we are right back to our pain. Some of us might even be unaware that we do this, our coping habits have become so ingrained in us that we don't even recognize that we are doing it anymore. And so finding your coping mechanisms will take time and self reflection, you have to ask yourself "Is there something, (even something that isn't sinful) that I frequently run to when life gets too hard for me?"

It is really important to discover what you utilize to numb yourself in your life because, even though it isn't always wrong to distract yourself from pain for a time, especially if you are in a situation that you can't change, ultimately you need to understand that whatever your coping mechanism is that you think will help you, it can only alleviated your pain for a moment, but it can't actually heal your hurt. And this is the problem with cynicism as a whole. Yes, pain takes time to heal, especially deep emotional pain and so we shouldn't think that God will heal us overnight or think that we have to focus on our pain constantly until it is gone. We need to keep living our lives even in the midst of trial, and that's why having distractions isn't necessarily a bad thing. But when we instinctively deal with our problems by ignoring them and we never address our pain because it's too hard for us, time won't heal our wounds, it will fester them. For me, using cynicism helped me cope with my trauma a little bit, but ultimately it could not get rid of all of my pain. I noticed that at best, I was numb, but at worst I would find that I could be "triggered" randomly by certain events and people and all that pain and anger that I was trying to bury would rise to the surface and spill out on the people around me.

As someone who does counsel others, I can tell you that I have never seen anyone be completely successful in their use of cynicism or distractions. When I am counseling people I always take notice of certain phrases like "I don't care anymore…" "It doesn't bother me…" "It is what it is…" "I'm over it…" These are usually red flags for someone who is trying to numb themselves to past pain or trauma through convincing themselves that they don't care. But saying that something doesn't bother you doesn't make it true. I convinced myself that I didn't care about the approval of others, and that my experience in Afghanistan hadn't changed me, but that didn't make it true. I realize now that so many of my negative habits, anger issues, and even a good portion of my depression stem from that shame that I feel for never really measuring up and trauma that I experienced in my past.

Have you tried to become numb as a coping mechanism? If so, can you see how doing this has impacted you?

Avoiding the Pain of Disappointment?

The final reason that I will mention in this lesson, is *avoiding the pain of having your hope disappointed.*

Proverbs 13:12: "Hope deferred makes the heart sick, But when the desire comes, it is a tree of life." There are very few things in this life that are more painful than sincerely hoping that something will happen, only to have that hope taken away from you. In the passage we read earlier about Elijah in 1st Kings 19, what led him to that despair was he had sincerely hoped that his country would change. At the time of his ministry, his nation had become inundated by idol worship and wickedness. In the previous chapter, he had a major showdown with the false prophets of his nation, and God delivered him in an amazing way and these false prophets were put to death. You can imagine just how happy Elijah was to witness this event, and how much joy he felt to see his greatest hopes and dreams coming true. But then in chapter 19 reality reared its ugly head. The king and queen of his time were the most wicked monarchs that Israel ever had, king Ahab and queen Jezebel. And even though the prophets were dead, these two remained, and in the beginning of the chapter, Jezebel orders Elijah to be killed which made him flee for his life. You could only imagine the disappointment of having so much of your deepest hopes come true, just to watch it all come to nothing. He probably thought "What was it all for. Nothing has changed and now I can't even go home because the queen wants me dead." That is why in 1 Kings 19:14

he says to God "I have been very zealous for the LORD God of hosts; for the children of Israel have forsaken Your covenant, torn down Your altars, and killed Your prophets with the sword. I alone am left; and they seek to take my life."

Elijah, the greatest prophet in the Bible, had been brought down by cynicism. He was unwilling to hope anymore and had completely thrown in the towel. This wasn't a prayer for help, this was a declaration of hopelessness. He is telling God that he was the last faithful Israelite left, that he was being hunted down and when he was dead, the last light of hope for Israel would be extinguished. The above Proverb explains to us why Elijah felt the way that he did, when your hope fails, it can make your heart sick. The heart for the Hebrews was the very center of their being, it was literally the seat of their deepest passions and desires. When your heart was sick, that meant that the mechanism that allows you to have passion or hope is sick and won't work. It isn't that you can't hope, it's that you literally lost the will to hope. This happens when you have been so hurt by disappointment that you really believe that hope is nothing but trouble. That it would be better to just assume the worst, then to get your hopes up only to have them crash down around you.

Have you ever had your hopes let down like this? _____

_____

_____

This is made even worse when you consider the cynical culture that we live in today. If you look around at the media you can see that we are saturated by cynicism. It seems that most people would rather mock and criticize others rather than have hopes and dreams of their own. That is why it is so interesting to me, that the fasting growing faith in our culture is not a belief in anything, but a lack of belief in anything. So many people in my generation don't have any real positive faith, they call themselves spiritual, but if you really pressed them about their specific beliefs you would see they don't really have any. It is always easier to mock someone else's beliefs than to be vulnerable and stand up for what you believe. I remember in high school that I would make fun of people who had high hopes and big dreams. I would cut them down in my own mind and I refused to take anything seriously. When you do this, it protects you from all fear of failure and rejection, if you never try, you can never fail. This made it easy for me to deal with the pressures of high school, but it also destroyed my ability to hope. It emotionally crippled me and without any real hope for the future, it made my life seem more and more useless. And as bad as I was in high school, I became even worse in the marines.

In the marines we used to quote Dante's Inferno "Abandon all hope ye who enter here." We said this because in our training, we were literally taught not to hope for anything. They did this by constantly getting our hopes up with empty promises of vacations, supplies, and even promises of going home early, only to take that hope from us at the last minute. They also were sure to put us through constant training that made us utterly miserable. This was done to give us a one track mind. If you have a divided mind when you are in combat it can cause problems, it is better to develop soldiers who don't hope for anything and therefore can adjust to any situation, than to have people who are always thinking of home, or demanding better conditions. It is good to have people who can just sleep in the dirt in horrible situations and just take it without being bothered.

During my deployments I was amazed at all I could survive without. I would go months without running water, electricity, showers, good food, family... All the while being shot at on a weekly basis. Some would think that this would make a person want to commit suicide, but ironically it didn't. In fact, most veterans commit suicide when they come home, not when they are over in combat. And even the people who do commit suicide over there, it is usually over something that happened in their family or personal lives, not what was happening to them in country. What studies have shown is that people from around the world in horrible poverty and abuse still have lower suicide rates than in the United States. The reason for this is largely because the things that people absolutely can not go without are hope, and love.

You see, even in the most horribly impoverished countries, they have strong communities that are bound together in their pain, and so even though they don't have much, they have each other. This also provides purpose for their lives, that even though they didn't have much, each person has a vital role for their families and community. They also have hope that we don't understand. You see, if you are living in poverty and you feel miserable, you can say, "Well, of course I'm miserable, look at my life..." And this can sometimes provide hope, that things can get better, and your misery could go away. The same was true for us veterans, we may not have had much over there, but we did have each other, we felt understood, and needed; and even though we had miserable lives, we had hope that when we went home, everything would be better.

And as long as there is a hope that things could get better, no matter how faint that hope is, and as long as you feel like there are those around you, who love you, support you, and ultimately enjoy you, you can keep going. But look at our country. If you have money and security and you still feel empty, hollow, and massively depressed, where is your hope that things can get better? When we were over there, we would imagine how awesome it would be to come home, and then we made it home and found that all of our problems were waiting for us. Our personal problems didn't go away, our depression continued to grow, and so our hope evaporated.

Beyond that, even though the Internet has united us more than any generation before us, we are also more isolated than ever before. We don't have strong community anymore, we only have superficial relationships built on hypocrisy. Meaning, that we have a lot of people who know about us, but we have barely anyone who really knows us. So even though we have a lot of "friends" we have hardly anyone who we can really depend on and who truly understands us. For veterans, ironically, it was being over in combat that made us feel understood, because there were tons of people around us going through the same exact stuff. But then you get home and all you can see is how much you have changed and how little everyone else has, it can make you feel very isolated and alone. It is a very unnerving feeling to come home and feel like a stranger. You realize everyone else is the same, but you are so different, you don't know if you have a place in your community or family anymore. When we feel isolated, like no one understands you, you can feel like you have no one you can trust or love. Then, if you have no hope that things can get better, it can seem that the only option for you is suicide. If this is where you are at today, we'll talk more about the hope we have in Christ later, but the encouragement I can give you right now is that there is hope and love for you, if you look in the right place.

Have you ever given up on hoping? _____

_____

_____

In Hebrews 6:18-19 it says, "Therefore, we who have fled to Him for refuge can have great confidence as we hold to the hope that lies before us. This hope is a strong and trustworthy anchor for our souls. It leads us through the curtain into God's inner sanctuary (NLT)."

This passage really points out for us the solution to the problem of cynicism. You see, the reason that we ultimately choose cynicism is because of the pain that exists in this cruel world. It is amazing to think about, but it is actually the cynics in this world that are more in touch with reality than most other people. A true cynic looks at all the joys of life and rightfully says that this life will ultimately let you down. Whether you put your hope in your career, relationships, health, finances… All these things will ultimately let you down. That is why it is so hard to talk to depressed people, unfortunately a lot of what they say is true, outside of God. The entire book of Ecclesiastes is written to address this issue. Solomon takes all of the great hopes of this life, success, wealth, fame, pleasure, marriage, children… And he talks about how each of these things failed him and left him empty and cold. What the writer of Hebrews is telling us, is that if we want to be set free from cynicism, and if we want the ability to have amazing hope that will not fail us or let us down, we need to put our hope in the right place, Christ. It is only in our relationship with Christ that we have an ultimate, and unshakable solution to all the problems that produce cynicism in us. Let's go back to our first quote of the lesson from Lamentations 3:15-20 to see this clearly, where it says, "He has filled me with bitterness and given me a bitter cup of sorrow to drink. He has made me chew on gravel. He has rolled me in the dust. Peace has been stripped away, and I have forgotten what prosperity is. I cry out, 'My splendor is gone! Everything I had hoped for from the LORD is lost!' The thought of my suffering and homelessness is bitter beyond words. I will never forget this awful time, as I grieve over my loss (NLT).'"

Jeremiah wrote this passage after he had watched his home, Israel, be taken over by the Babylonians after he had dedicated his entire life to trying to prevent this from happening. He told his people to repent and turn back to God or else this would happen, but all that his efforts ever did was make him hated by his fellow countrymen. His own family tried to have him killed and he spent a good portion of his ministry in prison; and it was from prison that he watched his city burn. And as he watched all of his hopes go up in flames, and as he witnessed the deaths of everyone he loved and cared about, he wrote Lamentations. What worldly hope would you possibly offer someone like Jeremiah? How would things possibly get better for him? And even though most of our life situations can't compare to the darkness of Jeremiah's life, ultimately all the worldly hopes we lean on are just as susceptible to death as Jeremiah's. And if we live long enough, we will see all of our hopes die, just like Jeremiah did. But, right after this cry of despair, Jeremiah writes this:

Lamentation 3:21-24 says, "Yet I still dare to hope when I remember this: The faithful love of the LORD never ends! His mercies never cease. Great is his faithfulness; his mercies begin afresh each morning. I say to myself, 'The LORD is my inheritance; therefore, I will hope in him (NLT)!'"

At the bottom of everything, in the deepest pit of despair that anyone could ever go through, Jeremiah says that he still dares to hope. Even though he feels hopeless and is experiencing grief that most of us can only begin to imagine, he still has hope and continues to press on because his hope is rooted not in this fragile world, but beyond it, in the everlasting, never changing, beautiful love of God. Jeremiah faced all of the primary reasons that we turn to cynicism, and though he faltered at times, he ultimately rooted himself in God and continued in hope.

Jeremiah knew what it was like to experience the weight of extreme emotions, but he learned how to control these feelings and trust in God. As someone who struggles with depression, it is amazing to read through Jeremiah's writings and resonate so strongly with how he felt. Jeremiah wasn't some perfect saint who never felt depression or fear, he felt all of these things just as we do. But what enabled Jeremiah to find hope in his emotions, was he learned to communicate his honest feelings to God instead of sulking in them like I tend to do.

In Jeremiah 15:18-19 he asks, "Why is my pain perpetual And my wound incurable, Which refuses to be healed? Will You surely be to me like an unreliable stream, As waters that fail? Therefore thus says the LORD: 'If you return, Then I will bring you back; You shall stand before Me; If you take out the precious from the vile, You shall be as My mouth. Let them return to you, But you must not return to them.'"

When I read this, I find so much comfort and hope. I have felt like Jeremiah so many times throughout my life. In times of suffering, or failing to sin, or deep depression... I have felt as though I had a wound that could never heal, and as though God had failed me. And when I felt these things, I bottled these emotions up thinking that it would be sinful for me to express these things to God. I didn't realize that God knows my heart and was already aware of my emotions, and even though I pretended like I didn't have these emotions, I wasn't fooling Him. I was instead giving these emotions power over me, and as I let them sit in my heart, they consumed me from the inside out. But, Jeremiah felt the boldness to express these things directly to God, and by doing this found comfort and strength in God. This comfort didn't take away his emotions, but it provided him strength and encouragement in the midst of his despair. Jeremiah was well aware that his heart could be deceptive (Jeremiah 17:9) and so when he felt these emotions, he sought truth in God. Even though he felt as if God had abandoned him in his pain, he still calls out to God in hope, trusting that God would hear him even though he couldn't feel it.

In the last couple years, I have learned from Jeremiah and countless others in the Bible, how to lament to God. Instead of attempting to repress my emotions, God has taught me how to express these emotions to Him and experience His comfort. In my foolishness I thought I could minister to myself, but I have learned that I don't even fully understand myself and the reasons I feel the way I do. How can I fix myself, when I don't even fully understand my problems?

Proverbs 20:24: "A man's steps are of the LORD; How then can a man understand his own way?"

The truth is, I don't really understand my own way, and the more I try to minister to myself, the more lost I become. But when I understand that it is only God who truly knows my heart, I can open up to Him and allow

Him to minister to me through His Word and His Spirit. And in order to allow God to minister to us, we have to learn how to trust God's word above our emotions. In my depression it is so easy to believe exactly what I am feeling. What I have to do is remember that through depression I am not seeing the world as it really is, but I am seeing the world through the grey veil of my negative emotions. The "truths" that I believe in my depression are almost always lies, and in order to find freedom, I have to learn to accept God's word as being true in spite of my emotions. When I feel that I am worthless, alone, or unloved. I turn to God's word and I read about His love and faithfulness towards me in passages like Romans 5, Romans 8, Jeremiah 31, Hosea 11, Psalm 23… and I pray for the faith to believe these things, even in the absence of feeling their truth. This is key to learning to cope with complex and powerful emotions, we can't shut turn them off, but we can learn to trust God over our feelings. So, I still express my emotions to God, but through praying to Him, I seek to have His Word be more to me than what I am feeling. If we don't learn how to do this, then either our emotions will crush us, or cynicism will turn our hearts to stone.

Other believers are also an invaluable resource for helping us. If you don't already have friends and accountability partners who you see regularly and who you trust and can go to in your time of need to express your struggles and your fears, and who can pray for you and encourage you in the truths of God, then you need to seek out relationships like this.

Proverbs 17:17: "A friend loves at all times, and a brother is born for adversity."

Ultimately only God's supreme love for you and His deep understanding of what you are going through can heal you, but God uses other Christians to come alongside us and encourage us towards Him.

Have you learned to pray your deepest emotions to God? Do you have other Christians in your life that you can confide in?_____

_____

Please read through the following Psalm and comment on how the Psalmist expresses his depression to God, how he acknowledges the reality of his emotions, but also sees their falsehood, how he asks for God's deliverance, and how he remembers God's faithfulness and goodness:

Psalm 42: To the Chief Musician. A Contemplation of the sons of Korah.

As the deer pants for the water brooks, so pants my soul for You, O God. My soul thirsts for God, for the living God. When shall I come and appear before God? My tears have been my food day and night, While they continually say to me, "Where is your God?" When I remember these things, I pour out my soul within me. For I used to go with the multitude; I went with them to the house of God, With the voice of joy and praise, With a multitude that kept a pilgrim feast. Why are you cast down, O my soul? And why are you disquieted within me? Hope in God, for I shall yet praise Him For the help of His countenance. O my God, my soul is cast down within me; Therefore I will remember You from the land of the Jordan, And from the heights of Hermon, From the Hill Mizar. Deep calls unto deep at the noise of Your waterfalls; All Your waves and billows have gone over me. The LORD will command His lovingkindness in the daytime, And in the night His song shall be with me— A prayer to the God of my life. I will say to God my Rock, "Why have You forgotten me? Why do I go mourning because of the oppression of the enemy?" As with a breaking of my bones, My enemies reproach me, While they say to me all day long, "Where is your God?" Why are you cast down, O my soul? And why are you disquieted within me? Hope in God; For I shall yet praise Him, The help of my countenance and my God.

Jeremiah was also not brought down by the despair of his circumstances. Even though his life constantly went from bad to worse, and he could have easily thrown his hands in the air and stopped trying to help those around him, he never did. Don't get me wrong, there were a couple times where he definitely considered it, but he always came back to his calling and sought to help Israel. But why was Jeremiah not crushed by his circumstances? And how did he not fall to the temptation to numb himself in cynicism? Jeremiah learned to find his ultimate joy in God alone. This is what enabled him to cope with unbelievable amounts of rejection and loss. He ultimately trusted God with the impact of his life, and he believed in God's faithfulness to use everything that he went through for good. Jeremiah hoped, because he believed that God wouldn't waste any of his sorrow, but use it for His glory.

Romans 8:28: "And we know that for those who love God all things work together for good, for those who are called according to His purpose."

The only way to keep from falling into the temptation of cynicism in the midst of loss and continuous pain, is if we can believe that what we are going through has a purpose. Not just a purpose for God's glory and the betterment of others, but also for our own sakes in our relationship with God. But if we numb ourselves out and just endure our pain, we will miss out on these wonderful promises. God will always accomplish His will, but if you choose cynicism over hope, you yourself will miss out on His blessings for you in the midst of your trial, and you will just end up more bitter and cold at the end of your trial as opposed to ending up closer to Him. Vaneetha Risner is an author who wrote the book *The Scars That Have Shaped Me* and in it she said something incredibly profound that has helped me in this area:

Vaneetha Risner, *The Scars That Have Shaped Me:*

We all need more of Jesus. One moment with Him changes us as it changed Mary, Martha, and Moses. The shift from wailing to worship has nothing to do with changing circumstances; it is we who are changed by encountering God, seeing His goodness and power, understanding His character... And seeing His glory is a far greater gift than rescue. Perhaps only when I am truly desperate can I hear the Lord's still, small voice. Perhaps suffering and sorrow are God's invitation to know Him better.

A SAYING WE HAD IN THE MARINES

In the marines we used to say "Pain binds." What we meant by that, is that deep intimacy and trust can be formed very quickly in the midst of intense trials and suffering. That is one of the reasons why everyone has to go through boot camp, and why I am still so close to my friends that I went to combat with. Shared trauma has the ability to draw people closer together than just about anything else. I do hate the fact that I struggle with depression, but it is through my depression that I am forced to find refuge and strength in God. In my time of cynicism, I gave up hope of getting closer to God or ever finding victory in my struggle against pride, lust, anger, insecurity… What I didn't realize is that in my cynicism I was missing out on God's greatest gift for me. God's greatest grace isn't freedom from sin, it is intimacy with Him. Freedom from sin is a fruit of being close to God, but it is only a fruit, it isn't the main goal. My issues, as painful as they are, force me to my knees and in that time of desperation, I reach out to God and draw closer to Him. Also, in my struggles, I remember that I don't serve a God who is immune to pain, but One who went through the same types of suffering that I myself go through. The apostle Paul saw pain as such a potential for intimacy with God that after he talks about all the great loss that he suffered in order to follow Jesus he wrote:

In Philippians 3:10-11 Paul prays, "That I may know Him and the power of His resurrection, and the fellowship of His sufferings, being conformed to His death, if, by any means, I may attain to the resurrection from the dead. "

We as Christians will always miss out on the amazing blessings of God's intimacy if we give in to cynicism. Cynicism blocks growth because it disables you from running to God in your pain and experiencing wonderful intimacy and joy in His presence. It also disables you from intimacy with others because if you just shut out your emotions, how can you empathize or show compassion to others? In our depression we can convince ourselves that we are alone and no one understands us. And to one extent that is true:

Proverbs 14:10: "The heart knows its own bitterness, And a stranger does not share its joy."

This Proverb does tell us that our emotions and experiences are ultimately our own and cannot be completely shared with other people. But, when we use this as a wall to say that those around us can't understand us at all, that is cynicism talking, not truth. When I got back from my first deployment, I told myself that I couldn't relate to anyone who didn't go to combat because they would never understand. But over the years I have seen that others can relate to me and my experiences through trauma and grief. Even though the cause of our trauma might be different, our experience in our emotions can be very similar. And the more we can see our pain as something to draw us closer to one another and not as something that divides us, the more we can learn to love and comfort one another. As we learn to express our pains to God and find comfort in Him, we can learn to express sorrow to other believers and comfort them as we are comforted.

In 2 Corinthians 1:3-4 it says, "Blessed be the God and Father of our Lord Jesus Christ, the Father of mercies and God of all comfort, who comforts us in all our tribulation, that we may be able to comfort those who are in any trouble, with the comfort with which we ourselves are comforted by God."

It is very important to not get the cart before the horse on this issue. Meaning that I must primarily seek comfort from God and secondarily seek comfort from others. The reason is that if I just go before other people and vent my feelings I can drag people into my emotions and self-pity instead of really seeking that correction and comfort that I need. Beyond that, people aren't perfect, and that means that while accountability partners and friends are capable of giving you amazing advice and comfort, they are also capable of giving bad advice and bad comfort, albeit with good intentions, just look at Job's friends. As we learn to express our feelings to God and hear from His perfect word, then we can begin to learn how to properly express our emotions to others as opposed to just venting, and we can also learn how to properly receive their comfort and counsel even though it will be imperfect. There have been a lot of times where I have just vented my problems to other people and never even gave them a chance to offer counsel or comfort, and there have also been times where I have received some bad advice from very well meaning Christian brothers and sisters. But through consistent accountability and prayer, I have grown a lot in expressing myself to others and in turn receiving their counsel and comfort for me. And I have also learned to sometimes "chew the meat and spit out the bones" of some advice as I compare their counsel to the Word of God. But even when I do reject some of their counsel I can still appreciate and be thankful for these people's care and attention in my life.

So, I'm not saying that we have to first receive perfect comfort from God before we share our grief with others and I am also not diminishing the importance of sharing our pain with other believers. No matter what you are going through, I do encourage you to share your hurts with other believers because sharing our grief is a vital part of how our Father comforts us and builds greater intimacy and honesty within His church. It's just that we always need to recognize that our ultimate healing will come from our relationship with God, and while He uses other people powerfully in this process, He is our ultimate source of hope and comfort.

Unfortunately, it is often more difficult to confess real hurt and genuine emotion with others than it is to confess sin. Most of the time, we just want to feel good, and share our best moments with God and others. And so when we are hurting, we hide our grief and depression, and sometimes isolate ourselves altogether. This is also a problem for us when we are listening to someone share genuine pain. For a lot of Christians, when we are trying to comfort those who are hurting, we try to fix them instantly instead of just being there for them. There will always be time to give real encouragement and advice to those who are hurting, but if we are unwilling weep with those who weep, we aren't showing genuine love, but instead we are actually damaging people in our haste to just fix them. Maybe what we really need to learn is how to sit with God and others in our sorrow, and feel "the fellowship of His sufferings." And as we experience that comfort in Him, we can share that same comfort with others.

Can you see how sorrow can bring intimacy? _____

_____

Jeremiah was also able to hold onto hope because he trusted God's faithfulness and not his own effort. If Jeremiah was going to hope based on what he had accomplished in his life, he would have definitely committed suicide. But, Jeremiah continued to live, not because he had to, but because he truly wanted to. The reason why he did this is because he supremely trusted in God's plan for his life. He dared to hope because he knew he couldn't see the big picture. He knew that the world didn't begin and end with him, but instead he accepted that he was just one tiny part in the plans of his Lord and God. Jeremiah never saw the fruit of his labor, but we know, that because of the faithfulness of Jeremiah, even though the Israelites went into captivity, they ended up coming back 70 years later. The writings of Jeremiah produced hope in the people of Israel, and because of that hope, it paved the way for Israel to remain a nation, and from that nation came the birth of Christ.

No matter what is going on in my life, I have to trust that if God is allowing my life to continue, He has a plan for it. I may not be able to see His plan, but by trusting in His character and love, I can keep going and trust my life's value to God. But if I give into cynicism and reject hope, I won't be able to be used by God and grow in my love for Him. In my cynicism I believe that I am alone, useless, and that everyone would be better off without me, but through Christ I know that I am loved, understood, and that God has a plan for my life.

Can you find hope in the reality of God's purposes and love? _____

_____

Finally, Jeremiah was able to endure a seemingly wasted life because he had a hope that passed beyond the walls of this world. Meaning that Jeremiah understood that his death wasn't the end of his existence, that there was a beautiful promise for him to be united with his God and Savior in heaven. For many of us, heaven isn't a hope that is very enticing. The reason is because heaven seems so ethereal and otherworldly that it is hard for us to be excited for it. For many of us, we are far more comfortable on this earth and so we prefer to root our hopes and dreams in our lives in the here and now. Because of this, when we do undergo trials and loss, we tend to become more cynical and even bitter at God because all of our hope is rooted in this world and not in eternity with God.

In Hebrews 11:13-16 we read, "These all died in faith, not having received the promises, but having seen them afar off were assured of them, embraced them and confessed that they were strangers and pilgrims on the earth. For those who say such things declare plainly that they seek a homeland. And truly if they had called to mind that country from which they had come out, they would have had opportunity to return. But now they desire a better, that is, a heavenly country. Therefore God is not ashamed to be called their God, for He has prepared a city for them."

For years I was terrified of the idea of heaven. I couldn't conceive of passing into eternity and I feared becoming bored with eternal life. Beyond that, heaven didn't really seem that fun to me. I had no desire to live on streets of gold, or to live in a city in the clouds. For me, I love movies, books, music, and food, and the people that I was closest to were my friends who didn't know God. And so the hope of entering into an eternity without any of those things seemed really dull and even frightening to me. As a result, whenever I suffered any amount of loss or disappointment I became massively depressed because I was only living for this life, I had no joy or anticipation of the life to come.

Over the years though, God has shown me that the true purpose of heaven is being with Him, not receiving any particular blessing. I was blinded by my own lust and selfishness and I couldn't see that it is my ultimate purpose to worship and glorify God for all of eternity, not for God to meet all of my wants and desires. And I also missed that God is so infinitely glorious, that only in loving and worshiping Him can my soul have eternal joy and satisfaction. No matter how wonderful God made heaven, if He wasn't there, it would get old and turn out to be more like Hell than anything else. I didn't see that heaven isn't about a place, but a presence.

Psalm 23:6: "Surely goodness and mercy shall follow me All the days of my life; And I will dwell in the house of the LORD forever."

David's heavenly hope was not about eternal health, maximum prosperity, or even eternal relationships. David's number one hope of heaven was about "dwelling in the house of the LORD forever." It's not like heaven won't have these things, (I do see now that my original understanding of heaven was very unbiblical and that heaven is going to be far more wonderful than I could have ever imagined and I would encourage you to read through Revelation 21-22 to see the full glory of what heaven will be like) it's just that these blessings are icing on the cake, God Himself is the main attraction. The more I saw as David did, the more I understood that my excitement for heaven is directly proportional to my joy in God. The more joy I experience in God, the more anticipation I will have to be in His presence. The less joy I have in God, and the more joy I have rooted in this earth, the less hope I will have in the promise of heaven. But when we have our hope rooted firmly in God and in heaven we will see that the hope of heaven is an incredibly powerful one. It is a hope that transcends the trials of this life, it is a hope that can be an anchor for your soul in the worst of storms and the greatest of losses. This is a hope that can even give you joy in your trials knowing that in heaven, every ounce of suffering that you experienced on this earth will be turned into eternal glory in the presence of Christ. This hope is an unshakable granite stone for us as Christians to lean upon and it will crush every ounce of cynicism in our hearts. And the more joy we have in our glorious Lord, the more powerful this hope will be for us. Heaven doesn't begin when we die, it starts right now in our relationship with God, and continues for eternity in the fullness of His presence.

In the book of Revelation 21:3-4 it says, "And I heard a loud voice from heaven saying, 'Behold, the tabernacle of God is with men, and He will dwell with them, and they shall be His people. God Himself will be with them and be their God. And God will wipe away every tear from their eyes; there shall be no more death, nor sorrow, nor crying. There shall be no more pain, for the former things have passed away.'"

Do you see the amazing hope that we have in heaven? _____

_____

The most amazing thing about this to me, is the way that Jeremiah was able to trust in God above his emotions and circumstances when he had far fewer resources than we have today. Jeremiah trusted in the character, the faithfulness, and the love of God so supremely, that it changed his life and gave him a foundation of hope that held him together through some of the most horrific events in Israel's history. And Jeremiah was able have faith like this, even though he had never tangibly seen God's love or faithfulness demonstrated the way that we have. Jeremiah had heard about God's faithfulness to deliver Israel in the past from physical dangers, but we have an example of God's love and faithfulness literally written in His own blood. We see in the life and death of Jesus the love and faithfulness of God in the most vivid way possible. And the more we study and understand these realities, the more hope we will have and that is what will free us from the poison of cynicism. Please read through the following passages and write down your thoughts:

Proverbs 14:13: "Even in laughter the heart may sorrow, And the end of mirth may be grief."

Romans 5:3-8 teaches us, "We can rejoice, too, when we run into problems and trials, for we know that they help us develop endurance. And endurance develops strength of character, and character strengthens our confident hope of salvation. And this hope will not lead to disappointment. For we know how dearly God loves us, because he has given us the Holy Spirit to fill our hearts with his love. When we were utterly helpless, Christ came at just the right time and died for us sinners. Now, most people would not be willing to die for an upright person, though someone might perhaps be willing to die for a person who is especially good. But God showed his great love for us by sending Christ to die for us while we were still sinners (NLT)."

Timothy Keller, in *Walking With God Through Pain And Suffering:*

> *Jesus lost all his glory so that we could be clothed in it. He was shut out so we could get access. He was bound, nailed, so that we could be free. He was cast out so we could approach. And Jesus took away the only kind of suffering that can really destroy you: that is being cast away from God. He took that so that now all suffering that comes into your life will only make you great. A lump of coal under pressure becomes a diamond. And the suffering of a person in Christ only turns you into somebody gorgeous.*

A quote from Joni Eareckson Tada:

> *Most of us are able to thank God for His grace, comfort, and sustaining power in a trial, but we don't thank Him for the problem, just finding Him in it. But many decades in a wheelchair have taught me to not segregate my Savior from the suffering He allows, as though a broken neck—or in your case, a broken ankle, heart or home—merely "happens" and then God shows up after the fact to wrestle something good out of it. No, the God of the Bible is bigger than that. Much bigger. And so is the capacity of your soul. Maybe this wheelchair felt like a horrible tragedy in the beginning, but I give God thanks in my wheelchair.. I'm grateful for my quadriplegia. It's a bruising of a blessing. A gift wrapped in black. It's the shadowy companion that walks with me daily, pulling and pushing me into the arms of my Savior. And that's where the joy is... Your "wheelchair," whatever it is, falls well within the overarching decrees of God. Your hardship and heartache come from His wise and kind hand and for that, you can be grateful. In it and for it.*

LESSON FIFTEEN

ANXIETY

Anxiety weighs down the heart, but a kind word cheers it up. (Proverbs 12:25)

In today's lesson we are going to go over the sin of anxiety. Before we talk about anxiety, it is important to remember that, much like, cynicism, anxiety comes from a very useful emotion: fear. It isn't a sin to experience fear or anxiety, but it is a sin to follow these emotions and feed them. Fear was given to us by God to provide us with caution that can help us avoid pain and tragedy. So, when you walk up to a steep ledge, fear will kick in and cause you focus on the ledge and exercise caution so you don't fall over it. Or, when you were in school and you had a test coming up, you would experience fear that would motivate you to study and prepare for the test. When someone doesn't have any fear we call them reckless. These are the people who do very foolish and dangerous things just because they can, and their actions usually end up hurting themselves and others.

But, much like depression, in anxiety we take the useful feeling of fear and we turn it into something harmful. Anxiety is fear on a whole new level, it is so powerful that it can actually paralyze us and take away our ability to function properly. Also, just like depression, people who struggle with anxiety won't always have a cause for their anxiety. Their anxiety becomes that narrowed focus that they view their world through and it steals all their peace. Andrew Solomon noted that extreme emotions tend to intertwine with one another, so you won't just feel anxiety, but you tend to feel depression, regret, anxiety, anger… All cropping up at various times. After going through a period of extreme anxiety, he said this about it:

And then the anxiety set in. If you told me that I'd have to be depressed for the next month, I would say, "As long as I know it'll be over in November, I can do it." But if you said to me, "You have to have acute anxiety for the next month," I would rather slit my wrist than go through it. It was the feeling all the time like that feeling you have if you're walking and you slip or trip and the ground is rushing up at you, but instead of lasting half a second, the way that does, it lasted for six months. It's a sensation of being afraid all the time but not even knowing what it is that you're afraid of. And it was at that point that I began to think that it was just too painful to be alive, and that the only reason not to kill oneself was so as not to hurt other people.

167

Have you ever experienced anxiety like this?_____

_____

Beyond being a very unpleasant emotion to have, giving in to anxiety also has the adverse effect of creating the very problems you were trying to avoid and it can create separation between you and God.

Proverbs 10:24—The fear of the wicked will come upon him, And the desire of the righteous will be granted.

The first thing that this Proverb points out for us is one sinful aspect of fear or anxiety. When we read this we have to wonder, if it isn't sinful to be afraid, why is it that the fear of the wicked comes upon them? As we talked about in yesterday's lesson, our emotions tend to point us to the things we love the most, and fear is no exception. So the reason why the "desire of the righteous will be granted" isn't because only righteous people prosper, it is clear biblically that God "makes His sun rise on the evil and on the good, and sends rain on the just and on the unjust. Matthew 5:45. The reason why this is true is because the author is trying to show us through contrast, that the desires of the fearful turn away from God, while the righteous desire God alone.

For me, my fears usually have very little to do with my relationship with God, but instead they stem from my own cares and worries of this life. And the level of stress and anxiety that I experience over certain things is directly reflective of my overabundance of care for things of this world. Meaning that, while it isn't wrong for me to feel fear or worry over worldly problems or situations, when my stresses and fears consume me over a particular area of my life, it shows me that I have an unhealthy amount concern or care for worldly things and not enough of a concern for God. For instance, it's good for me to have concern for my relationships, but if I am in constant worry and anxiety over what others think of me, even to the point where I lose sleep playing past conversations over in my head and consistently stress out about how my actions or appearance are being perceived by others, it shows that I have an unhealthy concern for my reputation. It can also be a good thing to have concern over my job, but if my job consumes my life to the point where my mind is always wandering back to the office when I am supposed to be present with people that I love, my love for my work is too much. So as we scrutinize our lives, usually our stress and our fears can help us understand the areas that we value above God.

In fact, it is usually in my fear that I run to God, not because He is precious to me, but because I desire what He can give me. In other words, I see God as a means to what I want, and not my treasure and reward which is what He should be. And even when I do have fears about God, it usually stems from my own insecurity of trying to be good enough for God instead of loving God enough to trust that His grace and love are sufficient for me. So, whether my fears are rooted in my cares and concerns for this life, or in my relationship with God, when I feed these fears and I follow them they will always turn my focus away from God. We'll talk more on this later, but I hope you see the truth that the writer of Proverbs is trying to show us here.

Can you see how some of your fears are rooted in selfishness? _____

_____

ROOTED IN SIN, RESCUED BY LOVE

The second thing that this Proverb is trying to show us is that when we give into fear and anxiety, the things that we fear the most will come upon us. This isn't some sort of a curse from God, that if you have fear in your life, God will be sure to make that happen to you. This is instead an observation of reality. Using our previous two examples, when someone has anxiety and they come up to a steep ledge, far from being made more safe by their fear, the fear actually clouds their vision and makes them lose their balance. Or, if someone had anxiety about a test, they would be so nervous about failing, that they would study for hours and hours and not be able to retain any of the information.

This is a truth that unfortunately applies to every issue of life. If I am terrified of getting into a car accident, I will be so tense and jerky in my driving that I will probably get into an accident. If I am paralyzed by the fear of illness, I will be so scared of getting sick that I will become a hypochondriac and literally make myself sick. If I am so scared as a parent that my child will grow up rebellious or get into trouble, I will become so overbearing that I will drive my child away, and push them into rebelliousness. If I am terrified that I will die alone, I will either become overly needy in my relationships to the point where I suffocate other people and they will leave me. Or I will commit myself to the first person who pays attention to me and will most likely end up in a terrible relationship that I can't leave because I am so desperate for love that I ignore the clear red flags out of fear of abandonment. I can go on and on with examples, but I hope you see the point, giving into our anxiety tends to lead us to the very conclusion we were desperate to avoid.

Can you see how your fears have gotten the better of you? _____

_____

Anxiety also has a nasty habit of paralyzing us. We talked about this a little in our lesson on laziness, but our fears can keep us from ever trying and keep us constantly on the run from what we are afraid to confront. When we struggle with anxiety, what our fears tell us is that we can't do certain things, and when we believe those lies we put up mental blocks that freeze us in our tracks. The easiest way to see this is to look at someone who has a phobia. My sister always had the biggest fear of cockroaches, and when she saw one she would either freeze up, or scream uncontrollably and run for her life. You see, her fear was so extreme, that even though, rationally, cockroaches can't really hurt you, there was a mental block formed in her mind that told her that she couldn't handle a cockroach and so when one showed up, all she knew how to do was either freeze or run in panic. This also applies to all areas of life. So, if there is someone who has anxiety about confrontation, whenever conflict arises they will either shut down emotionally and not be able to respond, or they will flee from the conflict. If someone has a fear of applying for a job, they will set up mental blocks that tell them that they can't get hired and so they never even apply for the position.

Anxiety can even become so bad, that it can completely isolate someone in their paranoia. They will sit alone and over-analyze everything. They will be consumed with paranoia of how people view them, what their life will be like, and they will ask themselves a constant line of "what if" questions about things that they couldn't possibly control. Anxiety stops rational thought, and therefore becomes a barrier to dealing with issues and thinking things through. And so because in our fear we never learn how to fight, our only option is flight. We can run from past trauma, bad relationships, responsibility, conflict, and so on and so forth, but if we never learn how to deal with our problems, our anxiety will keep us from personal growth and from a lot of beneficial things that we need. As we talked about in our lesson on joy, the best things in life, like our relationship with God, our love for others, our careers… All need to be fought for and protected, fear will prevent you from doing that and so you will miss out on many wonderful things. I do want to mention that there are times when it can be good to avoid or flee from something, but in our anxiety we won't be able to appropriately evaluate our options, all we will know how to do is panic and run.

Have you seen anxiety paralyze you or put you in a habit of running from your problems?_____

_____

Our panic also has a very strange ability to revert us back to the people that we were. A really simple example of this is when we run into someone who we used to be close to. When you are close to someone you develop a bond of mutual trust and love, but sometimes we can move apart from friends and family members that we really care about. And when we run into these people that we haven't seen in years, all of a sudden we can find ourselves reverting back to the person we were when we last saw them. Subconsciously, the reason why we do this is because of fear. You had a particular bond with that person years back, and deep down you are worried that they might not accept the person that you have become. And so you revert back to the person that you were in order to ensure your chances of being accepted. I find myself doing this all of the time when I contact my old marine corps buddies. This is unfortunately really bad for me because I was a much angrier, lustful, and more cynical person back then.

This is a simple example, but this is true in other areas of our lives as well. When we enter into panic, we tend to revert back to old habits in order to cope, and we forget all of the growth that we have made. So maybe you have been doing really good with your finances, but all of a sudden a stressful situation will happen to you at work, and all of a sudden you literally forget how to budget and you start spending money like a teenager again. Or maybe you get into a stressful fight with your spouse, and all of a sudden you revert back to the way you used to deal with conflict as a child and you literally treat your spouse as if they are your parent. Or maybe you have been doing really good in your struggle against sexual sin, but your marriage is in turmoil and all of a sudden you are actively viewing pornography again. Anxiety can literally cause us to revert to our worst selves, and if we don't learn how to combat anxiety, we are vulnerable to this.

Has this type of reverting ever happened to you?_____

_____

So what is it that causes anxiety? Unfortunately, like depression, there are many different causes for anxiety, and it is impossible to provide just one blanket cause for every person. I will spend some time going over common causes, but just because I list these doesn't mean that they necessarily apply to you. In order to grow in any of our areas of struggle, it is important to take the time to reflect on ourselves and learn over time what the center of our own issues are so that we can call on Christ to be our solution. One of the main causes of anxiety is our issues with control. Meaning that fear usually comes about when we realize that there is something that is out of our control or understanding. So we respond emotionally with fear to try to put these things under our control. Now some of these control issues really are irrational, and so they are actually simple to confront and overcome. So, like with my sister's fear of cockroaches, if she really wanted to confront that fear, I could set up a situation where she could, step by step, confront a cockroach and see that they aren't dangerous. No matter what, she will always experience fear when she sees a cockroach, but over time, she can be trained to control that fear and function within it. So if you have anxiety over something, take some time to think through your fear, see if it is rational or not. Sometimes, just taking a small amount of time to think through our fears rationally will show us just how silly our fears really are. And when we do this, it can give us the courage to confront these things and overcome them.

However, much like depression, it is hard to counsel most people who have anxiety, because the truth is that we do live in a very scary, and out of control world. So if I am counseling someone who has a fear of rejection, I can't really say "Don't worry, there's nothing to be afraid of, that won't happen." Because the reality is that rejection is very real, and very painful. Or if I were talking to someone who has a terrible fear of dying in a car crash, I can't say "Oh, that could never happen to you." Because it really could. From a worldly perspective, all I could really do is maybe point out some irrational things that they believe, but ultimately all I can tell them is "Yes these things are scary and you can't control them, but it is far more scary to not confront these problems…" Or I could encourage cynicism and tell them "Yes you could be rejected, but who cares what other people think, and yes you could die, but so what, everyone dies, it isn't a big deal…" Both of these solutions can work a little, but ultimately they can't really help people all that much because their fears are rooted in reality. Jordan Peterson is a clinical psychologist and in one of his lectures he said, "I am not concerned about people who struggle with anxiety, I am more concerned with people who don't."

What he means is that it seems like the majority of anxious people aren't living in a fantasy land, but in reality. On the contrary, it is those of us who don't really struggle with anxiety who tend to live in a fantasy of our own self-deception. So when I witness a couple going through a painful divorce I tell myself, "Well, that must have been their fault, that could never happen to me…" Or if I drive by a terrible accident on the side of the road I say to myself, "They must not have been paying attention, luckily I am a safe driver…" You see, I am protecting myself from fear by deceiving myself about reality. In both of those instances that I tell those little lies to myself, I am convincing myself that I have total control over those things and so there is no need to be afraid. That is why a lot of our coping mechanisms for fear really have nothing to do with logic or reason, but as long as they make us feel in control, we feel peace.

So, for instance, a child who is afraid of monsters under the bed will fight their fears by using a night light or by hiding under the covers. Logically, if there was really a monster under the bed, neither of those things would help at all, but for the kid it isn't about reality, it's about control. We may make fun of that as adults, but we are still doing the same thing. We have all these safety nets and precautions throughout our life, and these may be good to have, but they don't make us impervious to tragedy. In our self-deception though, we trick ourselves into thinking that these precautions put us in control of our lives. And unfortunately, not only do these precautions not give us the safety we think they do, if we are run by our anxiety to try to control things, our "precautions" will bring about exactly what they were supposed to protect us from.

For me, the clearest area that I can see this alive in my life is in my relationships. Because I struggle with a lot of insecurity, I live in constant fear of letting people down and not measuring up. And so I spend my time trying to please everybody, but the more I try to do that, the more I realize that by pleasing one group of people, I am upsetting another group. Not only that, but I realize that what repels people from me more than anything is my insecurity and my controlling behavior. So in my attempt to please everybody, I end up pleasing nobody and my fears of letting people down come true. In marriage counseling I see how marriages can go wrong, and so I begin to fear where my own marriage is going. I become paranoid about my relationship with my wife and our growth together. And so in my fear I try to "fix" our relationship, but in so doing I make my wife panicked and I become more and more controlling which turns her off and creates the marital issues that I was trying to avoid. So far from keeping us safe, our fears and our attempts to control our fears, turn against us and make our problems worse, not better.

The reality is, no matter how much precaution I take, I am still out of control in many of the issues of my life. In the issue of my marriage, I have absolutely no control over my wife, if she wakes up tomorrow and decides to leave me, there is absolutely nothing that I can do about that. Beyond that, I have learned in my struggle against sin, I am not even completely in control of myself. I have so many negative and sinful habits that, outside the power of God, I am absolutely powerless to conquer, and these habits very well could cause enough problems to erode my marriage over time. The issue with the car is the same. I can't control other drivers, I can't control whether my vehicle is going to have a random malfunction, and when I honestly look at my driving habits, I can see that I am not exactly the safest of drivers. Reality outside of the existence of a loving God, is terrifying if we think it through. And the more important control is to you, and the more you realize the nature of reality, the more anxious you will become.

Do you see some of your anxiety stemming from your control issues? _____

_____

Another common source of anxiety is our upbringing. Unfortunately, fears can be transferred to others, and for a lot of us, most of our fears were given to us by our parents and our society. A good example of this can be seen in the book of Numbers chapter 14. In this section, the people of Israel were about to come into the promised land until they see that the land is inhabited by people who are far more powerful than they were. So the Israelites rebel against God and refuse to go in to take the land. But, instead of admitting their own fears, the men hid behind their wives and children by saying that they couldn't allow their wives and children to fall prey to the sword. God sees right through this deception and is furious that the men would hide their cowardice by using their children as shields, and so God decrees that He would wait 40 years for all those men to die, and allow their children to take the land instead.

Unfortunately, things haven't changed a whole lot today. Loving parents struggle deeply with fears of what can happen to their children. They love their children very much and want what is best for them, so they struggle with lots of anxiety over the dangers that their children will encounter. Because of this, these parents will try their hardest to keep all of these dangers away from their children by totally insulating them from reality. So they never expose them to reality, they keep them in the house, protect them from "bad influences," and whenever their children run into trouble, they will rush to their rescue instead of allowing their kids to solve their problems themselves. Sociologists have noted that this is one of the biggest reasons for the laziness and entitlement of the millennial generation. The majority of millennials were raised by parents who were consumed with fear. And so these parents installed fears into their kids of what might happen to them in the future.

They, unintentionally, painted the world to be a cruel and merciless place and themselves as the only people that their kids can depend upon. This caused a large portion of this generation to never learned how to confront problems or work through issues. You see, the fear originally belonged to the parents, but they, through their actions, passed this fear on to their children and made their kids completely dependent on them. Now, it is understandable that this comes from the parent's love, and it is far better than the parents who are negligent towards their children and never take care of them. But in our discussion on love we talked about how love must be balanced, love like this is unbalanced and codependent. So while it is better, it is certainly not good and it can have many negative side effects on kids. In fact, this is such a problem, that psychologists have diagnosed it and called it "affluenza." Just to clarify, I'm not saying that parents shouldn't teach their children caution. But there is a world of difference between the parent that lovingly explains the harsh realities of the world, while at the same time helping their kids cope with these fearful things and be independent, and the parent who explains the fears without ever helping their children confront these things and therefore makes their kids completely dependent.

Sometimes though, fears aren't installed for such noble reasons. Fear can actually be one of the strongest methods for controlling people. And so oppressive people will use fear in order to control people underneath them to get them to do what they want, and this can range anywhere from a pushy boss, to a full blown cult leader. In a lot of cults, the way that they get people to stay, even in horrible and abusive situations, is by installing deep phobias into them. They convince the people that if they leave, God will send them to hell, or that if they leave they will be raped or murdered by the wicked people who are outside of their group. They convince people that the only safe place is in the confines of the cult, and so even when people are miserable, they don't leave. This is an extreme example, but things like this can be practiced by oppressive boyfriends or girlfriends, or even parents. In order to control the ones that they "love" people like this will instill deep, and often permanent fears into those who are with them about the outside world. All the while, the motivation from these people is to keep their relationships under control and dependent on their authority.

For most of us, we can relate to having at least one relationship that attempted to install fears into us, but even if you can't relate to that, we are all subject to our culture. We live in a consumer based society, and what businesses have seen, is the best way to motivate sales is through fear. If I can convince people that they can only be safe if they have my product, I have created a never ending demand for my business. Politicians do the exact same thing. By bringing up great fears of the economy, border security, job security… I can convince people that the only way that they can be safe is if they vote for me. Unfortunately, even pastors can be guilty of this. Installing fears into their congregation to make sure that people will never leave, and that they will serve and tithe more. No matter what the motivation is, installing fears in people is a wicked and destructive thing to do to someone.

Can you see any fears that have been instilled into you? Have you ever done this to someone else?

_____

_____

The final cause that I will mention today is through trauma. The reason why some of us deal with deep anxiety is because we were given a vivid reason to be afraid. So maybe you never had a crippling fear of heights, but then you had a bad fall that really injured you. Or maybe you went through a really bad breakup or divorce that convinced you that all relationships are to be feared and so you have put walls up to defend yourself. Or maybe you are terrified of conflict because you were in a violent relationship where you were abused, either verbally or physically. There are many other examples that I could mention, but this is the easiest cause to understand and I hope you see the point. When you come face to face with the harsh realities of this world, it can be impossible to look away. And when that happens, it is easy for fear to consume you.

Have you had any trauma in your life that has produced anxiety? _____

So what is the solution to our anxiety?

Matthew 6:25-34: "Therefore I tell you, do not worry about your life, what you will eat or drink; or about your body, what you will wear. Is not life more than food, and the body more than clothes? Look at the birds of the air; they do not sow or reap or store away in barns, and yet your heavenly Father feeds them. Are you not much more valuable than they? Can any one of you by worrying add a single hour to your life? "And why do you worry about clothes? See how the flowers of the field grow. They do not labor or spin. Yet I tell you that not even Solomon in all his splendor was dressed like one of these. If that is how God clothes the grass of the field, which is here today and tomorrow is thrown into the fire, will he not much more clothe you—you of little faith? So do not worry, saying, 'What shall we eat?' or 'What shall we drink?' or 'What shall we wear?' For the pagans run after all these things, and your heavenly Father knows that you need them. But seek first his kingdom and his righteousness, and all these things will be given to you as well. Therefore do not worry about tomorrow, for tomorrow will worry about itself. Each day has enough trouble of its own."

Jesus' solution for us is certainly not what we would expect. What we would want Jesus to do, is like many teachers, give us a list of rules or strategies to put us in control of our own destiny and teach us how to get from life whatever we want. But He doesn't do this, in fact, contrary to what we would want from Him, He actually points out the fragility of life by showing us that we don't even have the power to "add a single hour to your life." Jesus points out our mortality, and our utter powerlessness to do anything about it. So far from giving us a feel good pep talk, Jesus makes us confront the harsh reality of the world. But at the same time He tells us how we can have peace in the midst of our lives.

The first thing that He does, is show us that our perspective is all wrong by saying, "Is not life more than food, and the body more than clothes?" As we talked about earlier, a big part of our fear problem is that we are not putting first things first. Jesus is forcing us to evaluate our lives and see how much worry is spent on things that are ultimately fading. How much time do I spend on stressing about my job, the way I look, my relationships… All things that, while they are good, they are not ultimate. My eyes are fixed on the constantly shifting waves of life, instead of focusing on my unchanging, all satisfying, all loving Lord and Savior. The more that Jesus becomes our first love, the more peace we will experience as His children. Why is that? He answers that question in the next lines by pointing out the loving nature of our Father in heaven: "Look at the birds of the air; they do not sow or reap or store away in barns, and yet your heavenly Father feeds them. Are you not much more valuable than they?" Jesus encourages His followers to look at the peace of the birds in the air.

He points out that they don't have any of the precautions that we have that make us feel safe and in control, and yet they have peace. Why? Because, unlike us, they trust in the power, and the love of their Heavenly Father. Whenever we are consumed by anxiety, it is the result of one of two things going below our notice. Either we doubt the power of God, or we doubt the love of God.

Job 42:2: "I know that You can do everything, And that no purpose of Yours can be withheld from You."

If you really believed that God was all powerful, that nothing happens outside of His sovereign decree and that no one, not even you, could thwart His will or plans you would see the reality of how out of control you really are. If God is all sovereign, that means that reality ultimately bends to His will and not yours. So all of our attempts to feel in control of our lives are exercises in futility, we can never wrest control out of God's hands. This doesn't mean that we don't have responsibility, the Bible is clear that while God is perfectly in control, we are held accountable for how we act.

Proverbs 16:9: "A man's heart plans his way, but the LORD directs his steps."

And so the Christian that has this truth in center focus acts knowing that his actions are important and they do have consequences, but he does this in peace knowing that God is in control and His perfect will is going to be done. So we should evaluate whatever situation we are in and look for appropriate solutions and precautions. And we should seek, through wisdom, to make the most God glorifying choice that we can make. But we must also humble ourselves and realize that there is a lot that is not in our control, and so ultimately we need to submit ourselves to God. While we make our plans we need to do this in faith, knowing that our plans don't put us in control, but we make our plans in submission to the reality of God's authority and love.

Please read and comment on the following passage:

James 4:13-15: "Come now, you who say, 'Today or tomorrow we will go to such and such a city, spend a year there, buy and sell, and make a profit;' whereas you do not know what will happen tomorrow. For what is your life? It is even a vapor that appears for a little time and then vanishes away. Instead you ought to say, 'If the Lord wills, we shall live and do this or that.'"

THE SERENITY PRAYER

This is why I love the *Serenity Prayer* so much:

> *God grant me the serenity to accept the things I cannot change; courage to change the things I can; and wisdom to know the difference. Living one day at a time; enjoying one moment at a time; accepting hardships as the pathway to peace; taking, as He did, this sinful world as it is, not as I would have it; trusting that He will make all things right if I surrender to His Will; that I may be reasonably happy in this life and supremely happy with Him forever in the next. Amen.*

It is so awesome to me how this prayer focuses on the truth that there are some things that are within my control, and some things that aren't. How much of our time do we spend worrying about things that we can't change while we ignore the things that we can? Or, how much of our time do we spend paralyzed by fear as we convince ourselves that we can't change things, that we actually can? This is most obvious to me when I stress out about the past or the future. Again, it's not that it is wrong to think about the past, if we don't think about our past ever we won't be able to learn from it. And it isn't wrong to think about the future, God wants us to be good stewards of our lives and that requires planning and discernment. But when we obsessively ruminate over the past and allow guilt and regret to consume us, we aren't learning from our past, we are being controlled by something that we can't change. Likewise, if our thoughts are consumed with "what if" questions about the future, which is by nature uncertain and outside of our control, we aren't going to be able to effectively plan for the future. Instead, our minds will come apart with fear and instead of planning and making rational decisions, we will stress-out and dwell in paralyzing fear and indecision.

This will also steal all potential joy in your present circumstances because you will be so worried about what was, and what could be, you can't simply enjoy what is. This is what Jesus is warning us about when He says: "Therefore do not worry about tomorrow, for tomorrow will worry about itself."

Each day has enough trouble of its own. It is only as God gives us the power to accept the things that are out of our control, and helps us see that the only thing that ultimately matters about your future, whether or not you will spend eternity with Him, has already been accomplished by Him; that we can gain the peace to enjoy and function in the present, the courage to learn from the past and change, and the confidence to plan for the future and make decisions, knowing that the future isn't in your hands, but in the hands of God.

Can you see the peace of accepting God's sovereignty in your life? _____

_____

But God's power is only comforting if God is all loving. There is nothing more terrifying than the idea of an all powerful tyrant. If God is all powerful, but selfish and cruel, this isn't good news at all. So, some of us may understand that God is all powerful, but we still look at our lives and we fear what God is doing. We think that He is out to get us, and so we are trying our best to wrestle our best interests out of His calloused hands. This is an aside, but this is the center of what we call the prosperity gospel. These are people who believe that we have to learn a formula or plan to make God give us a good life. If we don't do this, there is a massive fear that God will let the worst happen to us. But if we are good people and do all the right things, we can will into our lives the prosperity that we long for.

Not only is this not making God our central focus and goal, but it also stems from a massive lack of trust in God's character. What Jesus is saying here is that, yes you are ultimately out of control, but God is in control and His will for your life is far better than your will for your life. In other words, God knows what is best for His children, God wants what's best for His children, and God has all the power in the universe to provide what is best for His children. But, what is best for us is not necessarily physical blessings, but nearness to Him. And sometimes we will find nearness to God through fire and not prosperity. But when the worst happens, do we really trust that God is enough for us and that our relationship with Him is ultimately what is most important? Vaneetha Risner struggled in a time of trial and anxiety and felt God saying this to her:

Vaneetha Risner: The Scars That Have Shaped Me …I sensed God whispering again, Vaneetha, am I enough? If none of your dreams come true, am I enough?... If your suffering continues and you never see purpose in it, am I enough?'…

Jesus tells us, that if He alone is enough for you, and if you firmly trust in God's sovereignty and love, you can have peace in any situation.

Isaiah 26:3: "You will keep him in perfect peace, whose mind is stayed on You, because he trusts in You."

It's not that peace is necessarily an emotion like happiness, it is more like joy and it is a firm confidence rooted in our faith. By faith, we know that God's will is going to be done, and His will is what's best. We may not always feel that way emotionally, but we trust God by faith and have peace in the midst of our fears. It is a peace that is rooted in giving up our control to God, and trusting that He will do what is best, even if it is against what we would want. One pastor said that when he prayed, he would always pray his deepest desires to God because He knew God cared for Him and wanted to hear his heart's cry. But, he would always pray with his hands open, as a picture of letting go of his will for his life, and embracing God's, whatever it would be. And the more I seek to pray like this, the more peace I have in my life regardless of my circumstances, but the more I try to control my life, the more out of control and fearful I become.

I find it really interesting that the Word for anxiety in the Greek and the Hebrew is a word that means to come apart, while the Word for peace is all about oneness, wholeness, and completeness. When we are anxious, we come apart and are overwhelmed by focusing on many different things that are out of our control, but in peace we are focused on the only thing that matters and that is God. And in His love and unchanging nature we find rest, not in knowing the outcome, but in trusting the One who is in control. And when we study the cross of God, we see the wonderful love of God demonstrated for us that should prove to us beyond a shadow of a doubt that His will is better than ours. In the cross we see the One who had ultimate power and authority, someone who could have used that power to get everything He wanted without any risk or pain. But instead of using that power to dominate us, He gave up His rights and authority to become a fragile human being. The One who was ultimately complete and whole, came apart for you and me and He bore all of our sins and was crushed for us. The level that we allow these truths to settle in our hearts is the level of peace that we will have in our lives.

Please read and comment on the following quote from Vaneetha Risner in *The Scars That Have Shaped Me*:

In the Bible, Shadrach, Meshach, and Abednego were not guaranteed deliverance. Just before Nebuchadnezzar delivered them to the fire, they offered some of the most courageous words ever spoken. 'If we are thrown into the blazing furnace, the God we serve is able to deliver us from it... But even if He does not, we want you to know... that we will not serve your gods' (Daniel 3:17-18)

Even if the worst happens, God's grace is sufficient. Those three young men faced the fire without fear because they knew that no matter the outcome, it would ultimately be for their good and God's glory. They did not ask what if the worst happened. They were satisfied knowing that even if the worst happened, God would take care of them.

"Even if." Those two simple words can take the fear out of life. Replacing "what if" with "even if" in our mental vocabulary is one of the most liberating exchanges we can ever make. We trade our irrational fears of an uncertain future for the loving assurance of an unchanging God. We see that even if the very worst happens, God will carry us. He will still be good. And He will never leave us.

When we look at the cross, we also see the source of the courage that Jesus had in the midst of His fear. We see in the gospel accounts that Jesus experienced great stress before His crucifixion, even to the point where He sweat blood. But He overcame this fear with the faith that He had in His Father, as well as the love that He had for us. In our own personal fears, it is important to understand the peace that we can have in trusting God's love and sovereignty for us, but it is also important to understand the courage that we can have in Him when we face our fears for the sake of honoring Him.

For many of us, we struggle with stress and anxiety towards uncertain futures, and we also struggle with fear of following God. Many of us are gripped in fears of sharing our faith, giving up certain pleasures in order to obey His commands, walking in truth and honesty when we know it will cost us, choosing to fight sin when we know how costly and difficult this fight will be, and so on. And when we face all the various fears of our life, knowing that our greatest fears might come to pass, we must constantly remind ourselves of the prize that we have in

Christ. We have to evaluate our motives and make sure that we aren't facing these fears out of foolishness or personal vanity, but because God is worthy and we desire to honor Him no matter the consequences. This is the same heart that our Savior showed for us, He faced His fears and swallowed the horrific consequences because of His deep love for us. And the more we understand the all-surpassing glory of our great God, the more we will be able to face our fears with courage, knowing that even the greatest loss for His sake, is actually deep gain.

Pastor Timothy Keller commented on Psalm 108 in his book *The Songs Of Jesus,* and he talked about this kind of courage. Please read and comment on his quote:

> *"Steadfastness" (see verse 1) is courage—standing one's ground and doing right regardless of fears and consequences. Where does courage come from? Primarily it comes from wanting something more than your own safety. David wants all to see God's glory (verse 5). True courage is not "I can do it"—that is self-confidence. It is, rather, "This is more important than me." In the animal kingdom the mother undauntedly faces any size foe, not because she thinks she can win but for the sake of her young. David will face any foe for the sake of his Lord, whom he loves above all. He's not looking at himself. That is the secret of courage.*

_____

_____

PEACE?

Now, this may sound all well and good, but if we are honest with ourselves, we will admit that none of us have perfect peace. None of us value God supremely or trust God completely and so we all struggle with anxiety, some of us more than others. And while it is true, that no matter how godly we might be, we will still experience the emotion of fear and stress. The reason why our stress and our anxiety consume us is because we all lack faith in the sufficiency of Christ and the goodness of His perfect will. So how do we go from where we are, to where God wants us to be? Unfortunately, most Christians have an overly simplistic view of growing in this area. They just quote from Philippians 4:6-7:

> Be anxious for nothing, but in everything by prayer and supplication, with thanksgiving, let your requests be made known to God; and the peace of God, which surpasses all understanding, will guard your hearts and minds through Christ Jesus.

This is a beautiful quote, but unfortunately we can treat this as some sort of a magic charm. We think it means that if you just prayed to God about your issues, you would magically be cured of all of your anxiety. And so when people struggle with anxiety, they are told basically to get over it and pray more. Then, when they do this, and it doesn't take away their anxiety, they feel as if they are sinful and haven't done this right. This leads many people who struggle with anxiety to turn to cynicism. We talked about this in the last study, but if you struggle with anxiety all the time and it wears on you constantly, numbing yourself out can sound like a great solution. So instead of understanding that there is nothing sinful or wrong with feeling anxiety, they feel like they are sinning by experiencing these emotions and so they attempt to purge themselves of all their fear.

This is also where many people turn to substances and distractions for their anxiety. For so many people, one of the reasons why they turn to some of the negative habits that they have is to deal with stress and anxiety. We get sick of stressing out, and so we find ways to take our minds off of our problems and relax. But, as we talked about yesterday, when you turn to cynicism, by numbing your emotions of fear, you might also be numbing your ability to love or feel positive emotions like hope and joy. It is also important to remember that fear has an important purpose in our lives. If you actually were successful in purging yourself of all fear, you wouldn't be a better person, but you would be reckless and indifferent. If you turn to distractions to help with your stress, while doing this a little might be help a little bit, it is not a long term solution and can't ultimately heal you. If you are in a situation that is highly stressful and you can't really do anything about it, distracting yourself isn't a bad thing, just as long as you aren't doing this to avoid your problem altogether, but you are doing this in addition to dealing with your issues with God.

Have you had this simplistic view of peace before? If so, how has it impacted you?

_____

_____

_____

What we fail to see when we read the passage from Philippians, is that when Paul tells us to pray and let our requests be made known to God, he isn't speaking of prayer the way that we tend to think of it in Christianity today. If you read through the Psalms, you will see deep, passionate, honest prayers that are focused on God and are deeply meditative. For a lot of us Christians today, prayer is more or less just asking God for things, and while that is a part of prayer, it really isn't the center focus of it. Yesterday we went through my favorite Psalm in the Bible, Psalm 42. And I hope that you saw as you read through it, the bulk of the prayer wasn't asking God for things, but it was reflecting on what he was going through and seeking God in his turmoil. The psalmist wasn't praying to distract himself from his issues, he was seeking God in the midst of his issues. He was inviting God into his pain and seeking His Father's presence in the darkness of his suffering.

He never denied his hurt, or even tried to cover over his pain, but he poured it out with incredible boldness and sought discernment in his emotions, comfort in his pain, and help from God's grace. When Paul says to pray to God, he isn't just saying to do this as a one time thing and you will never struggle with anxiety again. He is encouraging us to cultivate a deep, personal lifestyle of prayer with our Father in heaven as we learn to admit to Him our deepest fears, seek wisdom from Him as to why we have these fears, and ask Him to help us understand His love and power that we might experience His peace.

Most of us deal with our anxiety by ignoring reality and distracting ourselves in a lot of negative ways. But God actually calls us, not to be naive, but to be completely unified with the reality of the world. You see, the problem with our anxiety isn't that we are thinking too much, but that we aren't thinking enough. We stress out thinking through our lives, but we don't spend any time thinking about the character, love, and power of our great God. Throughout the Bible we are told to "fear God," and many of us don't do this because we misunderstand what this means. We tend to associate fear with terror, and so it is hard imagining the benefits of being scared of God, after all doesn't "perfect love cast out fear 1 John 4:18"?

If You, LORD, should mark iniquities, O Lord, who could stand? But there is forgiveness with You, That You may be feared. (Psalm 130:3-4)

This Psalm should show us that our English understanding of fear is very different from the Hebrew understanding. Obviously God's attribute of forgiveness wouldn't normally move someone to terror, but this Psalmist says that God's forgiveness leads people to fear Him. For the Hebrew, fearing someone or something meant being in awe of it, and this awe could be negative or positive. So I could fear a rattlesnake by being in awe of what it could do to me and so I avoid it. Or I could fear my dad, and have a wonderful awe of his loving and firm character. To fear God is to be in awe of Him, to gaze upon Him and see Him in all of His glory. To marvel at the richness of His love and mercy, but to also see His awesome power and justice. The Christian who fears the Lord supremely, finds the confidence and peace to not live in terror of this world.

In the fear of the LORD there is strong confidence, And His children will have a place of refuge. (Proverbs 14:26)

This is the reason why so many of the prayers in the Psalms begin with focusing on the greatness of God. And even the prayer that Jesus taught us begins with centering our focus on His power and love with the phrase "Our Father, who art in heaven…" Jesus assures us that God is in heaven and is all powerful, but also that He is our Father, and loves us in a personal and intimate way. When we pray, we should wrestle with the harsh realities of our lives, but not before we first gaze at the reality of our great God.

Please read and comment on the following quote by Timothy Keller: *Prayer: Experiencing Awe And Intimacy With God:*

They (the apostles) went out and spoke the gospel in public with such a wonderful lack of self-consciousness that some thought they had had too much to drink (Acts 2:13). But their boldness was unlike being drunk in the most important respect. Alcohol is depressant—it deadens parts of the rational brain. The happiness you may feel when you are drunk comes because you are less aware of reality. The Spirit, however, gives you joyful fearlessness by making you more aware of reality. It assures you that you are a child of the only One whose opinion and power matters. He loves you to the stars and will never let you go.

_____

_____

One of the most important things that a Christian must develop is an honest and deep prayer life with God. This will be your strongest tool in dealing with negative emotions and experiences. And, as we talked about yesterday, as we learn to enter into this level of honesty with God, we will also learn how to have honesty with other Christians and seek counsel and comfort in our relationships with others. If we can grow in learning how to do this, it will take all of our tragedies and negative emotions and turn them from being the damaging things they have been into opportunities to draw you deeper and deeper into the loving arms of your Savior and the fellowship of His church. So even though your anxiety will ever fully go away, you will get better and better at controlling this emotion, and even find joy in how it forces you to humble yourself before God and seek to know Him more. So as we wrap up, I have left some last quotes to look through, but I also left Psalm 27 which is one of the best prayers dealing with anxiety written in the Bible, please read through it and see firsthand what a powerful thing it is to be honest and deal with your emotions before your loving Father.

The wicked flee when no one pursues, But the righteous are bold as a lion. (Proverbs 28:1)

The fear of man brings a snare, But whoever trusts in the LORD shall be safe. (Proverbs 29:25)

I sought the LORD, and He heard me, And delivered me from all my fears. They looked to Him and were radiant, And their faces were not ashamed. This poor man cried out, and the LORD heard him, And saved him out of all his troubles. The angel of the LORD encamps all around those who fear Him, And delivers them. Oh, taste and see that the LORD is good; Blessed is the man who trusts in Him! Oh, fear the LORD, you His saints! There is no want to those who fear Him. (Psalm 34:4-9)

You have put gladness in my heart, More than in the season that their grain and wine increased. I will both lie down in peace, and sleep; For You alone, O LORD, make me dwell in safety. (Psalm 4:7-8)

The LORD is my light and my salvation— whom shall I fear? The LORD is the stronghold of my life— of whom shall I be afraid? When the wicked advance against me to devour me, it is my enemies and my foes who will stumble and fall. Though an army besiege me, my heart will not fear; though war break out against me, even then I will be confident. One thing I ask from the LORD, this only do I seek: that I may dwell in the house of the LORD all the days of my life, to gaze on the beauty of the LORD and to seek him in his temple. For in the day of trouble he will keep me safe in his dwelling; he will hide me in the shelter of his sacred tent and set me high upon a rock. Then my head will be exalted above the enemies who surround me; at his sacred tent I will sacrifice with shouts of joy; I will sing and make music to the LORD. Hear my voice when I call, LORD; be merciful to me and answer me. My heart says of you, "Seek his face!" Your face, LORD, I will seek. Do not hide your face from me, do not turn your servant away in anger; you have been my helper. Do not reject me or forsake me, God my Savior. Though my father and mother forsake me, the LORD will receive me. Teach me your way, LORD; lead me in a straight path because of my oppressors. Do not turn me over to the desire of my foes, for false witnesses rise up against me, spouting malicious accusations. I remain confident of this: I will see the goodness of the LORD in the land of the living. Wait for the LORD; be strong and take heart and wait for the LORD. (Psalm 27:1-14)

WRATH

This will be our final lesson; I do hope that this book has blessed you and that you will continue to reflect on these topics in your life and seek to constantly grow in the grace and knowledge of God. But for our final lesson we will be going over the sin of wrath.

Psalm 4:4: "Be angry, and do not sin. Meditate within your heart on your bed, and be still."

I love this passage because it is one of the few passages that we have in the Bible that actually commands us to experience an emotion, but warns us not to sin. It is also beautiful because it even exhorts us to meditate about our emotions before God in order to avoid falling into sin. This should reiterate for us what we have discussed in our previous two lessons. First, that God isn't mad about us having emotions, but He does want us to be weary of making emotions our god and not submitting our emotions to Him. As we have gone over cynicism and anxiety, I do hope that you have seen just how deadly emotions can be when they go awry, and wrath is no exception. But before we get into what can go wrong with our anger, let's talk about how useful it can be.

Anger was given to us by God as a natural response to injustice. So, when we either see an injustice happen, or we see one about to happen, we should experience the emotion of anger in order to prevent injustice from happening, or to demand justice for wrongs that have been committed. And, like our other emotions, our anger is rooted in our capacity to love, meaning that the more you care about something the more upset you will become at the sight of injustice. This is why the Bible actually commands us to be angry at times, it would actually be wrong for us not to be angry at the injustices of the world. If I could look out at the world and witness things like, rape, child abuse, murder, war, extortion… And honestly not be moved by anger at all, this wouldn't make me benevolent, but actually apathetic and wicked. If we saw a parent who was never moved to anger when their child was being mistreated or abused, or would never discipline their child to protect them from developing harmful habits, we wouldn't call them loving, but neglectful.

Most people do not understand this and so they become very uncomfortable when the Bible describes God as being "wrathful." They think that love and wrath are polar opposites and can't possibly coexist, but they miss the point that it is anger that moves someone to be protective of the ones that they love. In fact, it is actually because of the fact that God loves perfectly that He has such wrath. If God didn't have the anger that He had towards injustice, He would cease to be a loving Father and instead be an indifferent lord. There are many corrupt and wicked world leaders that never experience anger at the injustices that their people face, and because of this, they do nothing to help their people. By never demanding justice, they actually approve of the wrongs that are committed and guarantee that they will continue.

Can you see the good that is in anger? _____

_____

But, we can also see very clearly in the world how damaging anger can be. Even if you ignore the global landscape and all the wars and violence that permeates this world, I don't think there is a person on this earth that hasn't been negatively impacted by a wrathful person. Whether it was the wrath of your parent, a bully at school, a bitter teacher, an explosive boss, or some other painful situation, we have all seen just how scary and damaging anger can be when it is tainted by sin. And if we got really honest with ourselves, we would also see how damaging our own anger can be to ourselves and those around us. I am someone who has been on the receiving end of explosive anger, and I am also someone who has spent many years consumed by bitterness and anger. I have seen firsthand the pain that anger can inflict on others, and how painful it can be to carry that burden of wrath in your heart every single day.

> *A man of great wrath will suffer punishment; For if you rescue him, you will have to do it again.* (Proverbs 19:19)

Have you been impacted by someone else's anger? Can you see your own issues with anger?

_____

_____

WHEN ANGER GOES BAD

But what is it that makes our anger go bad? The first reason comes from our pride. As we have talked about earlier, our emotions are tied to what we love most, and the major issue with pride is that because it is rooted so deeply in all of us, the person that we love most is ourselves. Because of this, we often get very angry at things that we shouldn't, and we are entirely apathetic at times where we should be angry. When we look through the Scriptures, I think that Saul is a great example of this selfish wrath. Saul was the first king of Israel before King David, but because of his pride and his unwillingness to submit to God, God rejected Saul as king and appointed David. During his time as king, Saul became consumed with wrath for David, many times trying to run him through with a spear. And when David finally had to flee for his life, Saul attempted to hunt him down and kill him. But his wrath didn't just pour out on David, Saul had wrath for anyone that hurt his fragile ego. During one battle, Saul made a foolish vow that if anyone ate food before they defeated the enemy army, that person would die. His own son Jonathan didn't hear that vow and at one point in the battle ate a honeycomb.

Saul was so consumed with his reputation, that he actually considered murdering his own son in order to avoid admitting that his vow was a foolish one. This is the illogical nature of pride, Saul can't see the evil of trying to murder David and even kill his own son, he is instead only angry that these two men made him feel insecure. In all these instances you can see that Saul isn't getting angry at things that are actually unjust, but in his pride he has made himself judge and jury of what is right and wrong, and anyone who crosses him or interferes with his plans, is deserving of his wrath.

Saul is a pretty extreme example, but I know I can see this same character defect running through my life. A simple example is when I am driving. I get so frustrated with people who are driving slower than I want, and I get furious at people who cut me off, or pass me in a rude way. What this proves is that I have made myself the standard for what is right and wrong while driving; as the comedian George Carlin put it "If you're driving slower than me you're an idiot, and if you're driving faster than me you're a jerk." That's a simple example, but when I think through a lot of the confrontations that I have with other people I can see this principle very much alive in me. Because of my insecurities, my pride is so sensitive to disrespect. I can see it in almost everything, even when people aren't intending to disrespect me, I still get very angry very quickly to defend my fragile sense of self worth. In fact, when I look through my experiences with anger, I can see that the majority of the time that I get really angry, it has nothing to do with something that is truly unjust. Meaning, that when I hear about another school shooting, or when I think about the oppression of others throughout the world, I am not really that moved by anger, but when something as simple as someone snubbing me happens, I am consumed by my own wrath. You see I am filled with wrath that is almost entirely selfish, and so my anger is no longer helpful, but harmful to myself and those around me.

Can you see how your wrath comes from pride? _____

_____

However, not all of our anger comes from our pride, sometimes we are angry for right reasons, and yet we still fall into sin. In order to explore this issue more, we are going to take a look at the life of a man named Joseph. Joseph was the son of Jacob back in the book of Genesis. Jacob was told by God that he had been chosen to be the father of the nation that God would work through. God changed his name to Israel and he had twelve sons through four different wives. Jacob's favorite wife was a woman named Rachel and before she died she had two sons, the older was named Joseph, and the younger was named Benjamin. And even though Joseph was one of the younger children, he was his father's favorite child. He constantly doted on Joseph, even putting him in charge of his older brothers and most famously giving him a coat of many colors. This favoritism poisoned this family, consuming Joseph's brothers with wrath, and even making Joseph cocky and arrogant. During this time, Joseph began to have dreams that he would rule over his family. Instead of being humble and keeping these things to himself, or even finding a diplomatic way to say this to his family, Joseph gloated to his brothers and even his father about how he had dreams of ruling over them. Joseph did this multiple times to his family turning their anger murderous.

A little while later, Joseph's brothers were tending a flock a little ways from home, and Jacob told Joseph to check up on them. Right when they saw Joseph coming though, their anger flared up and they stripped Joseph of his cloak and tossed him into a pit to leave him for dead. After they did this they began to eat lunch, even with their brother crying for help from out of the pit, and a group of merchants on their way to Egypt passed by. The brothers then decide that they should sell Joseph off to slavery in order to make some money, and after they did that, they lied to their father and told him that Joseph was eaten by a wild animal.

When we look at this story we can see how wrath, even though it was justified, completely ruined that family. The brothers actually did have a right to be upset about what was going on in their family. When Jacob played favorites with his own children, he was being incredibly wicked, but they allowed their anger to control their lives and turn them into people who would sell their own brother into slavery and then trick their father into thinking he was killed. The first thing that we see that the brothers did wrong was they allowed bitterness to grow in their hearts.

> *Looking carefully lest anyone fall short of the grace of God; lest any root of bitterness springing up cause trouble, and by this many become defiled;* (Hebrews 12:15)

When we think about wrath, most often we think of explosive wrath, we think about the end of the story where the brothers strip Joseph of his cloak and throw him into a pit. But what this passage is telling us, is that like all sin, wrath begins in the heart like a root, and then grows up in us causing us to do all sorts of evil things. So even if you aren't the person who grows violent when they don't get things the way that they want, you may still be eaten up by wrath in your heart.

I think that Jesus gives us an even better metaphor in Matthew 18:23 where He tells a parable that compares wrath to a sort of debt. You see whenever an injustice happens to you there is a cost, and whoever wronged you just started a tab in your soul. And the more often someone wrongs you, the debt only grows bigger and bigger. So maybe the first time somebody wronged you, you could overlook it, but the more often injustice keeps happening, the more you will feel the wrath burning you from the inside out.

In marriage counseling I see this all the time. Maybe in the beginning of the marriage, the wife asked the husband to take out the trash, and even though he said he would, he got wrapped up in other things and he never ended up doing it. The next day, the wife would see that the garbage was still in the can and so she would get frustrated in her heart, but would just take out the trash herself and maybe make a passive aggressive statement and then let it go. But then after years of marriage, this becomes the routine. And without the wife even knowing it, a debt of wrath begins to accumulate in her heart, until finally she can't take it anymore and so she begins to lash out at her husband. Sometimes this takes the form of constant nagging, sometimes it can take the form of passive aggressively cutting down her husband, and sometimes it can take the form of explosive yelling.

All the while, what the wife is unaware of, is that the husband is now growing a debt of wrath towards her at the same time. With each cutting comment, nagging remark, and explosive fight, the husband begins to become more and more wrathful and vindictive towards his wife. And so he begins to lash out at her in much the same ways that she is, but both parties are unaware that they are equally to blame. The wife won't understand why the husband is angry because in her mind "He shouldn't be mad, he started it by ignoring me." And in the husband's mind, he isn't to blame because, "If she would have just communicated to me what was bothering her, than it would have never gotten this far." And things will keep spiraling out of control and getting worse and worse until either they will get divorced, or they will remain married but separate emotionally.

This was only a basic example, but there are an infinite number of causes for this type of relationship break down. The main takeaway here is that when we are in situations like this, things can't get better because what we fail to see, is that our wrath itself has become our solution to our problem. Meaning, in our hearts we know that injustice is happening, and we know that the scales of justice must be balanced. So our bitterness, nagging, and explosive rage are our ways of making things even. The issue is debt can't be paid off through "getting even," it can only be made right when the price is paid. If we look at this metaphor, if someone actually owes me a debt, me beating that person up doesn't actually make us even, also, that person doing good deeds for me also doesn't pay the debt. The only way to pay the debt is if that person actually gives me what they owe me. And here is the biggest problem with our root of bitterness, no price will ever be sufficient to get rid of wrath.

This is an aside but, we all need to understand that in our anger we aren't very good at confrontation. There are some people who simmer beneath the surface. They hold things in and grow bitter, but they lack the courage to actually confront the person that they are angry at. Because of this, they turn to passive aggressive tendencies, nagging, and character assassination in order to feel better about themselves, but none of these things will actually get rid of their bitterness, it will just make it grow. Unfortunately though, many Christians, both men and women, think that this is a righteous thing to do. They think that it is godly to hold their tongue and "take the high road," but what they are actually doing is stewing in their wrath. Now, sometimes it can be good to give a little space when confrontations become too heated. But examine yourself and make sure that you aren't separating to avoid the confrontation altogether, but instead to give space so that the confrontation can be more gentle and fruitful.

Can you see passive aggressive tendencies in yourself? _____

_____

On the other side of the coin though, are the people who are great at confrontation, but terrible at being compassionate and gentle. Someone like this can certainly tell you what is on their mind, but they will usually come across in an abusive and harmful manner. Also, in their rage, they will say things that aren't even true, just to hurt the person that they are talking to. People like this tend to think that they don't struggle with bitterness because "they get it all out there," but in the end, their bitterness remains and they will be just as damaging in their next confrontation as they were in their previous one.

Do you struggle with explosive anger?_____

GUILTY!

For me, I find that I can be guilty of both of these. Sometimes I can be a jerk and be pushy in my conversations with others as I express what I am feeling in a really harmful way. And sometimes I can be passive aggressive and pretend like nothing is wrong even though in my heart I am really hurt and upset. But no matter where we are on that spectrum, we need to change and discover that there is a way to solve our bitterness problem, but like our other emotions, we ultimately have to deal with our wrath before God. We will talk more about this later on.

Our wrath blinds us from the truth that there is no lasting way to deal with bitterness in the presence of the person that we are angry with. Sometimes we think that "if only that person got what was coming to them, then I would be happy." "Or, if they would just say they were sorry, or if they would just finally change, then I could forgive them." No matter what happens in the future, the pain of the past remains, it is that pain that must be addressed first, otherwise there can be very little hope for the future. This not only applies to relationships today, but to all relationships and hurt throughout your life. They say that time heals all wounds, but that is just completely false. The truth is, time heals all properly dressed wounds, but when you don't properly take care of a wound, it festers and becomes infected. This is exactly what has happened to us. Because the truth is that all of our "accounts" of wrath began when we were just children.

For a lot of us, we can probably see tons of injustices from our past, some of us have far more than others. And with the pain of our past, we have so much wrath stored up in our hearts that it extends out into all of our current relationships. And the most insidious thing about our roots of bitterness, is that roots are under the surface and therefore hidden from sight. For me, I used to think that I wasn't an angry person, but that I just had a very unfair life. But the people who are closest to me showed me that this wasn't true at all. The truth was I was a very angry person who found a way to bury my anger, until something would "trigger" me and I would react violently in my wrath.

A good example of this is my issues with my deployments. I thought that I was "over" what happened to me in Afghanistan, but my family pointed out to me that whenever someone brought up the topic of the marines, or Afghanistan, my mood would completely change and I would get noticeably angry. You see, just like my other emotions, I tried to bury my wrath, but that root of bitterness thrived in those dark conditions and soon, I didn't even know why I was so angry, I was just angry at the whole world. It is never good to obey your emotions, but we should always pay attention to them. Meaning, that when you have an extreme emotional reaction to something, this is more than likely a remnant of some past pain that you have never dealt with, and now it is dealing with you. It is very possible that you may think that you don't have any anger, and in reality you have a big root of bitterness in your heart that lies dormant until it is triggered. And the more you pay attention to your emotional state, the more you can see the deception in your heart.

Can you see the roots of bitterness in your own heart? _____

_____

The second issue that these men fell into, is they used bitterness to cover up pain. In our previous lessons we talked about how cynicism, or rejecting hope and emotions can be a destructive remedy to past pain. But what happens when you try to shut down these negative emotions and you never end up succeeding? For me and my friends, we tried our best to shut off our emotions of regret, fear, pain, helplessness, and so on through cynicism and, for some of them, through self medicating with substances and sex. But what we found, is that you can't fully shut down these emotions, they remain dormant and constantly come like massive waves of emotion. And so, if you can't silence your emotions through shutting them down, maybe you can instead turn to an equally powerful emotion on the opposite end to drown them out: anger. One reason why so many combat vets are so angry, is because they are literally using their anger to overcome their more negative emotions.

We can see Joseph's brothers doing the exact same thing. They have turned to their wrath to ignore the obvious feelings of hurt and insecurity that they were all struggling with. You see, it is much easier for them to hate Joseph, then for them to reflect on the serious questions of life like "why doesn't my dad love me?" We see this really clearly in the fact that Joseph's brothers should have actually hated their father and not Joseph for their problems. It wasn't Joseph's fault that he was favored by Jacob, Jacob himself made that decision and through his bad parenting, Joseph became just as much a victim of his father's sins as his brothers. But you see them irrationally hate Joseph, and even after he is gone, the brothers all try to please their father for the rest of their lives.

The truth that they refused to see is that they were far more hurt then they were angry, and we can do the exact same thing. So maybe you have gone through a bad breakup or divorce, and you have turned hateful and bitter towards your ex because the real pain that you are running from is "Was some of this my fault?" Or "Maybe I am a jerk and that is why they left…" Or maybe you had parent's like Joseph's who either abandoned you or never really showed you that they were proud or that they cared. And so you begin to hate your parents because you don't want to think "Was I really such a bad child that they couldn't love me…" At the end of the day, we turn our wrath outwards towards others because the truth is, that the person we are most upset with is ourselves. It is always easier to hate and blame others than it is to look at ourselves, but as we talked about before, once bitterness takes root, it can be almost impossible to get rid of. And when we turn to bitterness for this reason, the amount of negative issues that we have can be far more horrible than facing our fears and pains.

Have you ever turned to bitterness to cover up pain?_____

_____

_____   _____

The simplest issue with doing this is how exhausting bitterness can be. Being bitter and angry all the time is not fun at all, it steals all your peace and forces you to spend your time reliving your painful memories to fuel the fire of your hatred. I spent years in my hatred, and I found that my anger would never leave me. I would spend days at a time feeling constantly upset. After every little thing that someone did to me, I would relive that event over and over again until I would literally get headaches from being so angry. I found myself becoming explosively angry at the smallest things, and so I pushed away friends and family members. The saying is definitely true "Bitterness is the poison that you drink hoping that the other person will drop dead."

Another problem that comes from this is that, if you give in to this enough, you will develop a wall that will prevent you from all true intimacy, and from ever seeing any fault in yourself. For example, let's say that whenever you get into a relationship that turns south you immediately cut that person off and say that it was "all their fault." If your only response to relational difficulties is to cut people off and hate them, then it will be almost impossible to develop any real relationships, because real relationships have issues that need to be worked through. It will also repel most people from you, because they will see that you are unable to change or admit that you are wrong. Real relationships require change and compromise, people that are unable to do this, won't be able to ever have true intimacy with another human being. The only way that someone like this can build anything long term is if they are in an unhealthy relationship with someone who always lets them get their way.

Another issue is that when we cover over pain with anger, it can be very easy to project unresolved issues. So, maybe you had a bad relationship as a teenager where you gave all of your heart to someone and they ended up betraying that trust by cheating on you or dumping you for no apparent reason. So, in order to deal with that pain, you taught yourself to hate that person. But now, you are consumed by paranoia in all of your current relationships. You are constantly afraid of betrayal and so you end up sabotaging every romantic relationship you come into, not realizing that you are projecting the person who originally hurt you onto people that have done nothing wrong to you. Or maybe you had an abusive parent, and now you find yourself constantly rebelling against all authority in your life. And the second you get close to someone, whether it be a friend or a love interest, you project your parent onto that person and you rebel against them even if they are trying to help you. Or maybe you had a parent that you felt you never quite measured up to. Now you find yourself hating your parent, yet secretly longing for their approval. This insecurity has turned you needy and very unsure of yourself. And now even though you may have a lot of people in your life that love you and respect you, you still feel like you aren't measuring up or doing the right thing. These are just a couple examples, but I'm sure you get the point.

The final problem that I will mention is that, when you do this, you might be setting yourself up for becoming worse than the people you hate. Judah becomes a really good example of this. Judah was one of Joseph's brothers, and he was actually the one that made the suggestion of selling him into slavery. After they sold Joseph though, Judah ended up having children, and he became just as bad a parent as his own father. He had three sons who were incredibly wicked, one of them was so bad that God actually struck him dead while he was married to a woman named Tamar. The next son married Tamar, because it was customary in those days if someone died not having any children for the brother to marry his brother's widow and raise a child with her in his name. But he refused to accept this responsibility, and God struck him dead as well.

Judah could have logically seen that his sons had turned out wicked and repented, but instead he blamed the woman and said that she was the cause of their deaths. In an attempt to love his children, Judah ended up becoming a worse father than Jacob and refused to see the clear truth of his sons. I encourage you to read the story on your own, but Judah actually has an amazing conversion through a very disturbing set of circumstances. But if God wouldn't have intervened in his life, Judah would have certainly been turned into an irredeemably wrathful man. Think about it, Judah grew up always feeling unloved by his father. Because of this insecurity, he ended up marrying a pagan woman and had three wicked sons that he never disciplined. This caused his sons to become so bad that God had to strike them dead, and now Judah was not only a failure as a son, but a failure as a father.

This self hatred once again turned outwards, because that is the only way he knew how to handle disappointment, and so he put all the blame on this woman Tamar. His hatred became so bad that when they even thought that Tamar had been unfaithful in her vows to Judah, he ordered that she be burned alive. Thankfully he didn't actually do it, but you can see Judah had become so wrathful that he ordered someone, not only to be killed, but literally burned alive for wronging him. I have seen this many times when children hate their parents, some of them actually end up becoming worse than their parents. Their hatred blinds them from what they are doing, and as it consumes them, they become worse and worse in all that they do.

Can you see the negativity of turning to bitterness as an antidote to pain? _____

The next thing that the brothers do that is wrong is they seek vengeance in their own power. You can see it really clearly in their story, but when we seek vengeance in our own strength it produces several problems for us. The first is that when you are consumed by personal bitterness and resentment, you are not a very good judge. As stated earlier, Jacob holds the most accountability in this scenario, and yet the brothers in their wrath took all of their anger out on their little brother without ever confronting their father. Also, the punishment certainly didn't fit the crime. Joseph was probably a pain as a younger brother, but that certainly was not deserving of life in prison. When we give into bitterness for a long enough period of time, we can paint people out to be monsters when they really aren't. After a time, it won't be enough for us to hate the wrong that they have actually done, we have to scrutinize everything that this person has ever done and begin to believe that they are a complete demon.

So maybe you had a friend that gossiped about you once in high school and ruined your reputation. So over time you gave in more and more to your bitterness until you re-evaluated your whole relationship with that person and as you pulled out everything negative that they had ever done you began to hate every aspect of their being. Even if you are confronted with some good memories with that person, your bitterness will pollute those memories and you will say, "All of that was just a front, now I see how they actually are…" The truth is, reality isn't that simple, people can't just be put into neat little categories of good and evil. Some of the worst people to have ever existed had some good qualities, and some of the most honorable people had their dark sides. But in our bitterness we ignore all that and we convince ourselves that this person deserves far more justice than they really do.

Next, is that when they sought vengeance themselves, it turned them into wicked men. Up until that point they were victims of a bad upbringing, but in this moment they themselves turned into men who were far worse than anything that Joseph or Jacob ever did. The depravity of selling your younger brother into slavery and then lying to your father about it is unbelievably wicked from anyone's standards, and yet these men did it. There is a very wise but simple saying that states: "hurt people hurt people." The victims of today often times turn into the monsters of tomorrow, and when we are consumed by our hatred we can turn into the very thing that we hate. But, the most dangerous part of our bitterness, is that we will be so blinded by hate, that we will be unable to see how wicked you are becoming. You will justify your actions by demonizing the person you are attacking. I'm sure Joseph's brothers would say, "Yes, selling someone into slavery and lying about it is bad, but Joseph had it coming, in fact, he got off easy…" In their utter hatred for Joseph they painted an unfair picture of him to justify their evil actions, when the reality is that there was no justification for what they did.

Finally, exacting vengeance on Joseph actually didn't make things better for them but worse. Like I said before, most of the time we are actually using our rage to avoid pain. The issue is, that if you ever actually succeeded in your vengeance, the distraction of rage would dissipate and you would be forced to look at what your rage was blocking for you. So after Joseph's brothers went and told their dad that Joseph was dead, their dad loved them even less because he blamed them for allowing Joseph to die. In their minds they had painted Joseph to be the monster that ruined their lives, and if only they could get rid of him, their dad would finally love them and they would be a happy family. But the selfishness of their father got even worse after Joseph was gone, and now, not only did they have less love from their father then before, but with Joseph out of the way, the only person that they could blame was themselves. And when you read the story you do see this family crumble under the weight of guilt, shame, and insecurity. Earlier we talked about what happened to Judah, but the other brothers didn't fare any better than he did. In our rage we can think that getting even will make us feel better, but all it will do is force you to come face to face with all the pain and hurt that you have been running from for so long. And at that point you can either own up to reality, like Judah finally did, or you can keep running and find someone or something else to blame.

Can you see the problems with seeking vengeance in your own power?_____

_____

In the midst of all this pain and brokenness, this story actually has a very happy ending. Joseph ends up going to Egypt and serving as a slave for a couple years. But during his time in slavery, instead of running from God and blaming God for his misfortunes, Joseph actually becomes more faithful to God and ends up becoming the most trusted slave in his masters household. However, even though Joseph is faithful, those around him continue to sabotage and hurt him. So through a series of very unfortunate events, Joseph ends up in prison for several years, until finally his faithfulness pays off and he is able to interpret a very important dream of the Pharaoh. Joseph, through the power of God, sees that the whole Middle East would go through a severe famine for seven years after a seven year period of prosperity. And he saw that this famine would be so bad, that if something drastic wasn't done, all the affected nations would starve to death. So Pharaoh puts Joseph in charge of storing up food for the famine, and just like that Joseph became the second most powerful man in Egypt and single handedly saved all of the Middle East including his family. But how was Joseph able to resist the power of wrath and not become consumed by it? We aren't told much about Joseph's spiritual journey, but we do get a small, but important clue in Genesis 41:51-52 when Joseph names his first two children:

> *Joseph called the name of the firstborn Manasseh: 'For God has made me forget all my toil and all my father's house.' And the name of the second he called Ephraim: 'For God has caused me to be fruitful in the land of my affliction.*

Joseph says that he found a solution to his wrath in God that not only enabled him to completely heal from the damage that was done to him, but also allowed him to see that everything that was done to him had purpose and in God, fruitfulness. As we have talked about with our other emotions, it is possible without God to have a small amount of victory over your emotions. And if all you are looking for is a relief from your emotions, there are methods that can help you do that. But what Joseph found is only possible in the arms of God, because it is only through God that the pain of your past can actually produce fruit as it draws you closer and closer to Him. But in order for that to happen, Joseph had to do something that is almost impossible to do, he had to "justify" God.

> *All the strength of Israel vanishes beneath His fierce anger. The Lord has withdrawn his protection as the enemy attacks. He consumes the whole land of Israel like a raging fire. He bends His bow against His people, as though He were their enemy. His strength is used against them to kill their finest youth. His fury is poured out like fire on beautiful Jerusalem. Yes, the Lord has vanquished Israel like an enemy. He has destroyed her palaces and demolished her fortresses. He has brought unending sorrow and tears upon beautiful Jerusalem.* (Lamentations 2:3-5)

This was written by the prophet Jeremiah as he watched Israel be plundered and destroyed by an enemy nation, and as you can see, he says that God is the ultimate cause of this event. It is so hard for us to get this level of honesty in our relationships with God, but if we agree that God is all sovereign, than we have to believe that all of our pain and suffering were allowed by God. But as Christians, most of us were never taught how to be honest like this with God in our prayer life. And so when we start to realize this, we can begin to grow bitter towards God but instead of being honest about it, we pretend like it isn't there. The problem is, if you harbor bitterness towards anyone, whether you admit it or not, that bitterness will always be a barrier to your relationship with that person. And if God truly is the only One who can heal our past pains, then our bitterness towards God will separate us from the only person who can actually save us.

I remember that when I came back from my first deployment I was so angry at God for what I saw Him allowing in the world. It really messed with my faith and caused me to doubt the goodness of God. I thought, if I was a loving father, I would never allow the amount of abuse and pain to occur to my children that I witnessed, and yet God allowed untold amounts of suffering to occur all throughout the world. And when I came face to face with this harsh and devastating reality, it really messed with my views of God, and produced in me a severe anger towards Him that I didn't know how to express.

Around that time though, I began to read through the books of Lamentations and Revelation and these books helped me to trust in the faithfulness of God even though I couldn't see it. In Lamentations, Jeremiah lays out plenty of quotes just like the one above that express his frustration with God allowing the things that He did to occur to Israel. Jeremiah didn't pretend like everything was fine, he was honest with God about his feelings which freed God up to comfort him. And so I began to pray to God about my frustrations, and I was honest with Him about my struggles to balance His goodness with what I had seen. And it was around that time that I read the book of Revelation. In that book I was able to see the end that God was working towards. I saw the plan that He had to make the world right and bring about a new creation free from sin and death, but the issue was if you read through Revelation, you see that things have to get a lot worse before they can finally get better.

At that point God allowed me to widen my gaze and realize that God is dealing with a very complicated situation. I realized that the real issue with the world isn't God but people. I realized that even though God has literally done everything that He can to reach out to mankind, we still don't want Him. And this became crystal clear to me when I finally read through Revelation 20. In that chapter Jesus finally establishes a perfect kingdom here on earth for a thousand years. During that time, all of the objections that we have towards God are finally answered. Those who say that they would follow God if only He showed Himself will be able to see Jesus in person ruling the earth. Those who say that if God dealt with all the corruption and evil on earth will see justice reign in this kingdom of perfect governance. And those who complain about the natural disasters of this world, from everything from hurricanes to cancer will finally see a world that is brought to Edenic conditions of peace and perfection even in the natural world. But even with all of this, it says that humanity will rise up and try to overthrow Jesus, and the amount of people that will participate in this rebellion will be more than the sands of the seashore.

When I read this, everything finally clicked for me. The obstacle to the peace and happiness of humanity has always been humanity. All this time I was blaming God for the issues of my life, not realizing that the reason for all the evil and wickedness in this world happened in spite of God's desire to give us a perfect life in Eden. God never intended pain and suffering, but because He wanted us to have a free will, He allowed for us to fall and corrupt His once perfect creation to our own harm. Beyond that, I realized that God didn't just allow for us to suffer, but He Himself entered into our suffering and died. God does allow evil and suffering, but He is not immune to it, He entered in to the depths of human suffering and bore it all for us. In our unjust wrath towards God we blame Him for the problems of our life, when it was the fault of man and not God. And yet, when it is God who has righteous wrath built up against us, instead of giving us what we rightly deserve, He became a man, lived the perfect life that we never could, and bore His own wrath for us. And it is when I began to understand the lengths that God went through to save me, that I finally began to have peace, I can trust that even though I don't understand what God is doing, I know that He is good and will do all things well.

Joseph realized this early on, and that is why you see that he has such peace and faithfulness in the midst of his suffering. It's not like Joseph only became happy after God blessed him, he was fully content in God in the depths of prison, knowing that God had a plan and purpose for everything that he was suffering through. Now we can look back and see the plans that God had. If Joseph had not gone into slavery and then to prison, he would never have been in the position to interpret Pharaoh's dream and then he would have never been able to preserve the whole nation of Egypt and even Israel which was the very nation that God Himself would be born into. This side of the cross, we have far more reason to be confident in the goodness that God has for us even in the midst of suffering. If God could take the most unjust action in human history, the crucifixion of the only innocent man to ever live at the hands of wicked and sinful men, and use that to redeem all of mankind, you and I can trust that God has important plans even for our suffering if we can only trust Him in our pain. The more we accept this, through intensive prayer and honesty towards God, we can let go of our unjust wrath towards our good Father, and run to Him to heal our hurts.

Therefore we do not lose heart. Even though our outward man is perishing, yet the inward man is being renewed day by day. For our light affliction, which is but for a moment, is working for us a far more exceeding and eternal weight of glory, while we do not look at the things which are seen, but at the things which are not seen. For the things which are seen are temporary, but the things which are not seen are eternal. (2 Corinthians 4:16-18)

Do you have any anger towards God? _____

_____

Next, the Words of Joseph also show us that he had found healing from the deep pain of betrayal that he experienced, and the regret for his past. It would have been completely natural for someone like Joseph to be consumed with self-hatred for being betrayed by his brothers. When someone that you love can betray you that deeply and with that much violence, it would be impossible to keep from wondering, "Am I really as bad as they say?" Joseph could have wallowed in a lifetime worth of self pity, wondering if he really was the reason why his brothers felt unloved and whether he really did deserve what was happening to him. We could also expect that Joseph would turn into his brothers, blaming them for all that had happened and become someone that was consumed with rage over the unfairness of his life. But we see, not only in the incredible perseverance and faithfulness that he demonstrated at the lowest parts of his life, but also through his complete forgiveness of his brothers, that he found a peace and a healing that his brothers never could.

Joseph says that God had made him to forget all the toil and all of his father's house. This didn't mean that he mentally blocked out his past, we know from the rest of the story that he did remember exactly what had happened to him. But instead what it means is that God gave Joseph the ability to remember his past, without the weight of the trauma crushing him. As we talked about before, when it comes to pain and trauma we would like to completely ignore it with cynicism, or we would like to bury it with our rage. But Joseph doesn't do either of these things, instead he did exactly the opposite of what we tend to do in our trauma, he turned to God and sought healing in Him.

For years, I refused to do this. I was so paralyzed by the thoughts of my past, that I did everything I could to forget all of it. But after I realized the massive personality defects that I had developed through my wrath and cynicism, I began to pray to God about my past. Books like Jeremiah taught me how to express the pains of my past to God and trust Him with my heart. Slowly, what I saw God doing was first, He showed me the truth of my guilt. So many of us don't want to think about our past because we are terrified to face those haunting questions like "Maybe this really was all my fault…" And when you face your past alone, you just might come to conclusions like that. But as you pray through these things with God, while you are guarded by the truth of

His Word, you will begin to find healing as God will show you just how much of your past was your fault. And how even in those areas that were your fault, God will show you His grace that covers you and makes you new.

God helped me see, that there was a lot of guilt and regret that I was carrying for things that weren't my fault. But He also showed me that there were things that I could have done better, and needed to receive God's forgiveness for. For Joseph, he would have to own that he was a spoiled and arrogant son and he needed to be forgiven for that by God. But he would also need to see that some of the blame fell on his father, and, that no matter how bad a brother he might have been, he did not deserve what his brothers had done to him.

It's amazing to me to see how many people are held captive by their pasts, thinking that abuse, neglect, betrayal, and abandonment were their fault, when they weren't. We hold on to these feelings because we are afraid to confront the truth. It is so disheartening to hear stories of people who were raped thinking that it was their fault for the way they dressed, or for the situations that they put themselves into. Or kids who were abused or abandoned thinking, deep down, that somehow, it was their fault for disappointing their parents. Or even wives, blaming themselves for being physically abused by their husbands. These are extreme examples, but I hope that you see just how damaging it can be when you bear guilt that doesn't even belong to you. You might have a life controlled by wrath because you were never able to confront these issues before God and see the truth of your circumstances.

And even if you do discover that there was some fault of your own in what happened, if you confront these things with Christ, you will be able to see His grace covering what you did and you will be given the opportunity to repent in Him and move forward. Sometimes though, the pain of your past can be so painful that even in prayer it will be almost impossible to see the truth of your circumstances. That is why fellow believers can also help point you to the truth of the Word and, by offering you a different perspective, help you see those truths that your powerful emotions reject. But, as with all other types of confession, be weary of who you talk to about these kind of things, always checking to make sure that the counsel you are receiving is biblical. It is so easy to find people who will just validate you no matter what and feed your wrath. We always need to seek people who love us enough to confront us with the truth, whether that truth is comforting, or painful, because it is only when we embrace the whole truth of our circumstances that we are brought closer to Christ. It is in this type of prayer, reflection, and confession that you can gain the kind of peace and healing that Joseph, and countless other believers have experienced in Christ.

Has God begun to give you peace and healing from the pain of your past?_____

_____

Finally, Joseph was able to live in peace because he found in God forgiveness for his brothers. It is clear throughout the Bible that forgiveness isn't something that we are recommended to do, but it is something that we are commanded to do.

> *For if you forgive men their trespasses, your heavenly Father will also forgive you. But if you do not forgive men their trespasses, neither will your Father forgive your trespasses.* (Matthew 6:14-15)

This was one of the biggest stumbling blocks for me in my relationship with God, I just couldn't see how I could forgive the things that had been done to me. For me, the reason why this issue was so difficult, was actually because I misunderstood what forgiving was. When you grow up in Christian culture, you hear a lot of strange terms used all the time, that you don't fully understand. Forgiveness was one of those words for me. I heard it used, but I had this idea that to forgive someone meant to forget, or to get over what happened. I found in myself a huge resistance towards doing that, it didn't seem right to me that I had to just let go of my anger for this person and excuse everything that they had done. But now I realize that I had the wrong definition for forgiveness all along, and this misunderstanding kept me from peace for many years.

What I was actually doing, was I was mixing the definitions for "excusing" and "forgiving." Excusing someone means to justify what someone did. Or in other words, it means that you don't find any fault in their actions, and therefore what they did has no consequences or personal cost to you. And there will be real moments in your life when you will excuse the actions of people who have wronged you, realizing that it honestly wasn't their fault. A simple example of excusing someone would be if you are at a stop light and someone in front of you won't go when the light turns green. You might be really upset with that person for holding up traffic and making you late, but imagine this person gets out of their car and lets you know that their car broke down. In that moment, your anger towards that person will go away, not because that person didn't slow up your day, but because they literally couldn't help it, and so you can excuse them from any wrong.

Another common mistake that I see in the ministry that I am involved with, is that we somehow think that explanations are the same as excuses. So if I am talking to a man who committed adultery on his wife, he might say that he was raised in a lustful culture, or that he was exposed to porn very early on, or that his wife isn't fulfilling him sexually, or even a more severe explanation of sexual abuse or something like that. Now, all those things are essential for me to understand where that man is coming from and to have grace on him for where he has been. But, while these things might explain his behavior, they do not excuse his behavior. When we are wronged by somebody, we need to remember James 1:19-20 So then, my beloved brethren, let every man be swift to hear, slow to speak, slow to wrath; for the wrath of man does not produce the righteousness of God."

When you have been wronged, be sure to be swift to hear that person out and listen to what they have to say. Because if that person really does have a good excuse for what they did, and you rush to anger and don't listen first, you might say or do something really harmful to that person that you won't be able to take back. Hear what they have to say first, and see whether they have a valid excuse, or if they only have explanations. The real world is often times very complicated though and there will usually be a mixture of excuses and explanations. So while some of what they did is excusable, there will still be some left over that is inexcusable. So whether there is only a little bit that was inexcusable, or the whole offense is inexcusable, how do you forgive what you can't excuse? Here is where we get into the true definition of forgiveness. To forgive someone doesn't mean to justify what they did, but instead it means to recognize the cost of what someone did and, without excusing it, give the authority of judgment to God.

Which means that forgiveness is also different from reconciliation. We'll talk more on this later, but forgiving someone just means that you give your wrath to God and allow Him to be the judge, while reconciling means that you are actually repairing the relationship. So forgiveness is commanded and happens between you and God, sometimes, independent of the person who offended you. Reconciliation on the other hand happens directly between you and that other person, and is the act of restoring the relationship. Which means that reconciliation is a mutual act, it takes both parties to accomplish this step. The person who did the wrong must be willing to own what they did, make amends if they can, and make positive steps towards changing their behavior, in short, they have to repent. While the person who was wronged, must be willing to begin forgiving that person before God so that they don't continue to lash out in wrath against the person who did them wrong. Without both parties working together on this, true reconciliation can never happen. You might be able to patch together a superficial relationship, but nothing will ever be the same. It is also important to see that while the Bible does command us to forgive, it does not command us to reconcile. Instead we are told this in Romans 12:18-19 If it is possible, as far as it depends on you, live at peace with everyone. Do not take revenge, my dear friends, but leave room for God's wrath, for it is written: "It is mine to avenge; I will repay," says the Lord.

So you can see here that once again we are commanded to forgive and "leave room for God's wrath..." But we are not commanded to reconcile, instead it says "as far as it depends on you..." Meaning, that you can only be accountable for yourself. If you wronged someone, you need to move in repentance towards God and try to make things right. But if the other person refuses to forgive you, no matter how much you try, you can't force the other person to reconcile. It is important to leave the door open and try to make amends, but sometimes it just won't always happen. And if you are the one who was wronged. You are commanded to move towards forgiving that person through God, but if that person refuses to apologize or change, you can't really reconcile with them. If we fully reconcile with people who aren't sorry, and who aren't making any moves to change, you are first of all setting yourself up to be hurt again, and secondly you are actually enabling that person's bad behavior. It doesn't mean that you can't have any relationship with that person, it just means that depending on the severity of the sin, you need to use caution in your relationship. And even if you do get close to this person, this issue will always be a sore spot and so there will be no true reconciliation unless the other person is willing to move in repentance. There are a lot of grey areas with reconciliation, so I encourage you to talk to your accountability partners, and possibly talk to a counselor on your specific situation before you make any permanent decisions.

Have you confused excusing, explaining, reconciling, and forgiving? _____

_____

_____

The life of Joseph gives us a very powerful example of how this works. Later on in Joseph's life, his brothers come to Egypt in search of food. At this time the famine was so bad that they were almost completely out of food, and so Jacob sends them out to purchase food and come back. At this point though, his family believed that Joseph was either dead, or just some no name slave in Egypt, no one thought that he could possibly be the second in command in Egypt. And so when they arrived, while Joseph recognizes them, they don't recognize him. So Joseph puts them through some different trials, tricking his brothers several times in really profound ways.

I encourage you to read through the story on your own time, but Joseph uses his little brother Benjamin, who was now the favorite son, to test his brothers to see if they had really changed. He feeds them dinner, all the while he favors Benjamin to see their reactions, and then, after a few more tests, he finally puts them in a situation where they could either leave Benjamin to die, or to take his place. When he does this, Judah stands up and offers to take the place of Benjamin, and right then, Joseph sees the man who once heartlessly sold him into slavery just to make some money, literally offer his own life to defend his younger brother. In that moment, Joseph knew that his brothers had changed and so he reveals the truth to them about who he was. After this, they bring their father up from Israel and they all begin to live together in Egypt. But, after his father dies, the brothers fear that Joseph will seek vengeance on them for what they did and so they beg Joseph to make them slaves and spare their lives, but Joseph responds like this: Genesis 50:19-20 Joseph said to them, "Do not be afraid, for am I in the place of God? "But as for you, you meant evil against me; but God meant it for good, in order to bring it about as it is this day, to save many people alive.

Notice what Joseph says, am I in the place of God? Joseph does not say, "Don't worry about it guys, it wasn't a big deal…" He acknowledges that they were evil in what they did, but he says that he isn't the right person to judge them, only God can do that. This right here shows us that Joseph had already done the work of forgiving his brothers before they ever came to Egypt. But how did he do this practically? Unfortunately we have a very simplistic view of forgiveness in the church as well. We think that just telling someone verbally "I forgive you." Literally means that the process is over and you have completely forgiven that person. This is not true. Forgiveness is a process that takes consistent effort, and depending on how deep the wound is that you received is how long this process will be.

But the first step in that process is admitting to God that you are angry. This sounds obvious, but for so many of us, we don't understand what forgiveness and anger are all about, and so we pretend like we aren't angry at all, while secretly we are eaten up by it. And even if we are willing to admit the truth of our anger to ourselves or other people, we won't admit just how severe our anger is and we will still struggle admitting this to God because we think that it is sinful. For years I struggled under the weight of wrath, not knowing how to tell God about the truth of what I was feeling. But once again, God blessed me through His Word by showing me many prayers that expressed deep rage towards other people. In fact, there is an entire category of Psalms that deal with this issue, they are called the imprecatory, or cursing, Psalms. And out of all of them, my absolute favorite is Psalm 58.

Break their teeth in their mouth, O God! Break out the fangs of the young lions, O LORD! Let them flow away as waters which run continually; When he bends his bow, Let his arrows be as if cut in pieces. Let them be like a snail which melts away as it goes, Like a stillborn child of a woman, that they may not see the sun. Before your pots can feel the burning thorns, He shall take them away as with a whirlwind, As in His living and burning wrath. The righteous shall rejoice when he sees the vengeance; he shall wash his feet in the blood of the wicked, So that men will say, "Surely there is a reward for the righteous; Surely He is God who judges in the earth." (Psalm 58:6-11)

When I first read this, I was so relieved, because I saw that I wasn't alone in the way that I was feeling. And the imagery that is mentioned here is actually far more brutal than anything that I would ever think of. This Psalmist has the boldness to come before God, and honestly express his desire towards the people that he was angry with. The sad truth is that when we try to handle our wrath in our own power, all it can do is consume us. We can not extinguish the flames of our anger, all we can do is repress our emotions until they either turn into cynicism or bitterness, and both are sins before God. So while it may be wrong that you feel the way that you do, it is more wrong to lie to God about the truth of your emotions and try to handle them on your own. Remember what the writer of Hebrews tells us:

For we do not have a High Priest who cannot sympathize with our weaknesses, but was in all points tempted as we are, yet without sin. Let us therefore come boldly to the throne of grace, that we may obtain mercy and find grace to help in time of need. (Hebrews 4:15-16)

That word "boldly" in the passage literally means to say anything. In my walk with God I realized that I didn't have that boldness. I didn't really trust God with my feelings, and so my emotion of wrath became a major barrier between me and God. I used to lie in my prayer life and say things like "God just be good to that person, I really love them…" when in reality I felt like the man from Psalm 58. That hypocrisy before God just made me feel more distant and shameful before Him. But, when I learned to confess my anger to God, I saw that my wrath, just like all my other emotions, actually had the potential to bring deeper intimacy and love between me and God.

I also found that as I expressed these things to Him, I felt a tremendous weight lift off of my shoulders. As we talked about earlier, wrath is a heavy burden to bear. In our hearts we stay angry to "get even" with the person who wronged us, but often times, we are hurting ourselves far more than the person that we hate. And even if justice does happen to that person, it still won't lift the burden of wrath from us because our hurt will still be there. But when we begin to move towards forgiveness by admitting our wrath towards God, you will see that He will begin to take that burden from you and give you peace. Yes, forgiveness is commanded of us, but like every other command that we are given, it is for our good as well as God's glory.

Please read and comment on the following passages:

Psalm 37:8: "Cease from anger, and forsake wrath; do not fret—it only causes harm. For evildoers shall be cut off. But those who wait on the LORD, they shall inherit the earth."

Proverbs 20:22: "Do not say, "I will recompense evil"; Wait for the LORD, and He will save you."

As we begin to confess our anger to God, the next thing that we need to do is begin to realize that God is just and He will judge righteously. As Christians, when we forgive, we are not saying that what other people did is no big deal and we should just get over it. We are instead acknowledging the evil of what was done, but also seeing that God alone is worthy of judging them. The passage that finally helped me understand this was Ephesians 4:32 And be kind to one another, tenderhearted, forgiving one another, even as God in Christ forgave you.

Here you see clearly that we are to forgive just as God in Christ forgave us. Now, how did God forgive us? Did He forgive us by saying "Don't worry about it, everybody makes mistakes…" Absolutely not, God did not just "let go" of His holy wrath. Instead God took all of His wrath against the sins of humanity, He became a man, and He Himself bore the wrath that was due to us.

> *For all have sinned and fall short of the glory of God, and all are justified freely by his grace through the redemption that came by Christ Jesus. God presented Christ as a sacrifice of atonement, through the shedding of his blood—to be received by faith. He did this to demonstrate his righteousness, because in his forbearance he had left the sins committed beforehand unpunished— he did it to demonstrate his righteousness at the present time, so as to be just and the one who justifies those who have faith in Jesus. (Romans 3:23-26)*

We as Christians were not forgiven by God shrugging His shoulders and just inviting us into heaven. We were forgiven because God, in His great love for us, allowed His only begotten Son, to endure all the wrath that we so rightly deserve. All sin has a cost, but we praise God that He paid the price that we could never pay, so that we could have the forgiveness that we could never earn. Unfortunately in the church today, since we live in a culture that values tolerance above any other virtue, we have watered down the message of the gospel in order to appease those around us. And so, we skim over the verses that talk about God's wrath towards sin, like these:

Romans 1:18: "For the wrath of God is revealed from heaven against all ungodliness and unrighteousness of men, who by their unrighteousness suppress the truth."

Romans 2:5: "But because of your hard and impenitent heart you are storing up wrath for yourself on the day of wrath when God's righteous judgment will be revealed."

John 3:36: "Whoever believes in the Son has eternal life; whoever does not obey the Son shall not see life, but the wrath of God remains on him."

Instead we focus only on the love of God, to the exclusion of His wrath. And while the Bible does have much to say about the love of God, we have to remember that it is actually because God is love, that He must also have wrath towards injustice. If God's love didn't have to overcome any obstacle, then ultimately what we have is cheap forgiveness that had no cost. That would also mean that Jesus died for absolutely nothing. If there was no wrath to overcome, than God could have forgiven us without a sacrifice. To take away the truth of God's wrath, is to ultimately put to shame the sacrifice of our Savior. It would also mean that all the horrible things that have been done to us, and all the people who committed these wrongs, will ultimately go un-judged by God. What this means, is that every wrong that you have endured, will ultimately go unanswered and you will have no vindication for you suffering.

When we look around the world and we see the utter depravity of mankind and the evil that we are able to inflict on one another, what kind of "loving" God could possibly see all of that and say "No big deal, none of that matters." For God to be all just, He has to judge all injustices perfectly, and that means God must have wrath. So what we believe as Christians is that every single sin will be punished perfectly by God. Either the people who have wronged us will find their forgiveness through the crucifixion of Christ, or they will answer for their sins before God one day. Not only that, but I hope that as we have been going through each sin, you have seen that to be consumed by any sin has extreme consequences for that person in the here and now, as well as for eternity. So even if it looks as if someone is getting away with wrongs that they have done, they are reaping the consequences of their sins. And for some things that have been done to us, Paul tells us in Romans 13 that the government also serves as a protection for us. Meaning that if someone broke the law when they wronged you, they are subject to the punishment of the law and there is nothing sinful with you pursuing charges in situations like that. But ultimately, these sins will be judged by God in perfection and when all is said and done, we will all praise His perfect justice.

"... Will not the Judge of all the earth do right?" (Genesis 18:25)

THE POWER IN FORGIVENESS

The beauty here is that it is in the reality of God's perfect justice that we can finally have rest from the destructive power of our wrath. For me, when I didn't understand God's wrath, I could not let go of my anger because I thought that if I did, that person would get away with what they had done. But when I looked at the cross, and I saw the lengths that God went to in order to be just, it showed me that I didn't have to hold on to anger to make sure that justice would be served, God would do that for me. And so, as I express my wrath towards God over what others have done, and as I find comfort in the reality of His justice, I can begin to move in the freedom of forgiveness.

But for some people, their problem isn't that they can't let go of what happened, their problem is that they try to excuse sins that they need to forgive. Because of the misunderstanding of forgiveness that exists in the Christian culture, sometimes we can fall into the trap of thinking that it is righteous to just excuse everything that happens to you, but doing this also has some pretty severe consequences. One consequence that I have seen is that when we excuse someone of wrong, we can take responsibility for things that weren't our fault. For instance, let's say that a wife finds out that her husband cheated on her, but because she wants to be "godly" she just drops the issue and pretends like it didn't happen. However, the issue now is that the adultery still happened, but the wife has excused her husband of all the guilt, so now who bears the blame for the wrong? The answer is that the wife will now absorb the guilt for what was done to her. She will depress herself with thoughts of how, "maybe if I were prettier this wouldn't have happened" Or "Maybe if I spent more time with him he wouldn't have sought attention elsewhere."

While everyone has wrong in marriage, and will have room to grow and do better in Christ, the wife's faults in no way excuse the husband, but because she already has excused him, she will subconsciously absorb the guilt. This can happen in a myriad of different examples, but the result will be the same, the guilty party will be declared innocent, and the innocent person will call themselves guilty. And for most people who try to do this, they won't be very successful and they will have a root of bitterness planted in them. This will also lead to enabling the behavior of people who wrong you. If you just excuse everyone who wrongs you and never hold them accountable to their actions, you have become a doormat, and you are ultimately enabling the behavior that is destroying that person and everyone around them, including you. There are other consequences that we could talk about, but I think you get the point, for both the person who struggles with wrath and the person who inappropriately excuses, we all need to learn how to properly forgive.

Can you see the importance of forgiveness?_____

_____

Now, as stated before, forgiveness is a process that will take time. Speaking to other believers can help this process along, but it is a mistake to believe that it's all gone just because you verbally said that you forgave them, or because you had a beautiful moment where you felt forgiveness. Both of these things are awesome to have, but they don't necessarily mean that you have fully forgiven that person. Be vigilant in your prayers, asking God for the strength to forgive this person, and when you feel that anger rising up in you, talk about that anger with God, be completely honest with Him and ask for the courage and faith to trust Him with judging that person. Also, don't fall into the trap of thinking that every time your wrath comes back, it is the fault of the person who wronged you and take it out on them. Forgiveness happens almost exclusively between you and God. And the more you cry out to Him, the deeper your intimacy with Him will grow, and the more peace you will gain in His presence. And this peace will grow not only as God gives you the grace to forgive, but also as God helps you heal from the pain and trauma of your past.

Is there anyone in your life that you need to forgive? _____

_____

Joseph began this process long before his brothers ever entered Egypt, and it was this genuine forgiveness that enabled him to eventually reconcile with his brothers. As we talked about earlier, reconciliation is a different step from forgiveness. Reconciliation is all about restoring a relationship with someone else, and this process is dependent on both the person who was wronged and the person who did the wrong. We see in the story that while Joseph had already forgiven his brothers, he used caution with them before he opened himself up to reconciliation. Joseph put his brothers through tests to see if they had really changed before he finally revealed his identity to them and reconciled himself to them. It is important for us to use this same kind of caution. As we talked about before, it will be impossible, and potentially damaging, to reconcile with someone who is not repenting. But even if both parties are ready to reconcile and they are both moving in the right direction, reconciliation is a long process. How long this process will be is dependent on many factors like, how bad the sin was, how much someone was hurt, how long the sin went for, how close the relationship was, and even how diligent each person is in their part of the reconciliation process.

The person who sinned must be diligent in their repentance. They need to be faithful in pursuing God, working on their issue, and doing everything that they can to make things right. And the person who was hurt needs to be diligent in their pursuit of forgiveness, really pressing in to God, and seeking that healing that only God can give. This person also needs to know, just as forgiveness is a process, repentance is also a process that will not be fully complete until we go to God. And so there needs to be patience and even more forgiveness as the person who wronged you will most likely fall short every now and then and will need more forgiveness on a regular basis. But if genuine repentance is happening, then permanent and practical change should be visible, if it isn't visible, or if that change comes to a stop, you may need to re-think reconciliation. This is a difficult process, but it is ultimately worth it. This will cause both of you to draw closer to God than you have ever been before, and to have a new and powerful understanding of His love and forgiveness. This will also forge a new relationship through this fire that will be stronger than the one you had before. But this only works, if both parties are really willing to hunker down and do the work that is needed of them.

Please read and comment on this quote from C.S. Lewis in *Weight Of Glory:*

> *To be a Christian means to forgive the inexcusable, because God has forgiven the inexcusable in you. This is hard. It is perhaps not so hard to forgive a single great injury. But to forgive the incessant provocations of daily life—to keep on forgiving the bossy mother-in-law, the bullying husband, the nagging wife, the selfish daughter, the deceitful son—how can we do it? Only, I think, by remembering where we stand, by meaning our words when we say in our prayers each night 'forgive us our trespasses as we forgive those that trespass against us.' We are offered forgiveness on no other terms. To refuse it is to refuse God's mercy for ourselves. There is no hint of exceptions and God means what He says.*

_____

_____

_____

I do want to quickly mention that, depending on the situation, sometimes sin can be so severe that even if there is a desire from both parties to reconcile that real reconciliation can never fully happen. An example of this would be if I cheated on my wife with someone close to us. Reconciliation is possible between me and my wife, but it is pretty much impossible for full reconciliation to ever happen between myself, my wife, and that other person. There are some other examples where this could be the case, but as we talked about before, it is really important to pray about these situations and seek Godly counsel because the issue of reconciliation can be very complex.

Is there someone that you are trying to reconcile with right now? If so, how is that process going? _____

_____

To finish off our final study, I want to spend some time focusing on the wrath of God and the eternal judgment of our loving Father. For some Christians, the topic of judgment is so unpopular that we don't even mention the existence of hell and say that it really doesn't matter how you live, God will forgive everything. When we do this as believers we are completely destroying the beauty of the gospel. We as Christians believe in a God who is so loving, that He could not ignore the wickedness of sin, but had to judge it. But this love that He had was so strong, that He chose to judge all this sin in Himself, and that by faith in His sacrifice alone, we can be completely forgiven, and be counted worthy of being with Him forever. Not only that, but we also have a promise that while in this world, God is saving us from all the sins that are in our lives. Setting us free from the weight of living for ourselves, and bringing us the joy that comes from living our lives unto the glory of our great and infinitely worthy God.

But, God also understands that genuine love needs to have a choice. If God forced everyone to receive His forgiveness from sin, so that we have to be in His presence forever. And if He forced everyone to receive His deliverance from all the sin issues of our lives, He wouldn't be a loving Father, but a dictator. And so, God created a choice for us. Instead of receiving the grace of God, we can choose to live for ourselves and reject God, and then to ultimately live an eternal existence outside His presence that we call Hell. If we don't want the forgiveness of God, and His perfect love that can actually satisfy our heart and bring us to the fullness of joy, we don't have to have it. You can spend the rest of your life trying to find your identity in your sins. And as the fire of your pride, lust, depression, anxiety, wrath, and other sins consume you in the here and now, you will be experiencing the first fires of your eternal home.

What we need to understand is that this is the central issue of salvation, either we will by faith accept God's forgiveness of our sins and stand in His righteousness, or we will have to stand in our own righteousness that we have worked for, which could never satisfy us or the wrath of God. And in doing so, we will suffer in the tormenting fires of sin that will consume us for the rest of eternity. The beautiful part of this, is it is also only in the perfect judgment of God that we have confidence in God's love. As we see that we ourselves were deserving of wrath, we will also see that God took our place in His infinite love and care for us. And when we see that, all of our guilt and shame will slowly melt away in the truth of God's forgiveness. It also shows that God's love is so beautiful that He ultimately offers choice. We know that God doesn't want to see any of His children suffer, but, being the loving Father that He is, He will not take away His children's right to choose. And so He allows people to reject His offer and suffer eternally in the fires of their own "righteousness" outside of Him.

Please read and comment on the following passage by C.S. Lewis from *The Problem of Pain*:

> *In the long run the answer to all those who object to the doctrine of hell is itself a question: "What are you asking God to do?" To wipe out their past sins and, at all costs, to give them a fresh start, smoothing every difficulty and offering every miraculous help? But he has done so, on Calvary. To*

forgive them? They will not be forgiven. To leave them alone? Alas, I am afraid that is what he does....
The damned are, in one sense, successful, rebels to the end; the doors of hell are locked on the inside. .
. . They enjoy forever the horrible freedom they have demanded, and are therefore self-enslaved.

DECIDE TO TRUST GOD'S LOVE

So, hopefully you have made the decision to trust in the love of God as the source of your salvation, and if you haven't, it is never too late to put your faith in Christ as your Lord and Savior. But even for us who are saved, while we have that confidence to know that we have peace with God and that we will spend eternity with our Savior; we also have the understanding that in this life we still have choice. Just because I am a Christian doesn't mean that I am not afflicted by my own sins. I daily need to choose whether I am going to walk after God and actively fight the sins in my heart, or if I am going to be complacent and allow sin to continue to grow up in my heart. As the apostle Paul put it in Galatians 6:7-9 Do not be deceived, God is not mocked; for whatever a man sows, that he will also reap. For he who sows to his flesh will of the flesh reap corruption, but he who sows to the Spirit will of the Spirit reap everlasting life. And let us not grow weary while doing good, for in due season we shall reap if we do not lose heart.

My hope and prayer for myself and for the body of Christ as a whole is that we would daily seek to grow in our love for God. That the issues that we talked about in this book won't be things that we think about once and then forget. But that we would daily seek to put to death our old nature that more and more of our lives would be for the glory of God. That we would pursue passionately the love and joy that is only in God, that we would continuously let go of the false pleasures of sin, and that in doing this we would show those around us the infinite beauty and worth of our God.

For this reason we also, since the day we heard it, do not cease to pray for you, and to ask that you may be filled with the knowledge of His will in all wisdom and spiritual understanding; that you may walk worthy of the Lord, fully pleasing Him, being fruitful in every good work and increasing in the knowledge of God; strengthened with all might, according to His glorious power, for all patience and longsuffering with joy; giving thanks to the Father who has qualified us to be partakers of the inheritance of the saints in the light. He has delivered us from the power of darkness and conveyed us into the kingdom of the Son of His love, in whom we have redemption through His blood, the forgiveness of sins. (Colossians 1:9-14)

Some last verses:

1 Peter 2:21-23: For to this you were called, because Christ also suffered for us, leaving us an example, that you should follow His steps: 'Who committed no sin, nor was deceit found in His mouth;' Who, when He was reviled, did not revile in return; when He suffered, Her did not threaten, but committed Himself to Him who judges righteously...

Proverbs 19:11: The discretion of a man makes him slow to anger, And his glory is to overlook a transgression.

Proverbs 14:29: He who is slow to wrath has great understanding, But he who is impulsive exalts folly.

Proverbs 20:9: Who can say, "I have made my heart clean, I am pure from my sin"?

Psalm 32:1-5: Blessed is he whose transgression is forgiven, whose sin is covered... When I kept silent, my bones grew old through my groaning all the day long. For day and night Your hand was heavy upon me; my vitality was turned into the drought of summer. I acknowledged my sin to You, and my iniquity I have not hidden. I said, 'I will confess my transgressions to the LORD,' And You forgave the iniquity of my sin."

Timothy Keller writes in *The Songs Of Jesus:*

> *(God) removes our objective guilt so it can't bring us into punishment (verse 5), and He removes our subjective shame so we don't remain in inner anguish (verse 3 and 4). The happiest, most blessed, people in the world are those who not only know they need to be deeply forgiven but also have experienced it.*